Sculpting Wood
contemporary tools & techniques

JA

ɔ

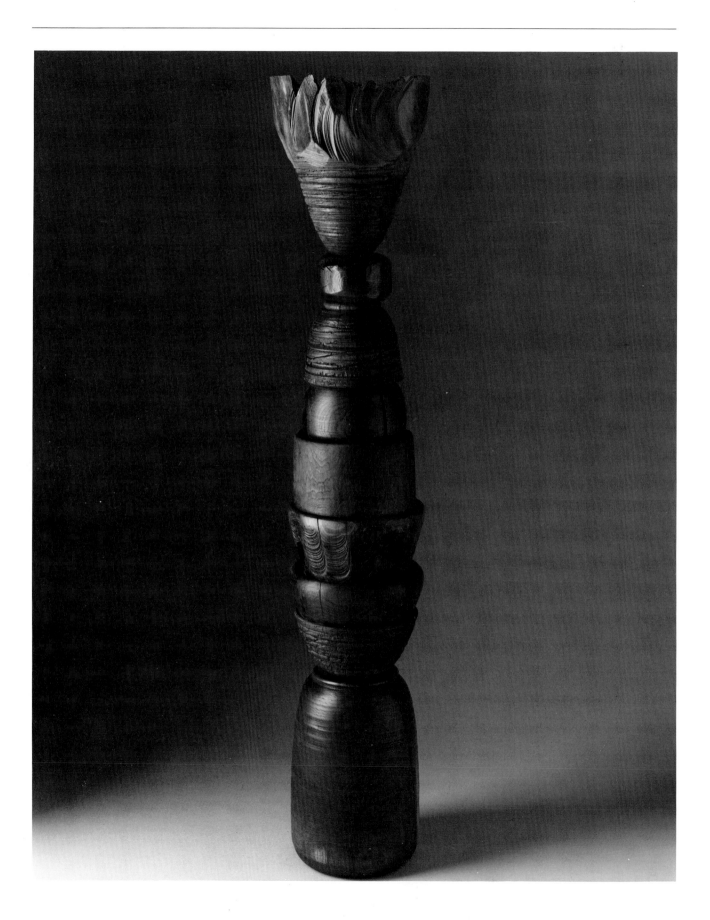

Sculpting Wood
contemporary tools & techniques

Mark Lindquist

Photography by Bill Byers

Davis Publications, Inc.
Worcester, Massachusetts

For my father and friend — Melvin

Unless otherwise noted, all works shown are by Mark Lindquist.

Every effort has been made to ensure that the information in this book, which is based on the author's experience, is accurate. However, the author and publisher take no responsibility for any harm which may be caused by the use or misuse of any materials or processes mentioned herein; nor is any condition or warranty implied.

Copyright 1986
Davis Publications, Inc.
Worcester, Massachusetts U.S.A.

Printed in the United States of America
Library of Congress Catalog Card Number: 86-70901
ISBN 0-87192-228-2 (pabk)

Designer: Greta D. Sibley

10 9 8 7 6 5 4

Frontis: Shogun, 1985–86. *Black walnut, 67" (170 cm) high. Photograph: Paul Avis.*

Front cover: Unsung Bowl Ascending, the author, 1982. Spalted maple, 16" x 18". Collection of Mrs. Edmund J. Kahn. Photograph by Paul Avis.

Contents

Preface

I have been aware of the work of Mark Lindquist for a number of years and have admired his seemingly intuitive approach to working wood. He combines energy, perception and ability acquired from a life-long association with wood and formal training in design. His creative nature keeps him at the leading edge of technique and design.

An exceptional command of joinery enables Lindquist to bring his pieces to fruition with unusual skill and excellence. He is highly organized and disciplined in his work. His studio is immaculate without the casual clutter generally associated with working wood.

Much of Lindquist's material is gathered by himself, the supply coming straight from the forest or from the refuse abandoned in sawmill yards. He has a spiritual feeling for the burls and spalted wood in his cache. A near-conversational relationship with each piece of wood forces him to wait until the proper time to give the wood new life and form.

From the essence of his art and craft, Mark Lindquist has distilled *Sculpting Wood*. This book should take its place in the library of all those who seek a better understanding of wood sculpture and turning techniques. It provides an opportunity to appreciate the greater meaning and satisfaction of working with wood. In *Sculpting Wood,* Mark Lindquist adds a new dimension to the woodworker's experience.

Dale Nish
August, 1986

Introduction

The wood sculptor has a rich heritage upon which to build. Nearly every culture has given us figurative wood sculptures. As early as 2650 B.C. the Egyptians were carving portrait panels, animal figures and funerary models. From Europe, we have a profusion of religious wood carvings from 500-1500 A.D. During much of the same time period, the Japanese Buddhist sculptors produced "ax-cut" or "split and joined" block sculptures. Tribal cultures from Africa, Asia, the Pacific, and the Americas have for centuries sculpted ceremonial wooden images. Along with these figurative sculptures a long tradition of furnituremaking spans the ages from the Egyptians, through the classical Greek and Roman cultures, to the art nouveau and deco styles of this century.

In this century, many important sculptors have explored the medium of wood searching for new levels of expression. Constantin Brancusi carved, sawed, chiseled and sanded old beams and planks, distilling form to its basic essence. Jean Arp carved reliefs and constructed assemblages of wood. Ernst Barlach created powerful narrative wood sculptures. Wood was used for constructivist sculptures by many other modern European sculptors including Joan Miro, Kurt Schwitters, Henri Laurent, as well as Louise Nevelson in the United States who used wood almost exclusively for her constructions. British sculptors Henry Moore and Barbara Hepworth used wood for direct carving.

Most modern wood sculpture has been done with traditional techniques using a saw, mallet and chisel. During the past several decades, however, wood sculptors have adopted more and more the techniques and technologies of wood artisans. Attention to joinery and imaginative use of power tools have strongly influenced the aesthetic directions of wood sculpture. Whereas in the past, there seemed to be a rigid boundary between the expressiveness of the sculptor and the sophisticated crafted technique of the furnituremaker, today we are beginning to see a common ground between "real art" and "craft."

Both sides have benefitted from this synthesis. Knowledge of contemporary tools and techniques has allowed the sculptor to create more efficiently and with more control. And the furnituremaker, hitherto considered a technician, has transcended the traditional boundaries of function to explore sculptural concerns of form and expression.

One important sculpting tool which has been overlooked for centuries is the woodworking lathe. Arp used a lathe for a few pieces, as have several other sculptors. But only beginning with the work of James Prestini in the 1930s has the lathe gained prominence as a tool for sculpture. As new machines become more readily accessible, as the technology increases the possibilities for scale and control, sculptors may continue to turn to the lathe as an important process in their repertoire.

Attitudes toward the nature of materials have also changed. Grain irregularities, bark inclusions and cracks are no longer viewed solely as defects to be filled or hidden. Burls and spalted wood, formerly neglected, now are recognized for their inherent beauty. Native woods direct from the forest are obtainable because of current chainsaw and portable mill technology. No longer are the options limited to the lumberyard.

This book is for all students of woodworking and wood sculpture, whether they come from a technical or artistic background. It covers the nature of wood, the making and maintenance of tools, the development of new technologies, aesthetic principles, historic influences and philosophical inquiry — all essential elements of wood sculpture. Since there are so many approaches to woodworking and sculpture, I do not even attempt to accommodate them all. I present my perspective so as to stimulate others to seek their own perspectives. After all, the best perspective for any sculptor is the one that affords personal satisfaction as well as pride of workmanship and a sense of accomplishment.

PART I   Wood for the Sculptor

CHAPTER 1 The Structure of Wood

The wind blows. The sun shines. The sky rains down water upon the earth. The forest perpetually runs through its cycle. Walk in the forest on any day and look at the new trees shooting up, the old ones sinking down. The rain falls. The trees gather water through their roots. They grow ever skyward, competing with one another for the precious sunlight which provides the vital energy for photosynthesis. The wind moves the plants, testing for weakness and distributing the seeds to the earth, reforesting. Wind, rain and lightening wrestle the old and frail giants and weaker trees to the ground. Insects and bacteria recycle the dead wood into rich soil — for the seeds to fall into, the rain to fall on, the sun to warm — producing new trees which will in turn yield to the same destiny. The elements are at work in concert, playing a perfect symphony.

The life of the tree is supported and governed by one main process: photosynthesis. In photosynthesis, water and carbon dioxide in the presence of light and chlorophyll combine to manufacture simple sugars, the food of the tree. But only a small percent of the water that the tree raises from its roots to its leaves is used up in photosynthesis. All the rest evaporates into the air, keeping the cell surfaces of the leaves wet, facilitating the exchange of carbon dioxide and oxygen.

In order to transport the great quantities of water needed for this process, the tree's structure is built around an efficient and intricate circulation system, starting at the roots and continuing upward through the trunk and branches

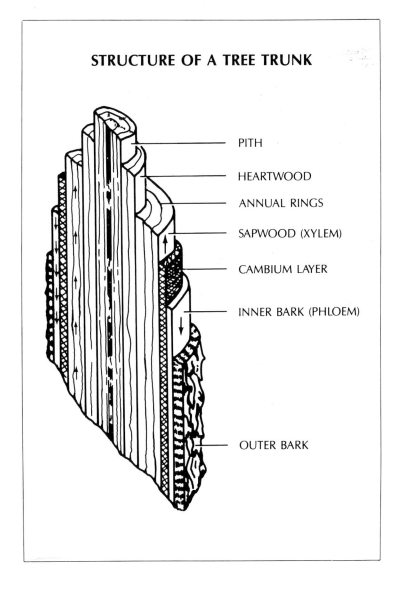

STRUCTURE OF A TREE TRUNK

PITH

HEARTWOOD

ANNUAL RINGS

SAPWOOD (XYLEM)

CAMBIUM LAYER

INNER BARK (PHLOEM)

OUTER BARK

ORIENTATION OF A BOARD IN A LOG

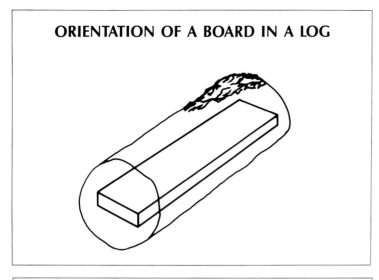

GRAIN OF A BOARD

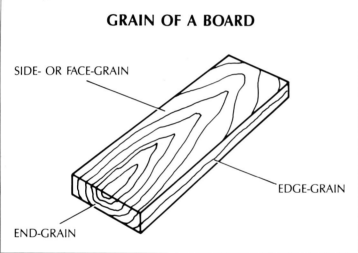

SIDE- OR FACE-GRAIN

EDGE-GRAIN

END-GRAIN

into the leaves. This system, individual cells connected to form water-carrying tubes, mostly determines the structure and physical properties of the material that we cut from the downed tree: wood.

The structural peculiarities of wood are also determined by the growth pattern of the tree. Most of the tissue of a tree trunk does not grow once it has been formed. Near the outside of the tree, a thin layer of cells called the cambium produces all the new cells, adding to the inside of the tree (the xylem), and to the outside (the phloem) near the bark. Cells are added at different rates and in different sizes according to the season of the year. This produces growth rings seen as the layers in a cross-section of the tree.

These layers of cells are largely composed of vessels which transport the water through the tree, and fibers which support it. As the tree grows older, the center of the xylem becomes clogged with gums and other substances and stops transporting water. This process causes it to darken in color, and it is called the heartwood. In addition to the vertical vessels and fibers extending throughout the tree trunk, rays extend outward horizontally from the center of the trunk to distribute liquids.

These structural properties and growth patterns in the wood produce its working characteristics such as strength, flexibility, tendency to crack or separate, and hardness.

GRAIN

The structure and growth of the tree also create the texture, porosity, consistency, density and structural direction of the wood. These qualities are loosely grouped under the heading "grain" (technically, "the stratification of wood fibers in a piece of wood"). For instance, there is dense grain, open grain, irregular grain, clear grain, wide grain, consistent grain. Grain also describes the direction of the cut as it relates to the direction of growth of the tree: cross-grain, end-grain, side-grain, diagonal-grain, edge-grain. The surface patterns and markings on a piece of wood resulting from the grain, colorations and the cut are also referred to as grain.

Both the structural grain and the surface grain are affected by the way the wood is cut. A piece of wood cut from the length of the tree will have the most structural strength because of the fibers and vessels running the length of the piece, and will expose a lengthwise and relatively plain surface grain. A cross section piece of the tree will be weak, and crack and check easily, but will expose interesting end-grain patterns of concentric rings. Diagonal cutting will expose oval concentric rings and produce a stronger piece of wood than cross-cutting but weaker than lengthwise cutting.

Wood carvings and bowls will expose all types of grain on their different surfaces and are positioned in the wood to best use the structural strengths and most attractive markings. For example, orienting a turned bowl with the lip toward the bark of the tree and the bottom toward the center will employ the structural qualities of the bowl to minimize the weakening effect of end-grain. This orientation will also expose the best variety of surface grain. The bowl surface changes from side-grain through diagonal-grain to end-grain and back as you move around the circumference.

Sawmills always cut lumber lengthwise, but in many different ways. "Turned log sawing" — or "plainsawing" — is the most common. In this method, the log is sawn to establish a flat side, then the flat is turned and the boards are cut perpendicular to the flat in different dimensions depending on the nature of the log and the desired lumber, often leaving a center beam which contains the pith.

Another common method in sawmilling is the "through-and-through" method: the planks are sawn by cutting through the entire width of the tree, leaving the natural edge of the tree on the boards. Boards produced by this method are called flitches.

"Quartersawing," rarely used by mills anymore, produces the most consistent, stable and tight-grained lumber possible. The tree is first sawn in quarters (length-wise), and then each quarter is sawn into boards having the bark side of the tree as one edge and the center of the tree as the other. These boards are edge-grain and make best advantage of figured wood, exposing the rays, and are often used by furniture-makers and violinmakers.

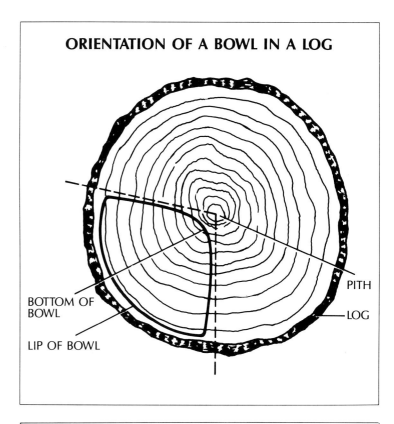

ORIENTATION OF A BOWL IN A LOG

PITH

LOG

BOTTOM OF BOWL

LIP OF BOWL

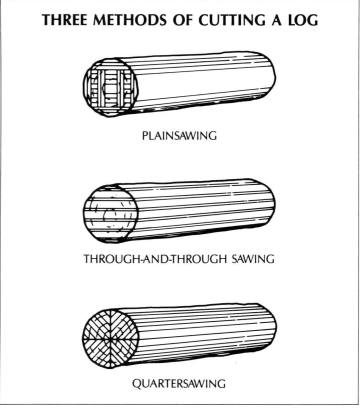

THREE METHODS OF CUTTING A LOG

PLAINSAWING

THROUGH-AND-THROUGH SAWING

QUARTERSAWING

FIGURE

"Figure" refers to the distinctive markings on side-grain wood surfaces. Any deviation from normal cellular structure results in irregularity of the grain. Certain kinds of irregular cell growth will occur consistently throughout a tree or a tree section producing a beautiful and rich grain pattern. Although rare, many of these patterns reoccur within a small proportion of the trees of a given species. There are innumerable colloquialisms which refer to these different figure patterns, such as curly, tiger, fiddleback, flame, quilt, bird's-eye, blister, mottle, dimple, stripe, ribbon, wavy, burly, knurly. Old time sawyers made up most of these labels to refer to special cuts and typically repeated characteristics in lumber. Figured boards were set aside for cabinetmakers and instrument makers who learned to ask for them by name. Today many sawyers are unfamiliar with figured woods, except perhaps bird's-eye and curly maple.

Figured grains such as bird's-eye are not related to burls. (A burl is a protuberance in the tree's growth rings — usually innumerable partially-developed buds, occurring on one spot on the tree. Burls are discussed in Chapter four.) Figured grain, such as bird's-eye, is due to sharp depressions in the growth rings, the same shape being taken by successive growth rings over a period of many years. It usually appears throughout an affected tree. Fungi, climate and soil conditions have all been blamed for producing figure, but scientists still are not sure what causes it. These trees give no outward sign of abnormal wood and so cannot be specifically hunted for. They are instead a "find" in a lumbering operation.

When light enters the cells of wood, it is reflected back. When a straight grained piece of wood is cut and sanded, all the cells are cut through at approximately the same angle and reflect light evenly. But when wavy or twisted figured grain patterns are sawn through and sanded flat, the cells are cut at different angles, exposing different cross section surfaces. The light hitting these surfaces is therefore reflected back differently according to the angle of the cell. The board shimmers, showing patterns of iridescence along the lines of the changing cell orientation. If the cell structure is extremely complex, as in some burls, the light is refracted and re-reflected, bouncing or echoing within the cells. This play of light produces an eerie, almost glowing quality. Curly, blister, quilt and tiger maple all have iridescent qualities to some degree. The consistency of cellular structure and reflective quality determines the quality and interest of each piece.

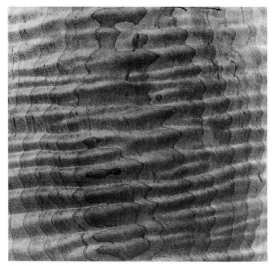

Curly maple.

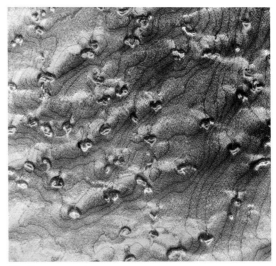

Bird's-eye maple.

Robert Whitley, Chariot Chair, Continuum Series.
Curly maple with ebony pegs, 26" x 36" x 29"
(66 cm x 91 cm x 74 cm).

CHAPTER 2 Commercial Harvesting of Lumber

Whatever beauties of grain, color and form the wood might possess, they will remain forever hidden and inaccessible to the wood sculptor unless the tree is felled and the wood cut into sections for use. With the advent of small chainsaws and even chainsaw milling devices, along with the increasing scarcity and expense of good quality milled wood, more and more woodworkers are harvesting their own wood. Still, the sawmill remains the most prolific producer of wood and for many, the most convenient and practical source. A basic explanation of sawmill procedure and operation will help the seeker of materials to understand the characteristics and limitations of milled lumber. Knowledge of the mass-production, cost-effective system which discards material at every step of the process will also enable sculptors with a good eye to find free or nearly free materials for their work.

HOW TREES ARE CUT

The first link in the chain between tree and woodworker is the lumberjack, or chopper. The modern chopper works when the weather permits all year round. Daily output varies from one chopper to the next depending upon skill, experience, stamina and equipment. Using wedges and the chainsaw, the chopper drops several trees an hour within an area designated to be "cleaned." Before the trees are hopelessly entangled they must be limbed.

Once the tree has been felled and trimmed, it is usually pulled out in as long a length as possi-

1

2

3

ble by a skidder — a bulldozer-like machine capable of pulling large "bundles" of logs at a time. The skidder driver wraps a chain around several logs, draws them close to the machine with a winch and drags the load to a landing or dock.

At the dock, the landing foreman studies the log and then divides it into sawable sections. These decisions are crucial for the most efficient utilization of the log. If a tree is twisted, the foreman may decide to make, for instance, a ten foot section from the butt area of the log because the first twist or lean in the tree begins at that point. The length of the next saw log will be determined by the possibility of eliminating the twist. If a tree is too badly twisted, the curve may simply be sawn out and discarded, left at the landing as waste. These landings are often excellent sources for material — much good lumber is left there. The mill has a "one-track-mind": anything other than a good straight saw log is not efficient.

After the saw logs have been sized, they are loaded onto a "cherry picker" (a log grapple truck) and taken to the millyard. Here the logs are unloaded, sorted as to size and type and left to sit until ready to debark.

Since the logs have been dragged out of the forest through mud and dirt, they have become very gritty and slimy. In this condition, they would quickly dull the saw blade. In the old days, the bark was peeled by hand using a long knife-like tool called a spud peeler. The modern debarking machine uses rotating blunt carbide

4

5

cutters to "maul" the bark off as the log itself rotates. This process is very quick and efficient but unfortunately destroys the outer edge of the flitch.

When the mud and bark have been eliminated, the splintery log is kicked up onto the next set of racks leading to a carriage. The log is "dogged" (held in place by lever or hydraulic operated spikes which prevent its moving on the carriage), and the carriage moves the log through the whirring circular saw. The log may be cut in several different ways depending upon whether the mill is sawing for pulp or production of pallets, railroad ties, dimension lumber or high grade furniture quality material. (See the diagram on sawmill cutting in Chapter 1.)

As the sawn board comes off the log it is either sent to a sorting area or, if the log has been sawn through-and-through, dropped onto a rolling conveyor which passes it through an edger. As the boards come through the end of the line process, stackers sort and pile the wood according to width and length. Hard and soft woods are sawn and stacked separately. The wood is stacked face to face and then delivered to the next station.

6

WOOD FROM THE SAWMILL

Timbers

Most smaller mills will saw a variety of timbers in sizes such as 4x4, 4x6, 4x8, 6x6, 8x8, 8x12 and so on, depending upon the call for different sizes. A recent trend in our area of New Hampshire toward building precut and planned log cabins has stimulated beam cutting. There is even a mill which deals only in shaping beams into roundish cabin logs complete with an insulating rabbet on top and bottom of the log. Post and beam construction has also become very popular again, and many mills saw pine, hemlock and oak beams specifically for this use. Often these larger beams are relatively inexpensive to use for turning material or for sculpture.

Pallets

Pallets are used for the transportation of products throughout every phase of modern industry. They provide the most efficient means yet developed of storing and moving quantities of objects. The pallet is simply a portable floor for temporarily stored objects, keeping them off the ground and holding them ready for quick transfer. Surprisingly, they are often constructed of cherry, bird's-eye maple and curly maple, as well as oak. Many mills do not grade their hardwood, and it all goes green into the production of pallets. Discarded pallets can be a surprising source of furniture-grade lumber.

Furniture-grade Lumber

Many mills produce beautiful lumber perfectly applicable for furniture and sculpture. These mills care about the material and the tradition and heritage of sawmilling; they respect the beauty of a fresh cut board. Many mills in Pennsylvania saw walnut trees (in precious dwindling supply) to make superb lumber for furniture. At these and other mills producing quality lumber across the country, prices are likely to be high, but good wood is obtainable.

Particle Board

To understand the attitudes of the workers and owners in many of today's sawmills, it is impor-

Above: *Cull pile at the mill.*

tant to realize that they are involved in providing material for the production of particle board. In this process, the nature and individuality of the tree are irrelevant; it is simply chopped up, mixed with glue and formed into a cheap low quality building material.

Waste Wood

Waste can be a valuable asset, and the mills are full of it. For example, when a log comes into the mill, a metal detector may be used to inspect it for nails, spikes, chains — any metal inside the tree which would destroy the saw. Usually, this information is marked on the outside of the log; sometimes the entire log is discarded into a waste pile. Most millyard owners and operators are more than happy to give away the cull just to make more space. If someone doesn't come along and rescue the material, many mills will either burn or bulldoze the waste into the ground.

In 1969, I stumbled onto a fantastic wood dump at Tom Johnson's mill in Henniker, New Hampshire. Down over the hill, for years they had pushed and bulldozed everything from giant four-foot diameter sugar maples to butt-end cuts of cherry to dozy old yellow birch logs. After a while, some of the millyard workers came over and poked fun at me, but by this time I was so pleased over the find that I joined in the spirit and laughed at myself too — their trash, my treasure.

The more I got to know Tom Johnson, the friendlier he got. After a while, he would even go so far as to tell me where he had thrown out the latest log. Pretty soon he would let me rummage through the log piles looking for burls and odd formations. Anything the mill didn't want, Tom would let me have. After a while, I made Tom a nice little bowl and gave it to him.

Above: *Waste log ends.*

CHAPTER 3

Drying Wood

Remembering that large quantities of water are required to support the life of the tree, and that the tree's structure is designed around the transporting of water, it is not surprising to find that a freshly felled tree is full of moisture. In fact, it may contain as much as 300 percent more water than it will after drying. This loss of moisture is the biggest change that will occur in the wood after milling and is inevitable. Whether the wood is worked wet or dry, whether drying takes place slowly or quickly, naturally or by man's intervention, the destiny of all wood is the loss of moisture content until it reaches a balance with the air of its environment.

THE DRYING PROCESS

When the tree has just been cut, the wood is said to be "green." In this condition, water is contained within the wood in two ways: within the structure of the cell walls (around the fibers which make up the walls) and within the cell cavities (which form the water transporting system for the tree). The water within the cell walls is bound in, but the water within the cell cavities is merely contained therein and can often be seen running freely out of the tree after a cut. Working the wood in this condition may actually result in getting splashed.

There are two phases in the drying of wood. During the first phase, the water from these cell cavities evaporates into the air until the cavities are empty. There is little shrinkage during this stage, since the cell walls are still full of water,

maintaining their structure and size. The moisture content of the wood will decrease to about 25-30 percent depending on the type of wood. The wood will feel dry and may be called "dry." However, the wood has really just begun to dry, and because the cell walls are still saturated, the wood is weak and very unstable. Often, lumber that is termed "air-dried" at the mill is really only "dry," that is, no longer green.

I remember walking on a new floor a friend had installed in his house. It looked beautiful, as he had painstakingly finished it to a perfect sheen. I asked him where he got the wood. When he told me he had purchased the so-called "air-dried" hardwood at a local mill, I cringed inwardly. Sure enough, when I came back several months later, his floor was ruined — the boards had all shrunk, leaving gaps from 1/4" to 1/2" between them. Parts of the floor had also twisted and warped.

Simply drying wood in the air until it appears dry is not really "air drying." When a board or stock of any kind is "air dried" properly, it becomes "seasoned." There is a major difference between dried wood and seasoned wood, and that is the second phase of drying.

In this phase, the water that is bound up with the fibers of the cell walls is gradually released into the air. The entire cell shrinks (more in its cross-section than in its length) causing the uneven shrinkage of the entire piece of wood. This phase of drying is complete when the wood has reached its balance with the air and is no longer giving off moisture. After losing their moisture,

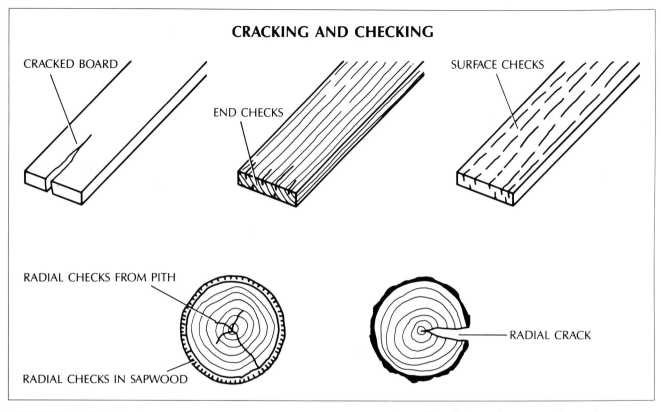

CRACKING AND CHECKING

CRACKED BOARD

END CHECKS

SURFACE CHECKS

RADIAL CHECKS FROM PITH

RADIAL CHECKS IN SAPWOOD

RADIAL CRACK

the cell walls have become tightened, stronger, harder and much less flexible. Whatever shrinkage, warpage, cracking, or twisting that can occur should have occurred by now. However, the wood will never be totally stable; it will always be affected by its environment, giving off and taking in water, shrinking and swelling, as the humidity in the atmosphere changes.

HOW DRYING AFFECTS WOOD

Wood may be worked in any stage of dryness (green, dry or seasoned), but an understanding of the very predictable side effects of drying is necessary to avoid disappointments.

As the wood dries, it shrinks unevenly, which causes cracking or checking. Cracks are separations in wood resulting in visible gaps, usually running lengthwise in a board. Checks are mi-

Left: *Will Horwitt, 1981–83, #19. Wood and paint, 86¹/₂″ x 80¹/₂″ x 9³/₄″ (220 cm x 204 cm x 25 cm). In accepting the nature of the material, the sculptor uses the twisted and cracked board as part of the overall design, enhancing the character of the wood.*

SHRINKAGE

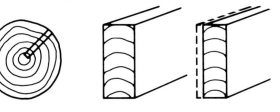

QUARTERSAWN BOARD

THICKNESS SHRINKS WITH VERY LITTLE WARP

PLAINSAWN BOARD

WIDTH SHRINKS CAUSING CUPPING

SAWN OR TURNED CYLINDER

CROSS SECTION BECOMES OVAL

nor cracks, evident in the end-grain of most boards. Since the cells of wood are relatively open at the ends and closed on the sides, drying occurs most quickly through the end-grain, causing checking an inch or so into the board.

As a log dries (and so also, the resultant lumber), shrinkage occurs mostly within the lines of the annual rings. Radial checking and cracking originate from the center of the log, the pith, due to this shrinkage.

Cracks also occur when certain areas (sapwood, for example) dry more quickly than others. Predictably, the pith of a log or board will crack, or is cracked to begin with, being the dead part of the tree.

Proper, careful drying will minimize cracking and checking, though not eliminate it entirely.

Another side effect of drying is warping. If lumber is not properly dried, it will almost always warp. Even properly dried lumber will

Right: Lapping Wavelet Bowl, 6" x 8" (15 cm x 20 cm). Collection, The Metropolitan Museum of Art, New York. Ordinarily a crack in a bowl would be considered a defect. Here, the crack becomes a focal point offsetting the "wavelets" above.

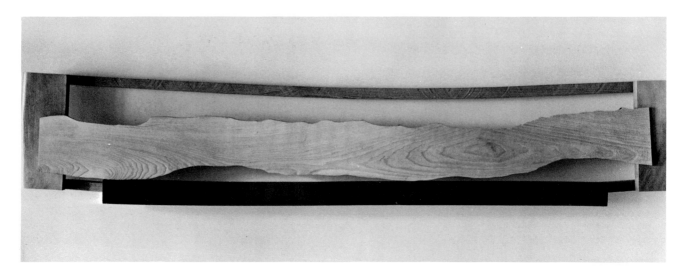

WARPING

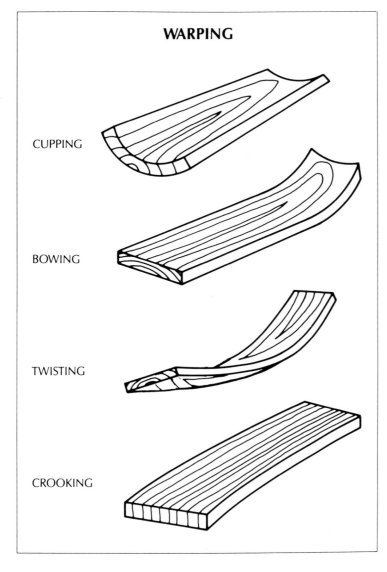

CUPPING

BOWING

TWISTING

CROOKING

warp. There are several predictable forms of warp which must be considered when selecting wood and particularly when working it.

The most common form of warping is called cupping, which is a curve across the width. A twisted board will not lie flat — the four corners of the board are not within the same plane. A bowed board sags along its length. A shifted board has warped out of square. A kinked board bends due to a knot or imperfection in the wood. A crooked board has uneven shifts throughout its length.

METHODS OF DRYING

The two main methods of drying wood are air drying and kiln drying. Another method which I have used is microwave drying.

Air drying is the time-honored technique of drying lumber, the way wood dries in the forest on its own.

After the wood is cut into lumber or blocks, it is stacked with rows of sticks (usually 3/4" x 3/4" or 1" x 1" sawn boards or edgings) evenly spaced between consecutive layers of boards to allow air to circulate through the pile. This technique, called stickering, is vital to the air drying process. It provides for the flow of air around

Above: *Will Horwitt, 1981–83, #9. Wood, 14" x 102" (36 cm x 259 cm). Bowed, twisted, shifted and crooked boards are combined achieving a harmonious and interesting blend of formal and planar relationships.*

each board and keeps the boards flat, the weight of the top boards keeping constant pressure on the boards underneath.

The sticks are usually placed at approximately one foot intervals starting and ending an inch or two in from the ends. This spacing hinders checking because of the clamping action of the system. Stickering allows the boards to shift and shrink during drying but helps to control warping or cupping.

Air drying takes time. Because of the evenness of drying and the color and character produced by aging, most woodworkers consider this method the best. Through the years, many rules of thumb have been used for determining drying time: for instance, one year for the first inch in thickness, one and one-half years more for the second inch, two years more for the third inch — and so, four and one-half years for a $^{12}/_4$ (3" thick) plank. Another rule of thumb commonly stated: a year per inch. Neither of these, nor any other, can possibly be accurate, because of the obvious differences in densities of different species of wood, and climatic variables. The only accurate way to air dry for the minimum amount of time necessary is to use a moisture meter to measure the moisture content of the wood. It is impossible to over-dry wood by air drying, so I allow my wood to dry for several years outdoors and then indoors for another year at the end of which it is safe to assume that it is adequately seasoned. Very old wood which has been aged for decades is perhaps the best, as the wood oxidizes (acquires a sun-tanned like quality) and becomes rich and mellow.

Kiln drying is a man-made, forced method which greatly reduces drying time. Green wood is stacked and stickered in a large kiln in the same way as wood to be air dried. The kiln is an environment which carefully controls the air, temperature and moisture in which the wood is dried.

Kiln drying is accomplished in three stages. When the wood is green, high amounts of steam are introduced into the chamber while the air temperature is kept low. Next, heat is applied while the steam is reduced, and the wood begins drying. The third phase involves high temperatures, almost "cooking" the wood, with minimal steam. The sequence is followed according to a kiln schedule which has been deter-

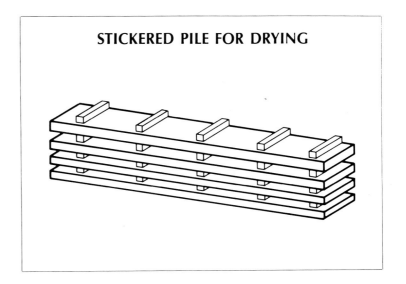

STICKERED PILE FOR DRYING

mined by scientific research.

Occasionally, the process does not work, or the load is rushed, and a "case hardening" occurs. The outer shell of the wood appears to be dry, but the inside is distinctly wet. Upon cutting an improperly kiln-dried board, the wood will usually "spring" or snap, eventually resulting in considerable movement or cracking.

I began experiments in microwave drying in the early 1970s, attempting to dry bowl blanks. I would turn the bowl green to an oversize wall thickness, then put the blank in the microwave oven. The technique unquestionably works, resulting in considerable warpage without too severe cracking. I found that cycling produces the best effect, using the microwave oven on the defrost setting. The waves are activated for thirty seconds, then off for thirty seconds, and so on. Since the wood retains heat so well, the intermittence is necessary to keep the piece from catching fire. Undoubtedly microwave drying can be applied to large lumber quantities, and perhaps already is.

Kiln drying and microwave drying both work. The wood is quickly and forcibly dried with predictable results. However, it seems to be a natural law of life: you can't have your cake and eat it, too. In the case of wood, it is color and character which are sacrificed. The quick drying precludes any opportunity for natural aging which produces a depth, lustre, warmth and richness not present in kiln dried wood. Kiln drying makes wood readily and consistently available, but air drying makes it special.

CHAPTER 4 The Forest~ a Source of Material

Traditionally, wood artisans and sculptors have used even-grained wood which has no irregularities or defects. This sort of wood is reliable, predictable and characteristically stable. With the exceptions of figured wood and burl veneer for decorative accents, furniture makers sought the straight-grained, almost bland, "perfect" wood. Furniture made out of straight-grained wood is less likely to crack or move over the years. It also works more easily and more quickly. In sculpture, even-grained wood gives a solid, smooth quality, like clay, with a consistency which is often desired.

I remember receiving a 2' x 2' x 4' block of Honduras mahogany from a furniture maker who had purchased it many years before as a sculpture block for figurative carving. Many years ago these large blocks of mahogany were readily available to sculptors in chunks which would stagger the imagination today. (Today if you want blocks of this size, you have to go out into the forest and harvest them.)

Back in the time of the straight grain aesthetic, defective wood was mostly cast aside, cut out and eliminated. However, Japanese woodworkers have always perceived and accepted the true nature of materials, harmonizing with it in their

Left: *Often the most spectacular wood finds are camouflaged by surrounding forest, as in the case of this dead giant elm burl tree.*

Above: *Swirl-eye burl, buckeye.*

work. Because of this attitude and also the relative scarcity of wood in Japan, the Japanese incorporated defects into their designs — a crack providing a point of interest, a split becoming a natural line to which to fasten or join another piece. The worker became skilled in adjusting to the idiosyncracies of the wood, rather than demanding that the material conform to idealized standards. After a time, twisted, deformed wood became the most prized, having symbolic significance and thus more character than straight-grained woods. But never was this difference blown out of proportion. Straight-grained woods had a place, and so did malformed woods.

In this country, the contemporary Japanese-American furniture maker George Nakashima has made perhaps the most significant contribution in this area of understanding wood. Mr. Nakashima developed an aesthetic arising out of traditional furniture-making concepts, combining his respect and appreciation for wood with architectural elements of design and engineering to create a harmonious statement of furniture/sculpture. Nakashima uses the rough, deformed aspect of the tree, the burl and the crotch as utility surfaces: table tops, desk tops, chair seats, etc., supporting them with clear, straight-grained wood appropriate for structural applications. There is a blend of good design, good engineering and aesthetic appreciation for the character of the material.

Defective wood that can be used for wood-turning and sculpture, traditionally discarded by the woodworker and the mills, can be roughly divided into three categories: damaged or distressed wood, spalted wood and burls. Throughout my years of turning and sculpting, I have used these kinds of wood almost to the exclusion of straight-grained, "healthy" wood.

DISTRESSED WOOD

Trees are easily damaged, but they have amazing capabilities for repairing themselves. When we get cut, our wounds heal. Minor wounds heal fast. Major wounds take more time and leave scars. So it is with trees. The scar tissue in

Above: *George Nakashima's showroom. Photograph courtesy G. William Holland.*

wood is often extremely intriguing and unusual. When properly placed within a bowl, sculpture or piece of furniture, it can become a focal point in an otherwise bland wood. Bark inclusions, scar tissue, knot holes and myriad other defects become possibilities for the sculptor who looks for expression within a work, expression of the nature of wood as well as of his or her own aesthetic concepts.

When a tree is scarred by animals eating bark, the hatchet of a young boy, a snow plow or a car's fender (among the infinite possibilities), the tree will also attempt to heal itself. After being ripped and twisted, the cells will often knit themselves back together in very beautiful and unusual grain patterns of swirls, rings and iridescences.

Above left: *Cherry burl natural top bowl with bark inclusion incorporated as a major design element. Collection, Mrs. Robert Skinner.*
Above right: *Melvin Lindquist,* Maple Burl Hollow Vase. *U.S. News and World Report Corporate Collection. The bark has been removed from the inclusion creating an interesting void on the vase surface and allowing a partial view into the interior.*

Once configuration of the repair has been established, the cells typically continue to reproduce in this fashion, until the problem has been over-corrected. If you have ever tried to splice an extension cord back together using electrician's tape, you'll have a good picture in mind of the result: the cord is smooth until the splice, where it becomes a larger bump of repair material, seemingly over-compensating for the small area of the splice.

If there are bark fragments that become imbedded in the tree during the injury, the tree will grow around the bark, enveloping it. Later, the cut wood will expose pockets containing the bark, called bark inclusions.

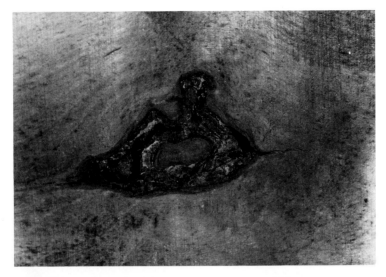

Bark inclusions also occur when two trees or sections of trees graft or grow together. After years of pressure and constant friction due to movement from the wind, the outer layers of two trees or branches that are in contact with each other will graft. The two trees or branches will grow together, but a layer of bark may be trapped within. This often occurs in a crotch section or fork where two parts of a large tree have come together. When this section of a tree is cut into a piece of wood, it is usually very unstable at this point due to the weakness of the bark. Occasionally though, the bark may be used as a decorative element in a piece.

SPALTED WOOD

If you've ever noticed a piece of sheetrock or plywood that accidentally got wet, you'll recall the edge where the water stain stopped, leaving an interesting pattern. The material soaked up the water like a sponge, and the water combined with chemicals in it to leave a stain in a seemingly arbitrary pattern. Spalting is like this but far more complex. Rich soil, a humid atmosphere, plenty of oxygen and the right type of dead wood combine to provide a suitable environment for the air borne spores of fungi to invade the wood. The process of change in appearance that the wood goes through as it decomposes in the presence of fungi, water and minerals, is called spalting.

Spalting occurs in three stages. A fungus first invades the wood (incipient decay), establishes itself (intermediate decay), and decomposes the wood fiber (advanced decay). Carbonaceous deposits mark the intermittent progress of each type of fungus as it advances into the wood to the point where the tiny filaments of two competing fungi clash. These deposits appear as distinct black or dark brown pen-like lines called zone lines. They are the visual manifestation of fungal activity in the material.

The structure and patterns of spalted wood are consistently unpredictable. Each piece is completely different from the next, even six inches down the same tree. That is part of the challenge of the material. One tree may have good workable spalted wood, while the next, although appearing the same, will be useless. So, working with the wood requires patience, faith, stamina and above all, experience. With each piece of spalted wood comes a new set of problems. Only by working the wood can one gain the experience and understanding necessary to appreciate this material.

Finding spalted wood at just the right point is crucial, because if the wood decays too long, it will be really rotten, unworkable and useless even as firewood. Found too early, it seems bland, too much like conventional wood, which, compared to the beauty of spalted wood, lacks visual interest. Spalted wood that is too soft will have very punky spots that are impossible to work and in combination with harder spots will not allow the piece to be turned. Spalted wood that is too hard will most likely check, because it's right between stages and is really unstable. One virtue of spalted wood is that the wood has already been allowed to age. Caught in the intermediate stage, spalted wood is relatively stable and resists checking.

Spalting occurs consistently in the following woods (under the proper conditions): birch, beech, maple, elm, gum, most fruitwood species. Most of the "white wood" hardwoods show good spalting. The process occurs at different rates for different trees and of course depends on climate and environmental variables.

White birch, yellow birch and grey birch spalt very quickly after felling or standing death of the tree; white birch usually starts showing some zone line formation within a year and a half; grey birch and yellow birch take a bit longer. Black birch spalts the slowest of all the birches because it is the hardest. When it does spalt, however, it is very beautiful and at the right point will still remain hard and work easily. Birches tend to spalt regularly and predictably with the grain because of the straightness of the tree's normal growth.

Beeches also spalt predictably with the grain, but the wood is often unstable and checks easily. Spalting occurs after two years in most cases.

Elm spalts rather quickly, also within two years. Frequently, however, it lacks character and looks anemic. But, if it's found at just the right time, and the wood has good figure in it,

some beautiful pieces may result.

Apple spalts, but it also cracks!

Oak will sometimes spalt but more often rots from the outside in. Occasionally though, usually in the southern states, you can find a splendid piece of spalted oak.

But the best of all spalted woods are the maples, especially old New England sugar maples. Within all of the old sugar maples are complex grain configurations with fantastic and beautiful patterns. The old-time makers of fine furniture and musical instruments coveted the beautiful figured maple wood that someone's grandfather had put aside for the generations to come. There are tiger maple, fiddleback, blister maple, curly maple, and burly maple, to mention a few.

Above: *A fresh cut spalted log, here being swept off after cutting, is always a delightful surprise.*

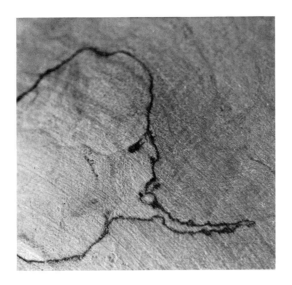 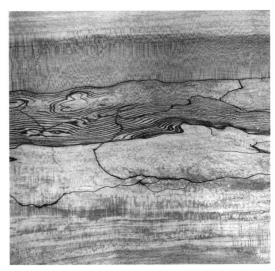

Because of all these different grain patterns and the hardness of the wood, sugar maple trees, especially the old ones, often contain remarkable patterns, designs and even pictures of recognizable objects in them.

Soft maple will spalt in anywhere from two to four years. Rock maple, or sugar maple, starts to spalt after two to five years. Once the process is working, there is a point at which it quickly speeds up, and the tree goes rotten all the way. Just before then is the time to get it.

I once found an old dead sugar maple full of maple sugar taps. I estimated it to be two hundred years old. It was full of tiger, curly and blister configurations, all magnificently spalted. The lines were so intricate that it looked as though an ancient Chinese calligrapher had penned his designs within the wood. The wood itself was still very hard; its texture was sensuously creamy, and the color of the aged wood was rich and golden. I was amazed at the beauty hidden within the old rotting hulk of the tree. There were maps of the world, animals, birds, fish, mountains, even a detailed "painting" of a rose — all done in fine lines like a pen and ink drawing. The most amazing thing was that the wood between the dark lines changed color from area to area, so that it seemed to be a carefully executed design with the most sophisticated combination of lamination and marquetry techniques.

But beyond the surface decoration of the wood, I was awed by the awareness of the depth of the design and the process which was causing it, by the realization that it was not like drawing and marquetry, but rather that artists' designs are an attempt to approach beauty which is constantly being created around us.

By far the most exquisite of spalted woods — and in my opinion better than the rarest exotic — is a piece of choice, aged, figured, pictorial spalted sugar maple. The iconography within the wood vividly expresses the tree's history: the storms, the sunny days, the cool moonlit nights, the sunsets, the snowfalls, the ever-changing New England weather. There is great beauty and mystery locked inside — secret memoirs, the last testament on its way to humus.

Experimenting with the expressionistic potential of spalted wood as a two-dimensional abstract design, I have over the years photographed exceptional pieces, producing a series of prints which I call the *Zone Line Series*. This photographic study increased my understanding of zone line formation — what to look for in cutting spalted wood — and also aided my recognition of the reoccurring themes within the infinite variety of spalting patterns.

My favorite zone line formation, which occurs regularly within the sugar maples, I call "landscape spalting" — perhaps wood's equivalent of picture jasper. Consistently, side-grain cuts show fungal areas of varying hues, of lighter and darker browns and tans, outlined and ac-

Zone Line Series. **Above left:** *Recognizable zone line imagery: The Man of the Clouds.* **Above right:** *landscape zone line formation, side-grain.*

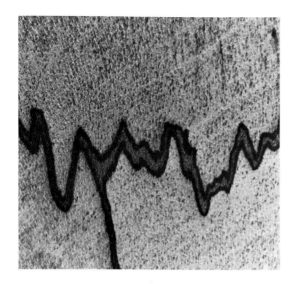

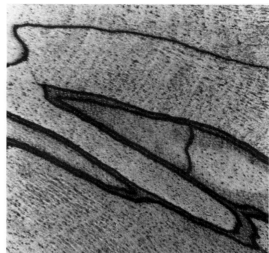

cented in horizontally oriented curves and straight lines. These patterns repeat themselves with variations throughout sections of wood, suggesting mountains, hills, fields or bodies of water, drawing the viewer into the wood, creating a sense of depth and space. An end-grain cut of the same log will expose entirely different patterns which are quite interesting in themselves but have no resemblance to the distinct landscape qualities of side-grain cuts. Exposed end-grain surfaces show radial butterfly wing-like formations or abstract patterns.

Another common recurring theme is double zone line formation — a pattern of two nearly parallel lines separated by a darkened portion, usually occurring within very bland surrounding wood. The contrast of the white wood with the dark black or blue-black zone lines is striking. This pattern most frequently occurs in elm in an intermediate to advanced stage of spalting.

Occasionally in sugar maples, a pattern of curved lines forms in a cluster resembling the petals of a flower. I call this pattern the rosebud zone line formation. Occurring frequently in maples is the web zone line formation, a stretched out grouping of tiny lines.

The presence of specific zone line formations in spalted wood is related to the grain structure as well as to all the other variables which influ-

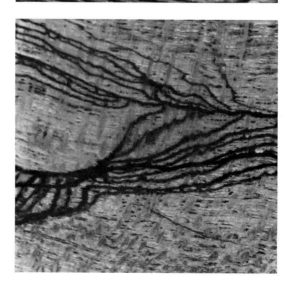

Zone Line Series. **Top left:** *double line zone line formation, end-grain.* **Top right:** *double line zone formation, end-grain.* **Middle:** *rosebud zone line formation.* **Right:** *web zone line formation.*

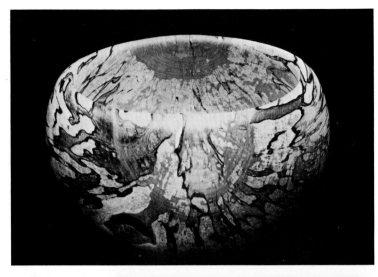

ence spalting and is usually not predictable. The actual cutting of the wood also affects the visual display of any given pattern. Within a log, sections having perhaps the same basic characteristics will present entirely different pictures when cut end-grain, side-grain, or quartersawn. Add the dimension of curve to the cut, and the pattern grows increasingly more complex.

The process of working spalted wood begins with finding the material. Think of the availability of the material: its cost is your time. The quality depends upon your perseverance and faith that the right piece is there, free for the taking. The journey from forest to drying shed to shop to the final resting environment in home or museum is mysteriously recorded in the wood itself.

Perhaps the real value of a finished piece can be suggested by the richness of the images it evokes. To work this wood is to experience — in a sense, rebirth. The wood that was saved from oblivion explodes into new life instilling the woodworker with a growing awareness of the material, of form, of work and wood. . .

BURLS

Burls are perhaps the most misunderstood and mysterious material in the woodworker's realm. Most woodworkers and suppliers who use these strange, unpredictable formations have very little idea of how they grow or what causes them. And, although burlwood has long been prized for veneer, lumbermen and forest pathologists trying to produce straight and sound stock for the mass-production lumber industry have always regarded the burl as a nuisance. But I find burls to be an extremely rich source of material for sculpture and turned and carved bowls and, most importantly, an inspiration for discovering new philosophies and approaches to woodturning.

Burls are protuberances on trees that come in all shapes and sizes. They are known colloquially as burrs, bumps, knobs or gnarls, and scientifically as galls. A burl is not a healing over of a broken branch, but an irregular outgrowth,

Top: *Spalted yellow birch fruit bowl.*
Above: Melvin Lindquist, Rosebud Vase. *Spalted maple, 6" (15 cm) high.*

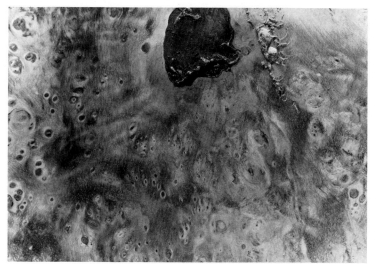

usually of fruit buds which have only partially developed. These buds grow slowly in thickness rather than length, causing the burl to become larger and more dense and creating unusual grain patterns. The grain of the burl is composed of conical elevations, each with a dark speck, the result of the partial bud development. The grain of some figured woods is similar to burl grain but is an entirely different phenomenon, even though some figured woods are mistakenly called "burly." The grain of figured wood is due to sharp depressions in the growth ring, repeated in the growth rings of successive years, and usually appearing throughout an affected tree.

Top right: *White ash burl quartered — showing cross-section, exterior and interior. Note bark inclusions and resulting voids where the burl has grown around the tree and in upon itself.*

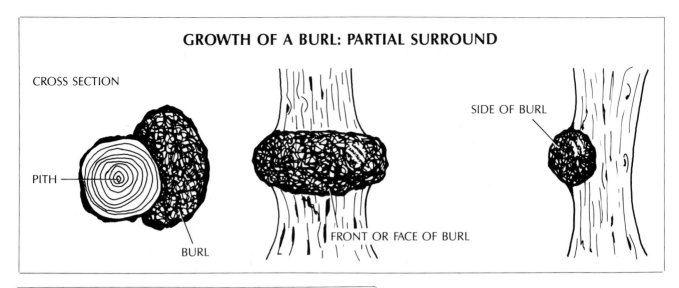

GROWTH OF A BURL: PARTIAL SURROUND

CROSS SECTION

PITH

BURL

FRONT OR FACE OF BURL

SIDE OF BURL

GROWTH OF A BURL: TOTAL SURROUND

BURL

FULL ROUND BURL

TRUNK

A burl may be a perfect half-sphere on the side of a tree or look like a wreath surrounding the tree, especially if it grows leaves on short stems as some do. Burls may be irregular, twisted and malformed; surfaces may be smooth or rough and fissured. A burl may grow at any height on the trunk or on a major branch of a tree. It may grow halfway around the trunk, creating a half-moon that makes a beautiful carved bowl, along one side of a tree or sometimes all the way up and around the entire trunk. This is the most exciting burl find — the "burl tree," a tree whose trunk has been entirely encompassed by burls growing into and around each other, forming a giant mass of burl growth and grain.

Burl forms offer many sculptural possibilities. Some burls are quietly round, whether shallow or deep, definitely suggesting a bowl. Others are twisted and convoluted, evoking a sense of animation. No matter how much energy shows on the outside, though, it is no clue to the incredible explosion of energy inside — a swirling, frozen pot of marbleized color, texture and structure, creating patterns too complex to understand or predict. It is one of nature's amazing mysteries — the starry galaxy within is greater than the form containing it.

Scientists are only beginning to understand burl growth. They believe that many burls are caused by injury to the cambium (the growth layer near the bark), either by fire or frost, or by something striking the tree. Burls have been induced on trees by mechanical injury, and by fire. Interestingly, when trees have been repeat-

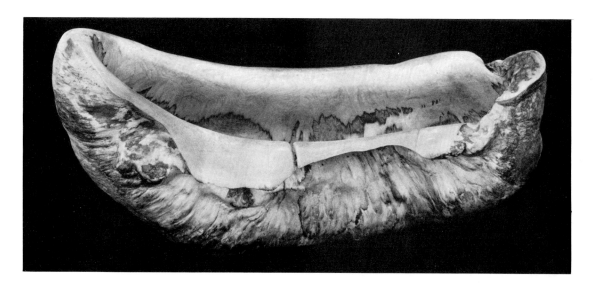

edly burned on one side, they form burls on the opposite side. Fungal or bacterial irritation of the cambium also causes burl formations, particularly the more gnarly, rough-barked ones. Some scientists suggest that a mutation or hereditary factor, combined with environmental conditions, is responsible for burl growth. This might explain why several trees of the same species growing in a particular area (which quite likely are related) may all grow burls.

Burls are generally divided into two categories: above-ground burls and root burls, either of which can occur on any tree. Root burls (called crown galls by scientists) may be caused by bacteria from infected soil entering the tree through plant damage. They tend to be less hard than above-ground burls because they form within a controlled atmosphere of soil and water. Usually a large round ball will form at the trunk base, and the roots grow out of the burl. Root burls form on cherry and white birch and gray birch in the East and are extremely common in California on redwoods and manzanita. Redwood root burls may grow to be twelve feet in diameter, nearly too big to handle. Most of the redwood burl tables made in California are constructed of root burls with extraordinary grain and pattern.

On the East Coast, maple and cherry com-

Top: Vessel Vessel/Arc Ark, *1978. Carved maple burl sculptural vessel, 12" x 5" (30 cm x 13 cm).* **Above right:** *An elm burl tree with burls growing intermittently along each limb.*

Above: *Typical Burls of North America: A. Poplar, B. Cherry, C. Black Birch, D. Grey Birch Root, E. Yellow Birch, F. Elm, G. Hop Hornbeam, H. Beech, I. White Birch, J. Swamp Maple, K. Oak, L. Butternut, M. Walnut, N. Ash, O. Spruce, P. Soft Maple, Q. Mulberry.*

monly exhibit above-ground burls. Next in prominence is the birch family, then oak, followed by elm, beech, ash, butternut, hornbeam and poplar. Softwood burls are rarer and not as interesting in grain pattern development, with the exception of California redwood and buckeye which have magnificent grain patterns. Softwoods will not take as high a polish as the hardwood burls.

Within the infinite variety of burl grain development are three main classifications: annual layering, dormant budding and a combination of these two growth patterns. In annual layering, the burl grows in much the same pattern as the tree, though much more rapidly, adding a thicker layer than the tree and causing a bulging and swirling form. Successive layers within a burl are inconsistent in thickness, with thicker layers toward the center of the burl rather than nearer the supporting trunk or branch. Where the burl "hangs" from the tree, there is apt to be a supporting crotchwood formation in the cell growth.

Dormant bud burls form through an explosion of early bud development that never quite makes it through the bark. All the buds sprout and clash within, causing more shoots to get started and early ones to become dormant. The buds never get past the stage of early development, growing more in width than in length, causing hard, dense wood. This type of burl is more prevalent in cherry and walnut and also occurs in certain elm, maple, oak and white birch species.

The third classification, which I call swirl-eye burl, is a combination of the other two. Often these are the most complex of all burl formation, especially when the patterns are balanced. It is as if the first two burl grain patterns have been melted and mixed together, then frozen. The dormant buds, or eyes, are combined with the rest of the swirly grain.

After working with hundreds of burls during the past fifteen years, I know that some grain patterns frequently recur within a given species. Yet on cutting into a new burl, I can still be surprised by an entirely new configuration.

Top: *Annual layering, fir burl.*
Above: *Dormant bud burl, cherry.*

PART II

Basic Tools and Techniques

CHAPTER 5 The Shop~ Basic Power Tools

Many sculptors I have known approach their work naively, interested only in the direction or idea they have in mind with no knowledge of how to accomplish their goals. Often, simple processes such as squaring or gluing boards are mysteries. Mastering the basic shop tools expands the sculptor's horizons, increasing both the selection of materials and the scope of the work that may be done through constructive techniques. These techniques are also used for many of the peripheral activities vital to the operation of a sculpture studio (such as making sculpture stands or packing crates).

The power tools comprising the wood shop must always be treated with respect and caution. Tool safety is a must for everyone, either expert or beginner, when approaching and using any power tool. When it comes to safety, everyone is a beginner. The most professional and experienced can have an accident due to a lack of caution or a minor deviation from established safety procedure.

Certain basic traditional **shop safety rules** (in addition to others specific to each tool) must always be followed:

☐ Do not wear loose clothing or jewelry which could catch in a machine.

☐ Wear non-skid shoes, preferably hard-toed to protect from falling tools or wood.

Right: Monument to the Unknown Potter, *1980. 4' (1.2 m) high. In this piece, the pyramidical base of figured oak was constructed using a splined mitered joinery. Collection, Mr. & Mrs. Richard Winneg.*

BAND SAW

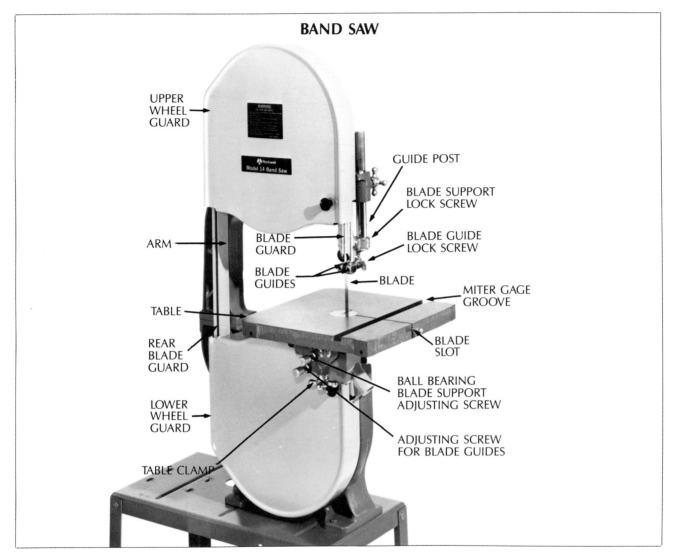

UPPER WHEEL GUARD

GUIDE POST

BLADE SUPPORT LOCK SCREW

ARM

BLADE GUARD

BLADE GUIDE LOCK SCREW

BLADE GUIDES

BLADE

MITER GAGE GROOVE

TABLE

REAR BLADE GUARD

BLADE SLOT

BALL BEARING BLADE SUPPORT ADJUSTING SCREW

LOWER WHEEL GUARD

ADJUSTING SCREW FOR BLADE GUIDES

TABLE CLAMP

□ Keep the floor clean — free from dust, trailing electric cords, wood scraps and other obstacles.

□ Keep long hair tied back and/or under a hat.

□ Wear eye, ear and face protection equipment.

□ Do not operate machinery if drowsy or under medication.

□ Do not force a tool to do what it was not designed to do.

□ Do not allow people to be near, or to distract you by conversation.

□ Concentrate!

□ Know each machine — its operating instructions, safety provisions and idiosyncracies.

Accidents can occur through ignorance. The best information for shop power tool use is obtained through demonstration and hands-on training by an accomplished instructor. Many

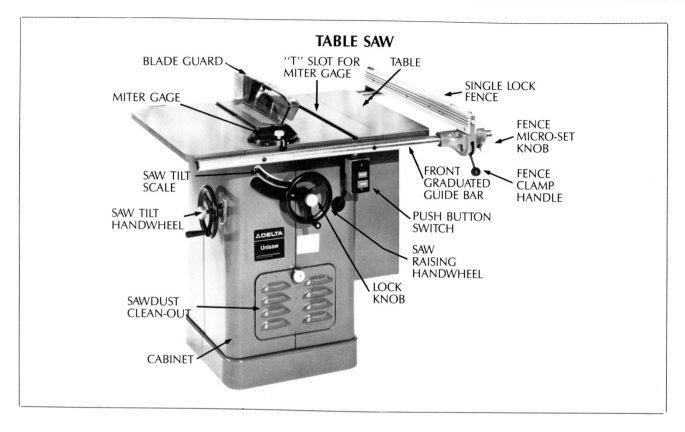

TABLE SAW

BLADE GUARD

"T" SLOT FOR MITER GAGE

TABLE

SINGLE LOCK FENCE

MITER GAGE

FENCE MICRO-SET KNOB

SAW TILT SCALE

FRONT GRADUATED GUIDE BAR

FENCE CLAMP HANDLE

SAW TILT HANDWHEEL

PUSH BUTTON SWITCH

SAW RAISING HANDWHEEL

LOCK KNOB

SAWDUST CLEAN-OUT

CABINET

schools and community institutions offer courses in cabinetmaking and tool use which are informative and useful. Receive the proper background instruction first; then begin to apply the principles and techniques to your work.

Above all, think safety before an accident occurs, and learn proper, safe procedures of tool use.

THE BAND SAW

The band saw is perhaps the most versatile of all saws. Although designed to cut curved and irregular shapes, it will also perform straight cuts. The band saw is useful in resawing or "splitting" boards since the very thin blade makes a narrow kerf. Kerf is the width of the cut caused by the thickness of the blade, its side-to-side wandering and the set of the teeth.

There are blades of several different widths available, but the most versatile, and the one I run almost all the time, is the 1/4" skip tooth blade. This blade has 5 teeth per inch with considerable set for quick cutting. The 1/4" blade will cut tight curves as well as straight lines.

Straight line cutting with the 1/4" blade requires a bit more control, but control may be acquired with practice.

THE TABLE SAW (CIRCULAR SAW)

The table saw is an extremely versatile tool for the sculptor. I've used the table saw in connection with my works, as well as in building benches, cabinets, stands, my studio and my house. When cutting waste blocks for turning and sculpting, it's nice to be able to "make wood" from scraps by resawing and ripping scrap stock. The table saw is particularly useful to those sculptors who use dimension lumber with construction techniques in structural sculpture.

I prefer a large professional 10" cabinet model table saw such as the Rockwell Uni-Saw or a smaller version of the same. The diameter of the saw blade determines the size of the wood which may be cut, and is used to indicate the size of the saw.

The table saw consists of three main sections: the cabinet or base upon which the saw rests, the table on which the wood moves and the

tilting arbor assembly which houses the motor, an arbor and the saw blade.

The table saw is used for cutting in three main categories: crosscutting, ripping and joinery cuts.

Crosscutting is achieved by using the miter gauge and allows for a variety of cross-grain cuts. Simple crosscutting is the cutting to length of stock. Production crosscutting is the same, utilizing the fence or other length measurement jigs for cutting several pieces to the same length. Miter cutting is cutting cross-grain at an angle rather than perpendicular to the length of the board, as in cutting for picture frames. Bevel cutting is crosscutting with the saw blade tilted. This is also called edge mitering. One use is for joining boards together at a corner. Compound miter is the cut combining miter and bevel cutting, achieving a compound angle cut.

Ripping is any lengthwise cutting of a board, utilizing the fence to achieve a board of a desired width with parallel edges. Resawing is the lengthwise cutting of a board, splitting it on edge, usually cutting with the blade in its uppermost position once from each edge. Resawing makes one or more boards of less thickness from the original stock. Bevel ripping is the lengthwise cutting of a board with the saw set at an angle, achieving a bevelled cut. Taper cutting is the lengthwise sawing of a board moved through the saw at an angle to the blade. This is accomplished by attaching an angle jig to the fence, and is used for cutting tapered legs for furniture.

Joinery cuts are achieved by using combinations of cross- and rip cuts and are used for making furniture or in construction.

Several types of saw blades are used for different purposes. The *crosscut* or *cutoff* saw is designed for cutting across the grain. *Ripsaws* are

Above left: *Author*, Brancusi Box. *Tiger maple, spalted sugar maple, cherry, oak, African blackwood, ebony, zebrawood, padauk, 12" x 6" x 18" (30 cm x 15 cm x 46 cm).*
Above right: *H.C. Westerman*, Homage to American Art (Dedicated to Elie Nadelman, *1965. Douglas fir, ash, and lead 48" x 30" x 30" (122 cm x 76 cm x 76 cm). Collection, Mr. & Mrs. Alan Press, Chicago. Photograph: N. Rabin.*

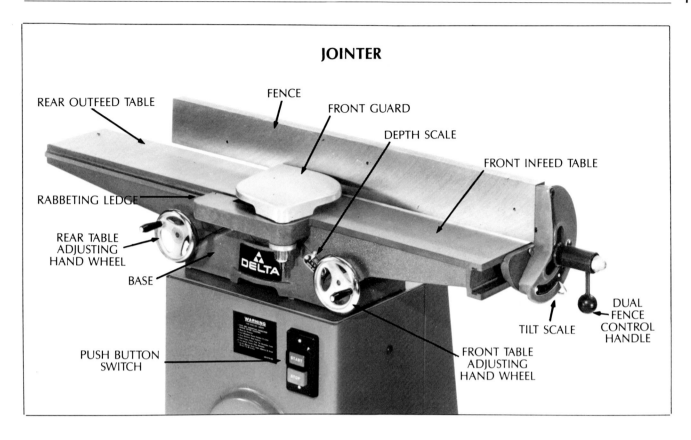

JOINTER

REAR OUTFEED TABLE

FENCE

FRONT GUARD

DEPTH SCALE

FRONT INFEED TABLE

RABBETING LEDGE

REAR TABLE
ADJUSTING
HAND WHEEL

BASE

DELTA

PUSH BUTTON
SWITCH

WARNING

START

STOP

FRONT TABLE
ADJUSTING
HAND WHEEL

TILT SCALE

DUAL
FENCE
CONTROL
HANDLE

for ripping (cutting with the grain). *Combination saws* are suitable for general ripping and cross-cutting. *Carbide-tipped blades* are available in the above three types and last longer due to the carbide facing of each tooth.

THE JOINTER

In woodturning and sculpting, I have found the jointer very useful for preparing stock for waste blocks and for building jigs to hold tools and work. Beside the need for even, flat and square surfaces when using wood in pieces requiring dimensioned boards, it is also good practice to use accurate and consistent material for the activities and applications (such as jig-making and waste-blocking) which the processes involve. Jointing assures accurate subsequent saw cuts and, also importantly, exposes the grain direction and patterns to easy observation. I will frequently run a board through the jointer just to see what is in the wood — what surprises are in there, what problems exist, which way the grain actually runs. The jointer is a useful basic shop tool, capable of performing many functions

which can help the sculptor in surprising ways.

Common jointer sizes (determined by the length of the knives which is the maximum planing width) are 6" and 8". Jointers come in all different sizes up to 24" wide for some industrial models. The bed of the jointer may be short for doing boards up to 8' in length, or longer for doing longer stock. Longbed jointers are practical as they will do both short and long stock with accuracy, but shortbed jointers take up less room and work very well for most applications, particularly edging and flat surfacing.

The jointer performs three main cutting operations: surfacing, squaring and shaping.

The jointer's primary function is surfacing: the preparation of a flat even surface from which to begin working. Usually, rough stock is first surfaced on the jointer to remove warp. (See "Preparing Stock For Use" Chapter 6.) Surfacing may be accomplished on the flat or wide side of the board, called facing, on the edge or end surfaces of the board, called edge joining or on an angle to these surfaces, called bevelling or chamfering.

The second most common function of the

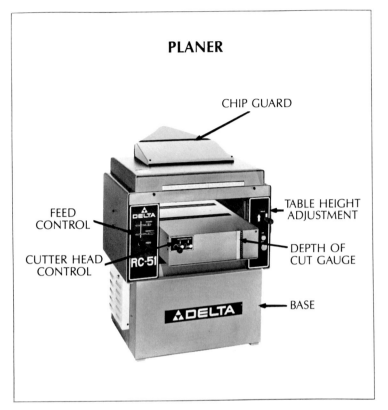

PLANER

CHIP GUARD

TABLE HEIGHT
ADJUSTMENT

FEED
CONTROL

CUTTER HEAD
CONTROL

DEPTH OF
CUT GAUGE

BASE

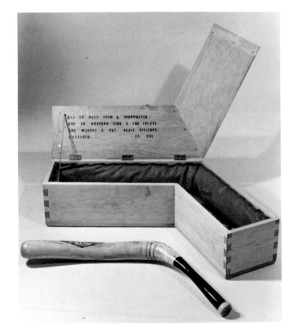

jointer is squaring or angling. The fence of the jointer is set to the angle at which the wood is to be cut. When set at 90°, the stock may be turned, achieving square sides (not necessarily parallel, however) by holding a flat surfaced side of the stock firmly against the fence while moving through the cutter head.

The last function of the jointer is used mainly by furniture makers to manufacture parts and is called shaping. This method permits certain profiles including the rabbet and the taper. The rabbet is used in several furniture making and cabinetry applications, as is the taper, particularly in making tapered legs.

Left: *H.C. Westerman,* Big Leaguer, *1978. Pine, walnut, oak, brass and calf skin, 36" x 7⁷/₈" x 22" (91 cm x 20 cm x 56 cm). Private collection. Photograph courtesy Xavier Fourcade, Inc., New York.*
Above right: *Georges Vantongerloo,* Construction of Volume Relations, *1921. Mahogany, 16¹/₈" x 4³/₄" x 4¹/₈" (41 cm x 12 cm x 10 cm). Collection, The Museum of Modern Art, New York. Gift of Silvia Pizitz.*

THE PLANER

The planer is designed to cut lumber to uniform thickness, and to smooth surfaces. A common misconception about the planer is that it will straighten crooked, warped or twisted boards. Because of the basic design and intent of the planer, this is impossible. The planer is designed to cut an even, uniform surface, parallel exactly to the surface which glides along the table bed, creating stock of uniform thickness.

A heavy cast iron housing or body contains the inner workings of the planer. The cutter head is a cylinder like that of the jointer, with slots to accept and hold three knives or planer blades. The cutter head is held by bearings at both ends. It is motor driven either directly or by gear or belt. The motor usually also drives feed rolls located in front of and behind the cutter head.

Since the feed rolls of the planer keep the wood firmly pressed to the bed as it moves along, any twist or warp will go through the cutter head unnoticed, and the cut will be parallel to the bed side surface. As the board comes out through the planer, it will snap back to the original twist. The result is a smoothly planed, twisted board. In order to achieve good accurate results in planing lumber, the jointer is used first to establish a flat surface. Then the planer is used to cut an even, parallel surface and to make the stock the desired thickness.

THE COMBINATION BELT/DISC SANDER (FINISHING MACHINE)

The combination belt/disc sander is designed for the sanding of parts which may be brought to the machine and worked while the machine itself remains stationary. The machine is made of two types of sanders: the stationary belt sander and the disc sander. The two are combined for convenience and efficiency.

The belt sander rapidly rotates a continuous abrasive belt around a course; a backing plate located in the middle does most of the sanding. The belt travels around two metal drums: one drives, the other idles.

The disc sander part of the machine is relatively simple and works well for end-grain sanding of stock. A circular metal disc is either at-

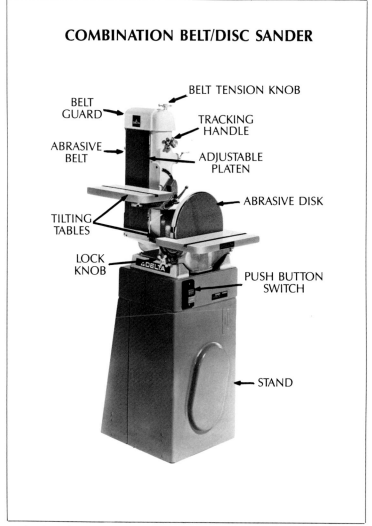

COMBINATION BELT/DISC SANDER

BELT GUARD

BELT TENSION KNOB

TRACKING HANDLE

ABRASIVE BELT

ADJUSTABLE PLATEN

ABRASIVE DISK

TILTING TABLES

LOCK KNOB

PUSH BUTTON SWITCH

STAND

tached to the motor or to a shaft driven by the motor. An abrasive disc is fastened by adhesive to the disc which rotates at approximately 1700 rpm. Outside curves may be sanded fairly accurately with the disc sander after a basic skill has been acquired. The machine is basically for rough sanding and simple shaping of exterior contours of pieces.

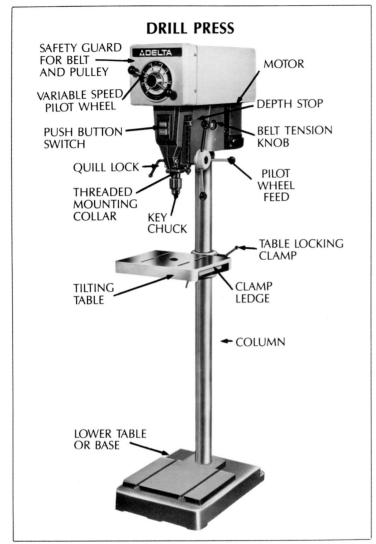

DRILL PRESS

SAFETY GUARD FOR BELT AND PULLEY

VARIABLE SPEED PILOT WHEEL

PUSH BUTTON SWITCH

QUILL LOCK

THREADED MOUNTING COLLAR

KEY CHUCK

TILTING TABLE

LOWER TABLE OR BASE

MOTOR

DEPTH STOP

BELT TENSION KNOB

PILOT WHEEL FEED

TABLE LOCKING CLAMP

CLAMP LEDGE

COLUMN

THE DRILL PRESS

Although the drill press is primarily designed for drilling, it is a very versatile tool. Through the use of drill press accessories, the machine can be used to perform several sanding and routing operations. Commonly available accessories are router bits, and sanding drums and discs of various sizes. These accessories are held stationary in the chuck, and the work is pushed into the cutter or sander for shaping, cutting, or sanding. A fence may be attached to the table (it may be merely a board clamped to the table) to serve as a guide for routing, etc. A mortising attachment is a square, hollow chisel, with a drill inside it. The drill, which protrudes slightly beyond the hollow chisel, drills a hole and the chisel squares it. The end result is a square hole called a mortise, commonly used in furniture making.

Drill presses are manufactured in many different sizes and models. However, the two most common types, the floor model and the bench model, share many of the same features, and work in the same ways.

The drill press consists of four main parts: the head, a heavy metal casting which houses the inner workings of the press; the column which supports the head, and on which the table moves up and down and rotates from side to side; and the base which supports all of the above.

The distance from the column to the center point of the drill determines the maximum diameter of a circle in which a hole may be drilled, and this figure is used to indicate the size of the press. For example, a press capable of drilling to the center of a 15″ circle is a 15″ drill press.

Variable speed drill presses range from 500–5,000 rpm, while belt drive presses have fixed intermediate, changeable speeds. Usually, wood drilling (boring) is done at speeds within a range of 1,000–3,500 rpm. However,

Left: *Drill bits. Back (from left): brad point adjustable counter bore bit, twist drill, boring auger, brad point drill, spade bit, power bore bit, Forstner bit, multi-spur bit. Front: countersink bit, counterbore bit, countersink bit with stop collar for setting depth, chamfer bit.*

large hole boring is slower in proportion to the size of the hole being drilled.

Many different types and sizes of drills and boring bits are available for use with the drill press. Twist drills are used for general purpose drilling in wood or metal. Spade bits are inexpensive, slower-cutting, less accurate bits useful when economy is important, or for rough work, such as drilling into a piece of wood that may contain metal. The power bore bit has a long brad point for easy starting and, like the spade bit, is best-suited to cutting soft woods. For the fast boring of deep holes where accuracy is not critical, a boring auger which clears chips quickly can be used. A brad point drill bores clean, accurate holes and can be used with a dowelling jig.

The multi-spur bit has a center cutter surrounded by a cutting edge of individual teeth and makes a relatively flat-bottomed hole. It provides quick and accurate cutting, does not clog, leaves the sides of the hole smooth and is well-suited to lathe work because it does not wander. The sawtooth edges sharpen easily. A Forstner bit has two cutting edges in the center and a sharpened outer ring. It is used for drilling shallow holes where accuracy, clean sides and a clean flat bottom are essential.

A countersink bit creates a pilot hole to receive a screw and a tapered countersunk hole to recess the head of the screw. To countersink a screw deeper to allow for plugging the hole, a counterbore bit is used. Some are adjustable, such as the bit shown top left in the picture which is a brad point drill with a smaller drill in the center that may be adjusted for length.

A chamfer bit has a tapered cutting point to create a tapered hole. Plug cutters are used to cut plugs for filling holes. There are many other kinds of drill bits for other specialized uses.

THE SPINDLE SANDER

The spindle sander is designed primarily for sanding concave or irregular interior surfaces. The basic machine rests upon a heavy metal base, or a cabinet type base. The shaft rotates and oscillates, much like an old washing machine and is designed to distribute the wear to the sandpaper evenly. The dual action movement has distinct sanding advantages.

The sanding drum, a cylinder backed with rubber for padding and cooler sanding, projects through a tilting table for sanding at any angle. The drum spins and moves up and down while the work is pushed into it. For interior sanding of many objects, such as a band saw box, the spindle sander is excellent.

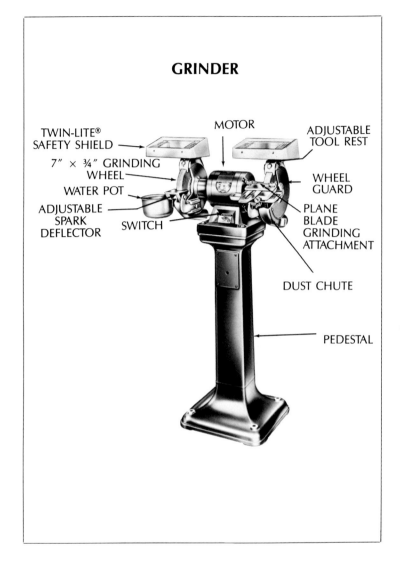

GRINDER

TWIN-LITE® SAFETY SHIELD

MOTOR

ADJUSTABLE TOOL REST

7" × ¾" GRINDING WHEEL

WATER POT

WHEEL GUARD

ADJUSTABLE SPARK DEFLECTOR

SWITCH

PLANE BLADE GRINDING ATTACHMENT

DUST CHUTE

PEDESTAL

THE PEDESTAL GRINDER

A pedestal or bench grinder is a necessity in most shops for grinding surfaces, for sharpening and for shaping metal parts.

The main tool, the grinder, rests either directly on a bench or on a pedestal stand as a free-standing unit. The motor, either high speed (3600 rpm) or low speed (1750 rpm) provides the power for the shaft which drives the grinding wheels which are located at either end of the motor housing.

Eye protectors must be worn at all times during grinding, and the tool rests must be kept properly adjusted. A good safety habit to develop is standing off to the side while turning the machine on, and allowing it to come up to full speed before stepping in front of it.

THE SHOPSMITH

Shopsmith is a trade name for a multi-purpose tool: a so-called "all-in-one shop tool." The primary functions of the tool are: table saw, drill press, 12" disc sander and lathe. Early 10ER models had band saw, scroll saw and 4" jointer attachments, but these are now rare.

The Shopsmith was originally designed and marketed in the 1940s. The first cast iron models (Model 10ER) were gradually replaced by a lighter weight aluminum model with minor design modifications. The new cast aluminum model is too lightweight to be used seriously as a lathe for doing pieces of 8"–10" or more in diameter. But it works adequately in its other functions or as a lathe for small work. My remarks about the Shopsmith apply particularly to the old cast iron Model 10ER. The original 10ERs are still out there — many were sold and occasionally you can find one in the papers or in a yard sale.

The Model 10ER Shopsmith makes a good beginner's lathe, and after graduating to a large lathe, the Shopsmith becomes a good backup lathe. Perhaps more importantly, the Shopsmith is an excellent stationary tool for holding various accessories. Even in the horizontal position, the spindle head is extendable (drill press fashion) and allows for a long extended quill with an accessory such as a drill chuck which will hold anything from a cotton buffing wheel to a foam

back sanding disc. I use the foam back sanding disc on the Shopsmith to finish bowl bottoms and for touch up and final finish work. The stationary foam back method is indispensable for finishing small parts of furniture, sculpture or boxes, and the Shopsmith is by far the most versatile of any stationary sanding tool.

The Shopsmith is a versatile and efficient tool for use where space is limited. However, individual tools are preferable as it requires time and energy to convert from one function to another. Each tool function when set up becomes a substantial and adequate (although not superior) tool.

DRILLS, AUTO BODY SANDERS AND DIE GRINDERS

The use of burl, spalted wood and other irregular woods in contemporary woodworking has been made possible largely by the development and use of new sanding techniques. New sculptural applications have been found for such tools as die grinders and auto body sanders, and the hand-held power drill, indispensable for its customary use in drilling, has now become essential as a sanding and shaping tool.

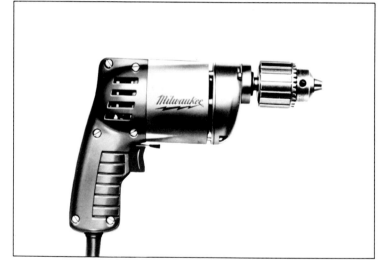

Drills

I have many different drills in my shop. I have a 3/8″ variable speed drill that I use just for drilling one or two sizes in wood for mounting faceplates for lathe turning, and another for driving screws into wood. I have a large Black & Decker that I use for boring large holes and power driv-

ing lag bolts. I use several other drills for the two basic sanding procedures in the finishing process: roughing or disc sanding, and finishing or foam back sanding.

● **Disc Sanding**

I prefer a high speed drill for rough sanding. I have three old AEG drills that run at two speeds: 1200 and 1800 rpm. The drill has a long extended neck which allows for full hand placement and extra control. It's a long pistol like tool and has a lot of power. The Milwaukee hammer drill is the only equivalent that I know about. The Milwaukee has additional benefits for the sculptor who wishes to experiment with power chiseling. Any high speed drill will work, however. Choose one based on availability, affordability, quality and personal preference. Then practice with it to achieve control and fluidity.

I use the locking disc system of rough sanding concave surfaces like bowl bottoms, and curved interior sculptural surfaces. The locking disc is a flexible backing pad holder fitted to a 1/4" shaft which can be chucked into the high speed drill. The backing pad has a metal or plastic fitting on the front which receives the fitting glued to the back of the sanding disc. The twist or screw lock device offers easy and quick changes of successive grits.

● **Foam Back Sanding**

To final shape and sand some of my work, I use a foam back sanding system which I adapted from the idea given to me by my friend Robert Whitley in 1971. The basic idea behind foam back sanding is to prevent the heat build-up that is usually caused by sanding. When wood heats up during sanding, the cells tend to clog up and close (become burnished). Foam rubber pads between the sandpaper and the power source prevent excessive friction because the foam pad gives under the pressure of sanding. Less heat is created, and the heat that is created is dispersed through the foam. The foam back pad also makes the sandpaper flexible so that it can conform to uneven wood surfaces. Depending on the degree of flexibility desired, there are two main applications of the foam back method: the

Above: Windsor Cloud Chair (Cumulus), *1978. Spalted maple, cherry burl, bird's-eye maple, padauk, ebony. The "Cloud Chair" was made as a sculptural statement about furniture.*

rigid back foam pad, and the flexible back foam pad.

Rigid Back Foam Sanding Pads A standard 6″ disc called a DA sanding pad, available at most auto body supply stores, is used for rigid back foam sanding. This pad consists of a flexible metal back with a core of industrial grade foam rubber covered by canvas. Pre-cut sanding discs are held in place with a spray disc adhesive (3M products). In some applications, such as the sanding of the band saw box exterior, the DA sanding pad is chucked into a stationary drill motor (such as the drill press of a Shopsmith, or another drill press), and the piece of wood to be sanded is held against the rotating disc. In other applications, the pad is attached to a hand-held drill and moved along the surface of the wood. In either case, the surface to be sanded must either be flat or an undulating plane which does not twist (as in the band saw box), as the stiff DA pad will not flex in more than one direction at a time to accommodate more irregular surfaces.

Flexible Back Foam Sanding Pads When more flexibility is required by the shape of the piece to be sanded, I use a rubber backing pad drill accessory which I have adapted to create my own flexible back foam pad. Rubber-backed drill accessories are readily available from local auto body supply stores and work perfectly because they are already adapted for use with a drill — a hard but flexible black rubber disc is mounted on a ¼″ shaft. Normally, stick-on discs are used with this type of pad. But, to keep the sandpaper and wood surface cool and to increase the ability of the sandpaper to conform to the surface, I add ½″ thick industrial foam rubber to the pad. I cut the foam rubber a little larger than the pad, glue it on with contact cement, allow it to dry thoroughly, then chuck the pad up in the lathe chuck, and turn the foam round by equilibrial sanding with the body grinder. I use 3M Feathering Disc Adhesive to stick the sandpaper discs on. I use 80, 150, 200, and 320 grit paper.

These principles can be applied to all sizes of sanding pads and discs. 3M products are easily obtainable because they are used in the auto body field and can easily be adapted to the foam back system. I buy 3M "stick-it" discs which are pre-cut and pre-glued to fit the 3M feathering "DA" disc. There are many backing discs avail-

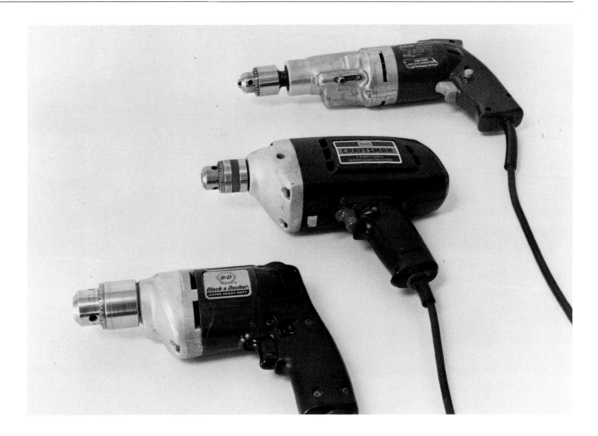

able which may be used as is and/or adapted. Through experimentation, you will begin to find and create many of your own accessories which will ultimately become indispensable to you.

Drills for Foam Back Sanding To power the foam back disc, the drill must be strong enough to take the considerable force and pressure applied during the sanding process. It should be easy to hold, properly balanced, not too heavy or too light and able to last under prolonged sanding periods where lesser drills might overheat. I prefer the industrial model 3/8" drills with variable speed and reversing made by Black & Decker, Milwaukee or Makita. They are strong, durable and lightweight, but they are also somewhat expensive. I've used consistently over ten years the Sears H.D. 3/8" variable speed reversing drill for sanding. I've had some problems with the motor over-heating under extreme load, and consistently the switches have become clogged with sawdust. But I like the balance, the weight and the cost. Every few years, I buy a couple on sale and use parts of worn-out ones to maintain them. What matters most is to have a drill that is strong, comfortable and af-

fordable. We seem to get used to what we have and use. Start with an inexpensive drill, and if you need to upgrade, use the first one at the faceplate mounting station; then buy an industrial model which you will appreciate all the more by that time.

Auto Body Sanders

Perhaps one of the most important sanding tools is the auto body sander. I began using the auto body sander for grinding and sanding metal sculptures and then made the transition to using it on wood. Experimenting with different grits and grades of sandpaper, I have found silicon carbide sanding discs in 60 and 100 grit to work best on wood. The 60 grit disc works well for roughing out, and the 100 grit disc smooths very well and takes the 60 grit scratches out. The body grinder is best suited to rough shaping but

Above: *Bottom: Black & Decker Heavy Duty Variable Speed Drill. Middle: Sears Craftsman 3/8" Variable Speed Drill. Top: AEG high speed drill.*
Opposite: *Milwaukee Auto Body Sander and silicone carbide 60 and 100 grit discs.*

in many cases can also be used for detailing. (See the Equilibrial Abrasion Method section, Chapter 9.)

There are many different makes of body grinders available today such as Skil, Black & Decker, Delta and Milwaukee. Each has advantages and disadvantages. I have a Milwaukee auto body grinder which I bought in 1969, and I prefer it to most other models, perhaps because I am used to its balance. Although it seems that the body grinder would be best suited to sanding large flat areas, in sculpting wood it is mostly applied to curved and rounded surfaces. Surprisingly, with practice and control, the sanding of very intricate and complicated surfaces is possible. A key element in developing control is in establishing a firm, anchoring hold on the grinder, pulling it in perhaps at the hip and then pivoting the body to move the grinder across the surface to be sanded. Bracing the sander against the body adds to the stability and allows for more even and accurate performance.

Die Grinders

The die grinder is most useful in refining sur-faces where a chisel or gouge, or a rasp might traditionally be used. I've used the die grinder most in situations where the rough work was done with the chainsaw and then the surface smoothed with the ball mill (as in the chainsaw carved vessel). Shaping is a back and forth process. First the roughing, then the smoothing.

Once you become skilled with the die grinder, surprising results can occur quickly. So quickly that perhaps the speed with which forms may be obtained is the one main criticism for the use of the die grinder. Often it's vital to proceed slowly, to take time to look, to study and perceive, then advance cautiously, yet with authority, knowing the right sequence of moves. The die grinder is a tool for those who already have the experience, the facility for arriving at form, but seek a method of getting beyond the "work" of getting to the point of being able to attend to the more important issues at hand.

There are many makes of high speed die grinders available for application to woodworking and sculpture including Skil, Black and Decker, Ingersol Rand, Milwaukee and Rockwell. In industry, the die grinder is primarily

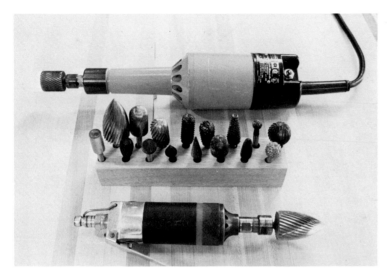

used for shaping metal in the tool and die process and for freehand sharpening of difficult-to-reach, intricate cutters. Since they have considerable power and are designed for freehand manipulation, die grinders are ideally suited for use in sculpting.

The die grinder is a long necked single speed drill, designed for forehand or backhand use. Normal speeds range from 15,000 rpm to 30,000 rpm. Most die grinder models have a collet chuck which applies even pressure to an accessory when tightened with the supplied wrenches. Most die grinders accept standard 1/4" shaft cutting accessories commonly referred to as power rasps, or ball mills.

Rasps and mills come in many sizes and shapes. Once when travelling through Florida, I chanced upon a used tool shop and found nearly a gross of ball mills and rasps made by Nicholson Tool Co. during the war. Nearly every conceivable size and shape was available. I was surprised to find, after I had purchased them all at a good price, that I could use only certain types, mostly the larger, simple, coarse bits. The larger the diameter (in this case, the largest was 1" in diameter), the larger the cutting surface, and the higher the surface speed, and the more accurate and strong the cutting.

One particular shape that has proved most useful to me is a rounded conical shape. Several different sizes and shapes of power rasps and ball mills are available through many different sources, and each is suited to its own application. Experimentation and practice are necessary to determine the right tool for you and for the job.

The first die grinder I used was an electric die grinder. Eventually I found an air grinder — I was thrilled with the lower speed and more control it afforded. The high speed electric grinder seemed to have too much speed, too much torque, and if the bit became at all out of balance, the die grinder itself would vibrate uncomfortably. The air grinder has the right speed to torque ratio and is more comfortable. Somehow the sound is important too, more pleasing than the electric motor whine.

BLOWER SYSTEMS

Fine particle dust creates a health and fire hazard. Die grinding, rough sanding, foam back sanding and auto body sanding fill the shop with fine dust which should be removed through a blower system of one type or another. Even if you have a blower system, it's a good idea to wear a dust mask whenever possible.

Commercial blower systems can be expensive. I have put together an inexpensive system that works fine for my shop's dust removal needs. I've gone to junk yards and saw mills to find old blowers which I clean and repair. The best blower I have is a cast iron housing, squirrel cage blower. (Squirrel cage refers to the type of wheel within the housing. Most lumber mills use the paddle-wheel type which removes chips and shavings.) The squirrel cage blowers are designed to move air quietly and efficiently. I've found three excellent blowers on which I've put new 3/4 hp. 3400 rpm motors. Usually the blower wheel is 6–7" in diameter, and with the high rpm motor driven directly off the motor shaft, the blower has enough suction to clear a good size room of dust.

I use 6" galvanized stove pipe (with duct tape to seal the joints) to run lines to different areas of the shop to pull dust from a lathe or a sanding station. The most important needs for dust removal are in connection with free-hand sanding with the auto body sander and when using any type of sanding accessory with the lathe. I prefer the 6" stove pipe because it can be quickly and easily changed (added to or shortened for repositioning when a tool moves to another area of the shop). I run an electric cable along the pipe to within a few feet of the opening and attach a switch box to the pipe itself for easy access to switching.

I position an elbow at the end of the line on the ceiling at the point where the pipe drops down to the tool, and at the very end of the pipe where the opening meets the machine I also position another elbow. This second elbow allows for adjustment and pivoting to obtain the best position and angle for suction. The elbows also allow the pipe to be swung out of the way when not needed. At the other end of the line where the dust is blown out by the blower, I just let the dust go out into the woods by the shop. In places where dust is a problem outdoors, it must be collected.

Above: *Maple burl carved sculptural bowl, 1982.*
3" x 8" x 6" (7 x 20 x 15 cm).

CHAPTER 6 Preparing Stock for Use

All commercially available wood is cut to specific dimensions at the mill. After the initial sawing, the lumber is called "rough-cut." Rough-cut lumber is purchased oversize for the intended use to allow for $1/8$" waste on each side ($1/4$" total) for replaning or "dressing" of the board. If you need a $3/4$" thick board, you would buy a 1" thick or $4/4$ ("four-quarter") board rough-cut. If you buy a $3/4$" board already planed, you pay the $4/4$ rough price plus planing costs. Sizes, rough or smooth, are designated by $1/4$" increments.

PREPARING THE BOARD

Identifying Warp

As discussed in Chapter 3, wood shrinks as it dries, producing varying degrees of warp. In many cases little warpage will exist in stock that has been properly dried. However, warpage often occurs in figured or unusually grained wood — even when properly dried — because the twisting is inherent in the grain structure.

In using flat stock for construction of objects, it is best to work with good, straight material. The warp in a board, if it is not too severe, may be "straightened" or eliminated by sawing or milling the twist out of the stock.

Before beginning it is important to evaluate carefully the type of warp and the condition of the board. Begin by checking the end-grain. How are the annual rings located in the board?

Left: *A rough cut butternut 8/4 board.*

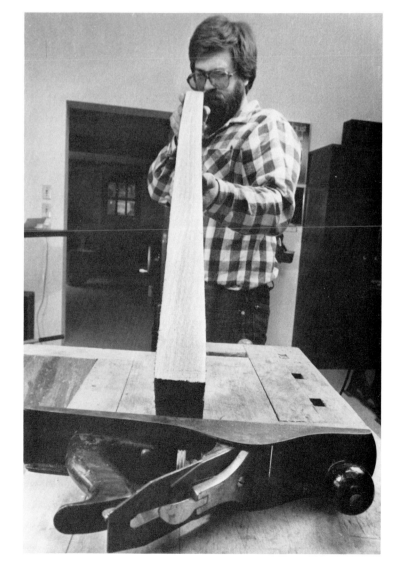

By reading the end-grain, visualize the board in the tree. Are there checks in the board? Locate any end-grain checks, possibly marking them with chalk.

Study the side-grain of the wood to see which way it goes. "Sight" down the board by holding it in front of either a light or dark plain surface in order to see the bow or twist in the stock.

Determining Grain Direction

One of the most basic problems in all woodworking is grain. Grain is determined by consecutive growth layers and by the way in which the layers are oriented in the board as it is cut from the log. The orientation of the layers determines the "direction" of the grain. Working in the correct direction produces satisfactory results, while working in the wrong direction can prove disastrous to the board.

Grain direction in lumber is like the fur on a cat's back. Stroking the fur on a cat's back in the wrong direction ruffles it up and makes the cat irritable. So it is with wood, too. It is vital to be able to "read" grain direction in wood. It may seem complicated at first, but reading grain is in fact easy to learn and becomes second nature with experience.

A warped 8/4 butternut board illustrates the sequence in removing warp. Notice the grain lines (annual layers) on the face or flat side of the board which have been darkened by pencil lines. If we chisel or plane into the grain, it will lift up. If we plane or machine with or across the grain of the wood, it will cut evenly, and the

Top right: *Cutting against the grain.*
Opposite top left: *Cutting with the grain.*

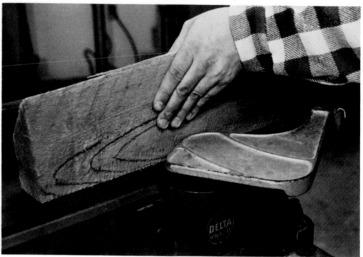

surface will be smoothed.

This simple principle may prevent many problems in working wood. Learn to see the grain in wood, even pencil the lines on the board. Think of the cat's back. If the wood tears or lifts, reverse directions. Proper cutting will make your wood "purr."

Once the board has been evaluated, a series of steps using the basic power tools may be employed to straighten it. The three main stationary tools — the jointer, the table saw and the planer — are used in combination. *Actual use of the main stationary power tools must be taught and supervised by an instructor. The instruction here is given to show sequence and procedure. Though guards have been removed to better illustrate cutting, they must be in place when duplicating these sequences. All safety procedures must be observed at all times. See Basic Shop Safety Rules at start of Chapter 5. Remember to wear goggles, ear and face protection, tie hair back and have shirt tucked in and sleeves buttoned (or short sleeves). Do not try to use these directions in place of an instructor. The only safe way to learn large power tool safety is under the supervision of an experienced teacher.*

Using the Jointer to Establish a Flat Side

The jointer is an ideal machine for surfacing and trueing stock. Used properly, the jointer will outperform any hand-planing techniques with extreme accuracy.

First, the jointer must be squared. Using a framing square or try square, adjust the fence so that no light can be seen between each side of the square, and the fence and bed of the jointer. Set the fence over to allow enough room for the board to pass completely through in its width. Using the depth adjustment handles, set the depth adjustment, by reading the depth of cut scale, to $1/32''$. Make sure that all adjustment levers are tight and secure, and all guards in place.

Now you are ready to establish the first flat surface of the board by running it through the jointer (jointing). (It is wise to practice this procedure by going through the motions several times with the machine off before attempting the cut.) Turn the jointer on. Place the board, with the grain direction properly oriented, on the bed

of the jointer. Hold the board firmly against the bed and the fence simultaneously. Keeping firm pressure against the fence, begin slowly moving the board into the cutter. Since the fence is square to the bed, the resulting cut will also be square to the surface which moves along the fence. Move along, actually taking a step or steps if required, while maintaining a constant pressure and pushing the board through the cutter. *Maintain a firm grip on the wood throughout the cut. Be careful to keep hands clear of cutter head at all times.*

Using the Table Saw to Cut the Board to Width

Once the flat has been established, the board may be sawn to width using the table saw. The board in the illustrations has a natural or flitched edge which will be sawn out. The point in trueing a board is to achieve uniform, parallel, square sides. Mark the desired width. If maximum use of the board is desired, determine the maximum width possible by using a cabinetmaker's rule to measure the minimum distance between the jointed edge and the flitch edge.

- **Setting up the Table Saw**

Squaring Blade to Table Like the jointer, the table saw must be squared in order to achieve a square cut. Using a framing square, place one edge on the table and one edge against the saw blade in its fully extended (maximum cut) position. Using the adjustment wheels, adjust the blade to the square so that no light may be seen through the crack between the square and the blade and table. Be careful not to allow the square to touch the teeth — work from the side of the saw blade only.

Setting the Fence Set the fence to the desired width (in this case 4") by measuring from the fence to the saw tooth rather than side of blade since the measurement must compensate for the kerf of the cut. Tighten the fence and remeasure. Usually, as the fence is tightened, it moves or changes slightly. Adjust and remeasure, adjust, etc., until the desired measurement is achieved.

- **Ripping the Board**

Hand positioning is all important when using the table saw. Remember, guards have been removed to better show the actual cutting but should always *be in place when you do it. Also*

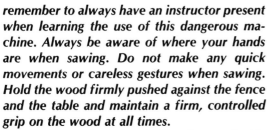

remember to always have an instructor present when learning the use of this dangerous machine. Always be aware of where your hands are when sawing. Do not make any quick movements or careless gestures when sawing. Hold the wood firmly pushed against the fence and the table and maintain a firm, controlled grip on the wood at all times.

Begin by gently easing the board, smooth side down and smooth side against the fence, into the saw blade (which, of course, must be sharp). Keep a sideways pressure against the fence at all times while slowly pushing the wood through the saw. Use the edge of the thumbs and tips of fingers to push and guide the wood. Push the board with your right hand keeping it close to the fence as you push the end of the board past the blade. If the board is less than four inches wide, use a push stick as soon as the end of the board gets within six inches of the blade. Use the left hand to keep the board against the fence, but never let your hand come closer than six inches in front of the blade. Let the board drop once it is cut. You should immediately sweep your right hand over the fence and back to your body. Then turn the saw off.

Squaring the Third Side
- **Using the Band Saw to Straighten Badly Warped Stock**

Now that the board has been ripped on the table saw with the jointed edge as a guide, it has two straight parallel edges. Now the third side must be flattened. If minor warps or twists are present, the board should be run through the jointer once or several times until a flat side is achieved. Then proceed below to "Flat Planing the Third Side." But in the case of severe bowing or cupping, a band saw may be used to saw out the warpage more easily than by laborious planing and jointing.

Again, "sight" the board, identifying the bow or warp. (A plane bottom gives a good, dark surface from which to judge irregularities in the lumber.) A line must be drawn to achieve a straight edge from which to begin working. Lines may be of two types: marked lines made by following a straight edge guide held on a surface and snapped lines made by snapping a length of chalk-covered string stretched between the two desired end points of the line.

Determine which side of the board has a concave surface and which has the convex surface. Following the illustrations, insert a push pin into point A, one end of the convex side of the board. Stretch the chalk line from point A to point B, the other end of the convex side, and snap. (Or use a straight edge and mark.) Next measure the shortest distance from the line to the concave surface of the board. Then mark the distance at each end of the board perpendicu-

larly from points A and B, creating points C and D. Snap or draw another line which will be parallel to the first line, if you have measured properly. When the lines are drawn, the curves can be straightened by cutting out of the board with the band saw.

Square the band saw blade to the table. Set the blade guide just slightly ($1/8''$–$1/4''$) above the board. Be sure that the guide is tightened and the saw is running true. ***Do not attempt this procedure without the aid of an instructor, or without first becoming familiar with the band saw by practicing straight cuts, curves and circles with scrap lumber.***

Begin by gently easing the wood into the cut, making sure to stay on the waste side of the line. Always leave the line so that you can just barely see it after the cut.

Keep a firm grip on the board, constantly pushing it through the saw with a consistent pressure on the blade. The blade may tend to wander, but compensate by moving the board from side to side. It may even seem like it's impossible for the blade to be cutting a straight line at the angle you're pushing the board through, but follow the line and an accurate cut will be achieved.

Once the saw is halfway through the board, move the hand, and guide through from the front end of the board. Keep hands clear of the saw at all times, and most importantly, do not make any quick movements. If the saw should go away from the line, do not back up without first shutting off the saw. Pulling the wood out

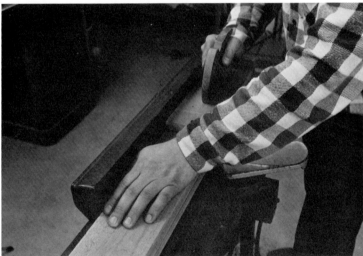

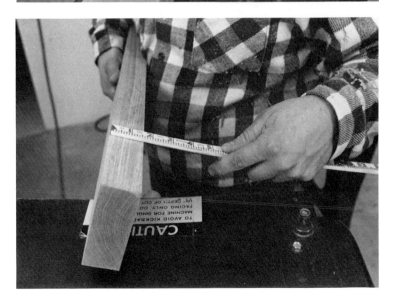

while the saw is running is liable to pull the blade off the tracks.

● **Flat Planing the Third Side**

Once a straight flat side has been achieved by band-sawing which is (or should be) square to the first jointed surface, the board may then be flat planed (face surfaced) on the jointer. This uses the same techniques as in the first jointing step, with adjustments to allow for the increased width.

Light cuts must be taken (shallow depth adjustment), and a push handle which hooks around the end of the board must be used to move the flat board through the cutter. Keep an even downward pressure on the board to avoid "chattering," while maintaining firm pressure against the fence.

Move along with the cut, keeping constant cutting action throughout. Be sure to go in the right direction with the grain. Check each successive cut; don't try to take too much at once. Gradually begin taking the kerf marks out until the board is smooth.

Sometimes the grain tears within a cut because the grain changes direction within the length of the board. In this case, attempt a light cut in the reverse direction, then make the decision as to which direction works best.

Using the Planer to Square the Final Side

Three sides are now square, with one remaining untrue to the rest. Used in conjunction with the jointer and the table saw, the planer is perhaps the most accurate and satisfying tool of all for surfacing lumber. The planer will not take warp out of a board on its own. Its rollers literally clamp the board to the bed, momentarily counteracting warps only to have the board spring back afterwards, sometimes even cracking. But, since we now have a flat, smooth surface from which to begin, the last irregular side may be planed to achieve a uniform thickness.

Use the planer only with proper instruction and under proper supervision. Review power tool safety rules — especially no loose clothing, hair pulled back, face and ear protection, clean and uncluttered work area.

After measuring the board thickness and presetting the depth of cut, begin by inserting the board into the planer, but do not turn it on. Adjust the depth of cut until the board no longer

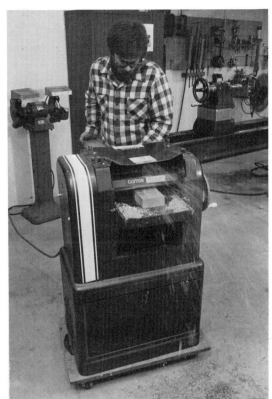

slides through the bed freely. Loosen or readjust enough of a turn to allow the board to be taken out. Count the turns or fractional turns of the wheel. Remove the board and reverse turn the wheel back to the point where the board was clamped between the cutter head and the bed, and go past 1/8 of a turn for the first cut.

Making sure of the grain direction, turn the planer on and feed the board into the rolls. Keep hands, fingers, foreign materials away from the machine, particularly rollers and cutter head. Observe the board being pushed out through the outer side. If the board gets hung up or stuck in any way, the beds may need light waxing. First clean with steel wool or light emory paper, then apply a light coat of paste wax and buff.

If the grain has not become torn during the first pass, turn the board end-over-end to plane the other side. Usually the grain reverses direction from side to side on a board. Once the board has been surfaced to the thickness desired, the last edge cut (the table saw cut) may be planed in similar fashion (if the board is not too wide or too thin) or hand-planed as illustrated on the following page.

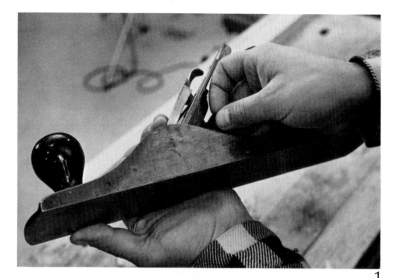

● Hand Planing

The jack plane is a very useful shop tool, whether or not you have a jointer. Properly used, a jack plane will yield very accurate and desirable results. It is important to sharpen the blade properly and lay the plane on its side when not in use so as not to dull the blade. A sharp plane will nick easily. When the plane will not be in use for a length of time, draw the blade back up into the body for protection.

Set the depth of cut of the blade at about $1/64''$ to $1/32''$, checking to make sure the blade is parallel to the mouth. If it is not parallel, use the blade angle lever to make adjustment. Make a practice cut. As you begin, lean into the wood, letting your body "get behind" the plane. Exert downward pressure at the start of the cut, moving through the wood and easing up and out of the cut at the end. There is a rhythm to planing, each shaving coming off and smoothing the surface. Be careful to plane at right angles; check occasionally with try square or machinist's square to be sure that you are cutting square.

If the grain rips or tears, reverse directions. If the problem persists, plane diagonally in the direction that works best. Be careful to clear the chips out of the mouth of the plane, and always cut with a clean blade. Let the tool do the work. Develop a rhythm and follow it through. Above all, keep that blade sharp!

5

6

7

8

Crosscutting to Length

Now that the board is dimensionally surfaced (consistent and square), it may be cut to desired length on the table saw. First make sure the miter gauge is square to the blade. There are two types of length cuts possible: simple crosscut and production crosscut.

In the simple crosscut, the board is firmly held with both hands against the miter gauge. (I like to attach a longer guide board to the gauge for greater accuracy.) Then slowly push the board through the saw blade, allowing the miter gauge to determine the angle of the cut.

The production crosscut is used to duplicate a cut exactly, producing several pieces cut to the same length. This technique is very valuable for constructing jigs, boxes, waste blocks all the same size and numerous other applications. Unlike the simple crosscut which utilizes only the miter gauge, the production cut uses the fence as well.

Never attempt to crosscut a board using only the fence as a guide. Freed from the board, the just sawn wood now between the saw blade and fence will literally eject, almost always with damaging results.

When cutting several pieces of stock to the same length, clamp a block to the fence (back from the blade) and set the fence with the block at the correct distance for the length of the board. Carefully push the board through the saw as in the simple crosscut. The gauge block clamped to the fence will allow the board to move freely through the saw without becoming bound between the fence and the blade and will also determine the length for successive cuts.

This system may be used in many different applications of the table saw. Jigs of any kind which improve accuracy or safety are not only necessary but make life much easier. Although the table saw is not considered a sculptor's tool, it is an asset to any shop. The saw is versatile, and very useful for the activities which surround the work itself.

BUILDING UP STOCK — STACKED LAMINATION

One of the most difficult problems facing the wood sculptor today is the expense of the raw material. Several years ago, huge chunks of mahogany, walnut, elm, etc. were readily available for purchase at a reasonable price. It was easy to buy a piece suitable for carving and create a sculpture from it without the addition of any other pieces of wood. Now, not only is it difficult if not impossible to obtain large blocks of wood, but the high cost makes the significant waste inherent in carving from a block undesirable. Stacked lamination allows for the building up of a mass along the general lines of the planned sculpture, producing minimal waste.

Because it presents a solution to the problem of expense and/or unavailable pieces of wood for large sculpture, the technique of stacked lamination has had a great upsurge in use by contemporary artists. Woodworkers and sculptors have used lamination for years, but usually attempted to make the laminations as unnoticeable as possible — almost apologetically — assuming that a solid piece of wood would have

Opposite above: *Isamu Noguchi*, Table, ca. 1941. *Carved avodire, laminated, 30" x 41" x 16" (76 cm x 104 cm x 41 cm) Collection, The Museum of Modern Art, New York. The Philip L. Goodwin Collection.*
Opposite below: *James Prestini*, Hand Sculpture, *ca. 1939–42. Black walnut, Cuban mahogany, Mexican mahogany, 7" x 5" x 3³/4" (18 cm x 13 cm x 10 cm). Collection, The Metropolitan Museum of Art, New York.*

been better. However, such notable artists as sculptor Isamu Noguchi, designer James Prestini and, more recently, furniture maker Wendell Castle have pioneered the possibilities inherent in laminating — the contrasting grains, the breaking up of form by joint lines, the different grains exposed by curved cuts, even the effects of joining different woods. Stacked lamination has progressed from a less desirable stand-in for large blocks of wood to a fully acceptable standard for creating large stock.

The mechanics of stacked lamination are simple: planks are sawn to a desired length, planed and checked for grain and defects; glue is spread on all pressure areas (surfaces to be joined), and the boards are clamped together. Each layer may be matched carefully in an attempt to give the impression that the joined chunk is all one piece. However, no matter how skillful the joinery, the grain patterns, which differ from board to board, will not match at the joints. Even if extreme accuracy is achieved in matching the grain, patterns exposed through carving on a diagonal will display grain discrepancies. The direction of contemporary lamination has been to take advantage of grain and color differences.

Large blocks formed by stacked lamination are less likely to check than large solid blocks of wood which are under greater tension. Even so, wood for stacking should be very dry to minimize the chance of checking after gluing. Surfaces must be carefully planed so that all areas being joined will touch and adhere perfectly. Careful planning of the design is vital, as valuable lumber is easily wasted in an afterthought.

With the exercise of careful craftsmanship in selecting, planing and joining the wood, stacked laminating will provide stable and infinitely variable masses to use for sculpting.

Above left: *Wendell Castle, Metropolitan Settee, 1973. Stack-laminated cherry, 60½" x 30" (154 cm x 76 cm). Collection, The Metropolitan Museum of Art, New York. Photograph: Bruce Miller, Rochester, New York.*
Left: *H.C. Westerman, Table, 1966. Laminated Douglas fir plywood, leatherbound books and steel, 51" x 30" x 30" (130 cm x 76 cm x 76 cm). Collection, Mr. & Mrs. Alan Press, Chicago. Photograph: N. Rabin.*

Combining several layers of contrasting woods will create interesting and beautiful graphic patterns in the overall design. Veneers used in combination with colored layers can enhance the design and form. Stacking offers unlimited scope in the area of design and presents a challenge to find and explore new combinations and techniques.

Stacking becomes a new form of sculpture — an additive step combined with the subtractive nature of wood sculpture. The joinery involved in stacking should not be confused with joinery that "adds up" to a finished piece; rather it is a means to the end of subtractive sculpture. Simply — it is a method of putting wood together to create a mass from which a form is to be released.

Stacked lamination may be done in two basic ways: making a solid rectangular block which may be carved in any direction; or stacking precut layers which correspond to a pre-planned object or drawing of a proposed object, thereby eliminating the waste and achieving a mass roughly the shape of the designed object. In the illustration that follows, a rectangular block is built up.

Selecting and Preparing the Stock

First, select good, dry wood. If the size of your finished object is predetermined, calculate the dimensions and number of boards necessary to build up the size block needed. Or, let the dimensions of your available lumber influence the size block to be stacked. Be sure to allow for some extra stock in the event that grain doesn't match, or a hidden irregularity shows up, such as a pitch pocket or bark inclusion.

Carefully prepare the surfaces for joining. Follow the directions in the section on "Preparing the Board" observing all safety precautions.

Be sure to study carefully the ends of each board, looking for checks and cracks. Cut the first end off at least an inch past the checks. The boards may then be cut to length using the "production crosscut" technique illustrated in the previous section. You could also use a similar technique with a motorized miter saw, basically a circular saw hinged to an arm which may be angled to cut miters and which pivots in a downward chopping motion. A hand saw or radial arm saw may also be used.

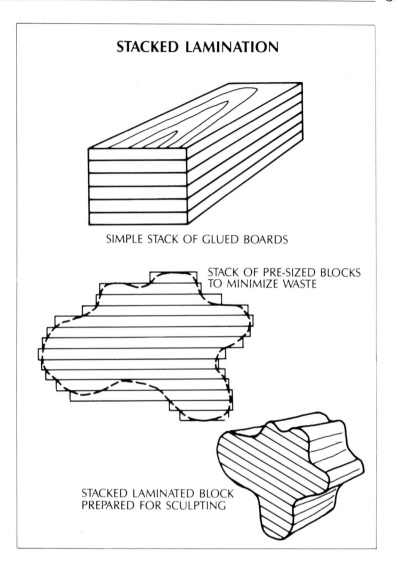

STACKED LAMINATION

SIMPLE STACK OF GLUED BOARDS

STACK OF PRE-SIZED BLOCKS TO MINIMIZE WASTE

STACKED LAMINATED BLOCK PREPARED FOR SCULPTING

Stacking and Gluing

Successful gluing requires four things: properly dried wood, proper preparation of surfaces, grain matching and good clamping. Before applying glue to the surfaces, it is important to do a dry run which allows gluing to go smoothly without pressure and anxiety. This way, if there are any problems, the clamps may be taken off and the problems rectified without panicking. All the clamps will be properly spaced and ready to go back on once the glue is applied. Use heavy-duty clamps. Space them evenly to achieve uniform pressure, so that when the glue is applied, it will be forced out of the space between the wood, bonding the surfaces to each other. Once the block is stacked dry, use a framing square and mark a large "x" as illustrated

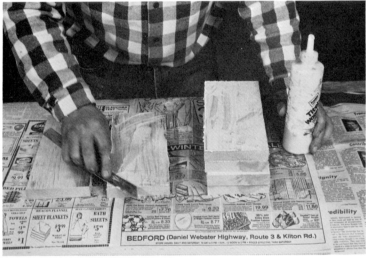

which will aid in realigning the block, and then mark the sequence.

After going through the dry run and correcting any problems, lay newspapers on the surface of the table. Have paper towels and a small dish of water handy for cleanup of the excess glue which will be squeezed out of the joint. You will also need wax paper to keep glue from getting on the clamps. Spread the glue on all surfaces quickly and uniformly with a feather stick. A feather (or spreading) stick is simply a very thin length of hardwood that allows quick even spreading of glue over flat surfaces. (Though a brush may be used, the feather stick works much faster.)

Stack the glued surfaces together and arrange the clamps in their corresponding positions. Make sure from the beginning that the pieces are aligned closely to their desired positions (using the "x" as a guide) as they will have a tendency to slide around once the glue is applied.

Wrap wax paper around the now glued block, position waste blocks to prevent clamping impressions, and position clamps. Applying gradually increasing equal pressure to all the clamps will inhibit movement. Apply pressure to the clamps — much like tightening the nuts on the wheel of a car — going from diagonal to diagonal until the pieces are uniformly clamped and the glue is oozing out of the joints. Tighten all clamps as much as possible to be sure that a pressure joint is achieved. If positioning is crucial, an oversize block may be used that has been drilled and pinned, machinist's jig fashion. Use a wooden mallet to knock the pieces back into place as they slide, gradually tightening clamps. Use correct room temperatures and drying time as specified on the container for the glue that you use.

Take the clamps off the block by gradually loosening, following the same diagonal to diagonal, little-by-little procedure as in tightening. Use a chisel to loosen and scrape off excess glue. (Do not use a special chisel, as removing the glue dulls a sharp chisel.) Once all oozed glue is removed, the block may be planed or jointed, squared up and sized on the band saw, ready for use.

Improper preparation of surface, improper pressure and uneven spacing produce a faulty glue joint which will eventually cause prob-

lems. If the joint has too much glue, it will allow the wood on either side of the joint to move, expanding and contracting, forcing the glue out of the joint. This process is often termed "cold creep." On an improperly glued surface, the glue line will invariably stick out, leaving an ugly line like a small scar which can be felt by rubbing the hand over it. If the glue sets before the wood is joined because of inadequate clamping within the drying period, the wood will eventually separate, leaving a gap between the surfaces. The gap will allow the wood to open and close, and will work its way farther into the joint, eventually causing a larger opening and a faulty joint.

A proper stacked laminated joint is achieved when the surfaces are properly prepared, being flat and correctly aligned, with the correct amount of glue between, and equal forceful pressure that squeezes nearly all the glue out of the joint. What actually occurs under the correct conditions is a knitting of the grains. Since wood is made up of countless tiny tubules that act as pores on the surface, the small openings (barely visible to the eye) receive the glue and fibers from the opposing surface because of the great pressure. The two surfaces are actually compressed into each other and mixed with the very small amount of glue necessary to complete the bond. Once this type of joint is made, it becomes stronger than the wood and is very unlikely to come apart.

Above: *Ernst Barlach, The Vision, 1912. Relief (oak). Collection, Neue Nationalgalarie, West Berlin.*

CHAPTER 7

Beginning Sculpture~ Learning to Carve

Among the most basic of the sculptor's tools are those of the woodcarver. Woodcarvers tend to use only carving techniques to achieve desired results. They work in absolutes — right and wrong ways of doing things. Most woodcarvers feel a great sense of accomplishment and satisfaction from their work. They enjoy putting a keen edge on their chisels, making the most efficient cut, and achieving a flowing rhythmical working pace.

Although sculptors will use any available means to create a piece, learning the skills and techniques of the woodcarver will help them work with confidence and freedom no matter what tools are used. After learning these basic skills one can begin experimenting looking for new solutions to problems. These can often turn into opportunities for personal expression or even a new style. For example, an accidental tool cut in a piece may become an inspiration for a new direction or special texture. But, first you must know the basic tools, materials and techniques in order to take advantage of the possibilities that present themselves.

CARVING TOOLS

Chisels
There are two basic groups of chisels: cabinetmaking chisels (which include chisels and gouges used in carpentry, cabinetmaking and furniture work) and carving or sculpting tools (carving chisels and gouges).

The general term "chisels" refers to hand tools

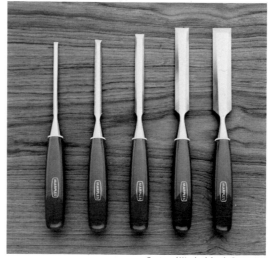

Cabinetmaking Chisels

Courtesy of Woodcraft Supply Corporation

with beveled metal blades for cutting wood. More specifically, "chisel" names tools with a flat blade, and "gouge" names chisels that have a blade that is curved across the width.

Cabinetmaking chisels are made in different sizes, lengths and shapes. There are *firmer chisels* for heavy work, standard bevel-edged *cabinet chisels* for general cutting, *mortising chisels* which are thicker with parallel edges for cleaning corners of mortises, *paring chisels, in-cannell gouges* which have a bevel ground on the inside of the tool for paring concave surfaces, and many other different shapes for different jobs. With the exception of the flat firmer and standard cabinet chisels, most cabinetmaking chisels are not used in carving, since there are corresponding carving chisels especially

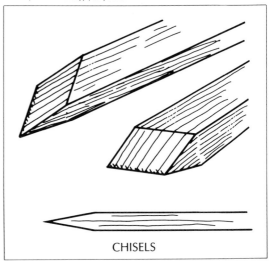

CHISELS

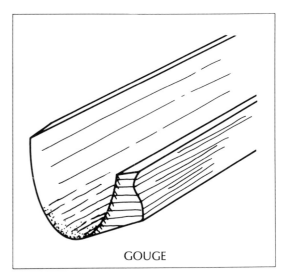

GOUGE

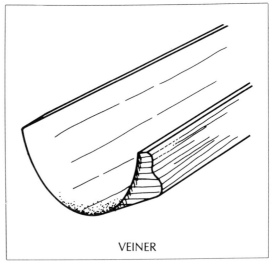

VEINER

adapted to the carver's needs.

Cabinetmaking chisels are flat on one side and beveled on the other, designed primarily for work on flat and uniform surfaces. Carving chisels, however, are gradually beveled on both sides allowing a smooth, continuous, sweeping cut on a curve. They also allow for the varying of the depth of the cut by carving with a rocking motion.

Carver's chisels and gouges come in varying widths from about 2mm to 35mm in increments such as these: 2, 5, 8, 12, 16, 25, 30, 35. Flat chisels are available in all widths in two types: *straight* with a cutting edge perpendicular to the length of the tool and *skew* with a cutting edge approximately 25° off perpendicular. The point of the skew is very useful in hard-to-reach areas.

Every width of gouge is available in different depths of curve, called sweep: from an almost flat 2 sweep gouge, to a deep curved 11 sweep gouge called a *veiner*. Greater sweeps are available in *v-parting tools* from 12 to 15 sweep. These gouges with straight sides forming a "v" are used for tight corners and for designs which employ the v-shape of the cut. *Bent gouges,* in the same sweeps as standard gouges, are curved along the length to make cuts on concave surfaces. *Spoon gouges* give access to hard-to-reach concave surfaces. *Back bent gouges,* with a convex cutting edge, and *fishtail gouges* are useful in special circumstances such as undercutting, cleaning out corners, and texturing.

There are many types, sizes and styles of carving tools. It is best to begin with a small selection

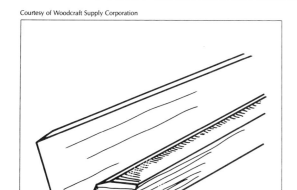

V-PARTING TOOL

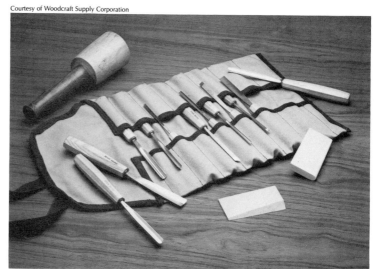

Carver's Chisels

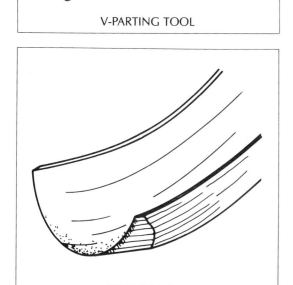

BENT GOUGE

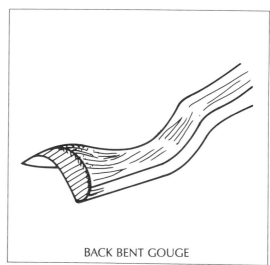

BACK BENT GOUGE

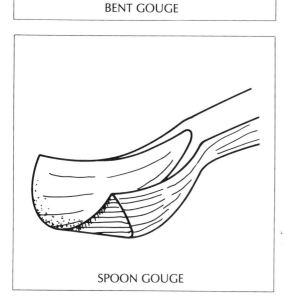

SPOON GOUGE

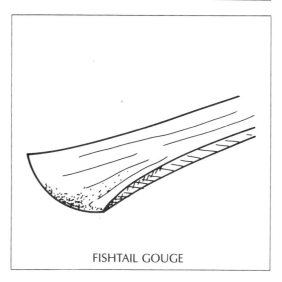

FISHTAIL GOUGE

Courtesy of Woodcraft Supply Corporation

of typical varieties, perhaps a starter set from a tool catalog. Experiment with them before purchasing more. Continued use will indicate the best sizes and shapes for each individual.

Lignum vitae mallets of three different weights are recommended. Mallets may also be made in different sizes and shapes.

● Sharpening Chisels

As each chisel and gouge is used, it must be sharpened. Sharpening requires knowledge, skill, experience and practice. It may seem mysterious and nearly impossible at first, but with perseverance the skills can be acquired. The keys to sharpening are consistency, steadiness and patience.

Determine the angle and direction, sweep and depth of cut for each chisel. Do not assume the angle that the tool comes with is correct. However, if it is, then duplicate it.

Begin by grinding a consistent flat using the face or side (if manufacturer's directions permit) of a medium coarse grinding wheel of a pedestal or bench grinder. Most grinders have two wheels mounted on either side of the motor: a coarse wheel and a fine wheel. Tilt the grinding table so the tool rests on it at the proper angle.

A certain amount of experimentation is necessary before a proper edge can be achieved: a uniform surface without shifts or inconsistencies from the heel of the surface to the tip of the cutting edge. Be sure that the tool rest has no bumps or gouges in it that would prohibit the tool from sliding evenly across its surface.

Using even pressure, slide the tool from side to side in towards the wheel. Rough-grind a flat or round depending on the chisel and desired shape; then repeat with the fine wheel.

It is vital that neither the tip nor any other part of the tool be burned, for burning takes the temper out of the cutting edge, greatly reducing the edge-holding capabilities of the tool. Many grinders come equipped with a water pot which hangs to one side of the wheel. If your grinder doesn't have a water trough, use an old coffee can or other container. Dip the tool in cold water between grindings to prevent over-heating. Frequent dipping insures safe grinding. If the edge turns purply-blue, you've heated it up, gone too far and must grind down past that point to good, unaffected steel.

Once the tool has been ground, it must be

Courtesy of Woodcraft Supply Corporation

Courtesy of Woodcraft Supply Corporation

honed with a sharpening stone. Perhaps the best sharpening stones are Arkansas or Wichita natural stones. However, artificial stones are usually less expensive and sometimes provide the convenience of different grits on each side. Also, artificial stones are usually oil-soaked at the factory. The two basic kinds of sharpening stones needed to sharpen most chisels are the round-edge slipstone and the gouge slipstone.

A cutting oil is necessary in most sharpening operations. The old-timers used to spit on their stones which they called "spit stones." The "old standby" cutting oil mixture is 50/50 kerosene and light oil. I prefer WD 40 lubricant. Japanese water stones are soaked in water and work well. Whatever the source, lubrication provides cool, floated cutting, which also keeps the stone free of chips. Kerosene is used to clean a clogged stone.

A flat chisel or skew is sharpened by honing in a cutting oil solution on a slipstone. The chisel is moved back and forth in a straight line or in a figure eight pattern. Hold the chisel at the desired angle and push it across the lubricated stone. Be careful not to change the position of the angle while sharpening. Down pressure is achieved with the index finger. Hold the chisel just as in chiseling.

A clean rag is useful to clean the chisel and wipe down the stone. Perhaps I "clear" the stone more than necessary, but I am always assured of a good clean cut.

The same sharpening process applies when sharpening the gouge using a gouge stone (a half

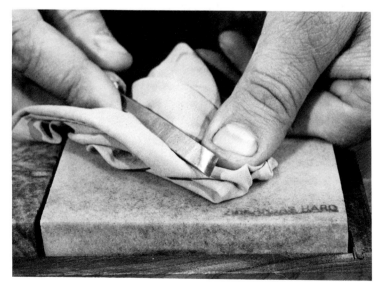

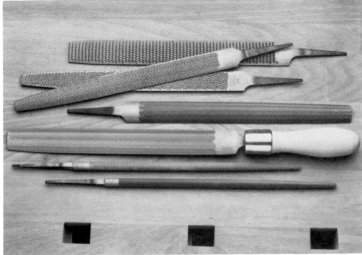

Courtesy of Woodcraft Supply Corporation

Courtesy of Woodcraft Supply Corporation

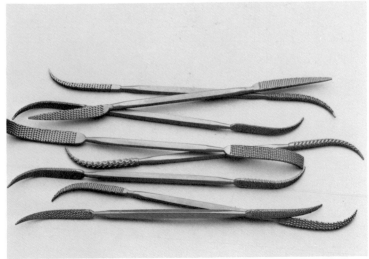

Courtesy of Woodcraft Supply Corporation

cone with a hollow inside) and regular slipstone. Holding the stone in one hand, the gouge in the other, work both together, rotating each, being careful to keep the stone at the proper angle. Use the round edge slipstone to hone the inside of the gouge, again being careful to keep the stone flat to assure a proper cut. When the gouge becomes dull and misshapen from continual honing, reshape on the grinding wheel by rolling it at the proper angle.

After each sharpening, excess oil, chips and dirt should be wiped off the stone. I then spray the stone with WD 40 and wipe clean. Care of the stone will insure long lasting use.

It's important to keep chisels safe and protected in a rack or tool roll. After spending so much time developing a good sharp cutting edge, it is wise to protect that edge. A conveniently located rack, either mounted on the wall or free-standing near the bench, organizes as well as protects the tools.

Rifflers and Rasps

Rifflers and rasps are specialized files used by sculptors to shape rounded forms and to smooth carved surfaces before sanding, breaking over the gouge-cut edges. *Rasps,* in varying coarsenesses, are used for working flat or convex surfaces. They have sharp individual teeth rather than the ridges of smaller teeth of regular files, and cut and remove more wood, leaving a rougher surface. The curved *sculptor's rasp* will carve and smooth concave surfaces. *Rifflers,* with their narrower blades and teeth on both sides will file hard-to-reach areas.

DESIGN CONSIDERATIONS

Design can be achieved through a studied mathematical approach or through an intuitive, natural approach. As is most often the case, though, design is a combination of the two.

In the mathematical approach, careful planning precedes the actual work: scale drawings are made, previously discovered principles of design are employed, function is carefully considered and often allowed to dictate form. A good example of the mathematical approach are the furniture designs of the Bauhaus, a school of furniture-making in Germany in the 1920s. The artists of the Bauhaus designed with emphasis

on function and geometric simplicity, conforming the materials to their designs.

Natural design happens as the responsive artist reacts intuitively to the material and also to the uncontrollable elements which are accepted and encouraged. A tea ceremony bowl is thrown by feel; it "becomes" through firing — ashes fall from the wood firing and create a specially glazed surface on one side, while the blast of the fire creates flashing on the other.

Experimenting with the mathematical approach, an artist may develop many designs that are practical, functional and correct. The problem is to recognize which of these have transcended mere correctness and have become "good design." The Marcel Breuer chair from the Bauhaus exhibits simplicity of form and practicality. His eye for form enabled him to recognize when deliberate mathematical experiments

Top: *Marcel Breuer,* Reclining Chair, *1935. Laminated bent birch plywood; upholstered pad, 31½" (80 cm) high, 53" (135 cm) diameter. Manufacturer: Isoken Furniture Co., England. Collection, The Museum of Modern Art, New York. Purchase.*
Above right: *Shiro Otani,* Tea Bowl, *1982. Wood-fired. Collection, the author.*

had achieved "good design." Successful design work evokes a timelessness — a quality which makes it seem as thought it has always existed.

The artist approaching design from an intuitive position makes decisions based partly on personal experimentation and partly on the influence of other artist's work. Principles of basic design must be learned, but ultimately the most important design elements come from within.

1

2

3

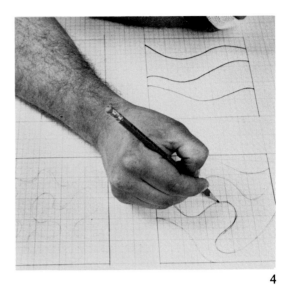

4

3-D PUZZLE FROM BLOCK

Designing the Puzzle

Shaping a three-dimensional puzzle from a block of wood according to the following method uses the mathematical approach to achieve an apparently natural and organic form. Following this exercise will introduce the student to controlled design, and familiarize him or her with the sculptor's hand tools.

In this exercise of beginning carving (shaping to be more precise), begin by designing a simple jig saw puzzle utilizing flowing lines. Use graph paper with a scale of $1/4" = 1$ to prepare a basis from which to begin. This grid makes possible precise and accurate measurement and transfer to larger scale — perhaps one of the earliest designing aids used by artists.

In our society, we are constantly bombarded with countless examples of design/graphics in the products we use and even more in the packaging of them. Consider the label of the Coca Cola bottle. The new Coca Cola logo has flowing lines, evoking feelings of smoothness, wetness, ocean movement, soothing motion. Practice drawing the Coca Cola logo on graph paper. Transfer the design. Make new designs which have similar feelings.

Block out several small squares as illustrated. Create simple flowing designs within each square. It is helpful when studying design to practice in this manner. Use many pages — perhaps even entire graph paper books — of design

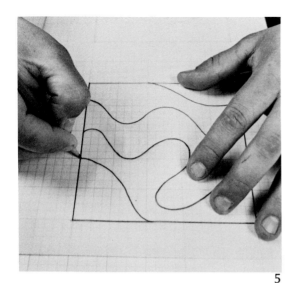

5

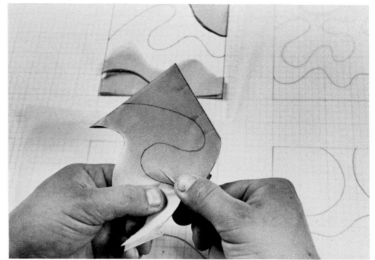

6

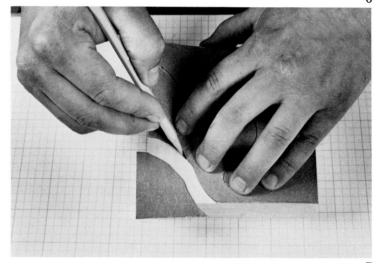

7

after different design. Go back over each design block and decide which ones are preferred over the others. Outline these in dark ink so that they stand out on the page.

Once a particular design catches your eye, blow it up to a larger scale. Draw a square four times as large and transfer the line drawing. Use a ruler to measure distances and plot the points of rises and falls in the lines as in a graph. Once the critical points have been established, connect the points with flowing lines. Go back and compare the blow-up with the original. Make any changes that are necessary within the new blow-up. Perhaps the curve might be improved, shortened or lengthened. Study, investigate, experiment, decide.

Select the design for the puzzle carving. Place a light piece of cardboard with carbon paper on top, under the drawing. Carefully trace over the drawing without deviating, accurately transferring the image onto the cardboard. Carefully cut along the lines with scissors, cutting out the jig saw shapes as illustrated, making a template for use in transferring the design.

Obtain or prepare a blank piece of stock (see section on "Preparing the Board") the same size as the design square or template. Place the template by lining it up on the square. Piece by piece, outline and remove, until the puzzle is transferred to the block. Use a try square to make perpendicular lines on the block sides to aid in sawing.

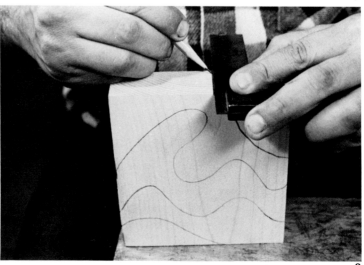

8

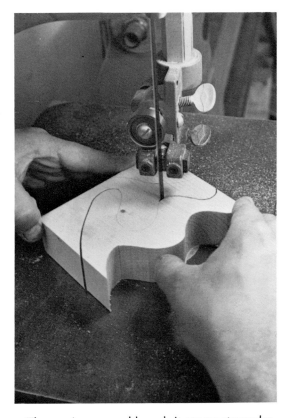

Using the Coping Saw

Now the block may be cut with the coping saw. The coping saw is a hand woodworking tool designed for cutting curves. The frame and blade together form a square "hoop" with the very thin fine-toothed blade as one of its sides. The frame is made of a tempered spring steel which of itself keeps pressure on the blade. The handle is threaded to adjust the tension. The blade may be adjusted at angles to the frame for greater diversity and control when sawing. Since the blade is so fine, a minimum saw kerf results in almost unrestricted circular cutting. The blade may be installed in either a push or pull position.

The coping saw, although it seems strong because of its versatile cutting capabilities, is indeed a delicate instrument requiring proper care and use. The tension on the blade must always be tight (achieved by adjusting the tension bolt and tightening the handle which locks the adjustment). The sawing must be done with steady, even, controlled movements. Jerky yanking will quickly kink the delicate blade.

When learning to use the coping saw, begin by making practice cuts through a thin piece of wood, first just cutting, then following a line. The saw cuts only in the direction in which the teeth face, so pressure is applied only on that stroke of the blade, easing up while returning for the next pressure stroke. It may seem awkward at first, but a little practice will quickly achieve facility. As the saw begins to follow the line, and the frame gets in an awkward position, loosen the handle of the saw very slightly and rotate the frame to a position out of the way of the cut.

Practice cutting thicker boards. First saw in a vertical plane, then practice sawing in a horizontal plane. Be careful to saw in perpendicular lines, developing good sawing habits.

As in all hand sawing, the very first cut sets the direction and attitude of the rest to follow. Begin deliberately setting the course, and advance with careful controlled strokes.

When sawing the puzzle, it is wise to hold the block in a vise or clamp to free both hands for sawing and to insure proper stability. Carefully cut along the center of the line following the curves, liberating each shape one by one.

This cutting process may be completed with the band saw for those accomplished in its use. See "Rough Cutting with the Band Saw" in the "Designing and Carving a Spoon" section.

Carving the Puzzle Pieces

After the block is cut apart, reassemble it and tape it together using masking tape. Then, clamp it in the bench vise, or similar holding tool, and use a small gouge to begin chiseling the edges of each puzzle piece from the center out toward the cut-line making small consecutive cuts. Experiment with different chisels, different gouges and gouge sizes. Always seek some sort of brace with the hand that holds the chisel by resting the hand on the work surface or bench. Hold the arms in and against the body at the elbows, using mostly wrist action while gouging. Bracing is extremely important in achieving a good, clean, well controlled cut. As each cut is completed, the chips will fold back. Be careful to go with or diagonal to the grain, minimizing tearing.

Continue shaping and working each piece, clearing the chips until a relief surface has been formed. Use the cut lines as a guide, letting each cut line be at the bottom-most part or "valley." There are infinite possibilities within the carving process, but in the beginning, make the block simple, with bold, flowing peaks and valleys. Think of the local landscape, perhaps the undulating forms of a snowscape.

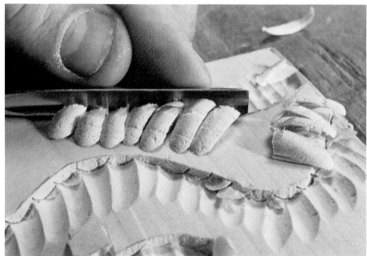

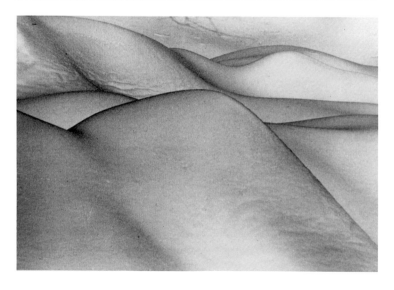

Rasping and Filing the Puzzle

Once the chiseling is completed, use a riffler or rasp as illustrated to merge the gouge cuts together. Continue forming the "landscape" as well. After the block top surface is shaped as desired, take off the tape and begin filing the edges of each piece. Wrap your hand around the part, and clamp or push down on the bench surface, while filing and shaping. Work the entire piece around, being sensitive to each curve, without disturbing the original cut lines. The puzzle must go back together again, after all.

Sanding the Puzzle

The purpose of sanding is two-fold: to shape and to smooth. Rough-sanding for shaping finalizes the form. Subtle, yet significant shifts in the flow of the form may be made by sanding while at the same time smoothing the surface before final sanding. (The rough sanding phase may be eliminated, if desired, by very careful use of the sharp cutting tool in the initial shaping of a piece.)

Sanding produces the degree of visual and tactile smoothness desired on the piece and prepares the wood for its protective finish. The final sanding phase is literally the first phase of the finishing process, for a finish is only as good as the final sanding of the wood.

Sandpaper is composed of multitudinous sharp, hard objects: grit. The movement back and forth of the grit against the wood, the softer surface, cuts the wood and gradually smooths the uneven top. The lower the grit number, the larger the individual abrasive particles and the coarser the cut. Sandpaper is always used in succession from low grit numbers to higher numbers in jumps of 40 to 80 or so. Each successive grit produces finer sanding lines while still being coarse enough to remove the sanding lines from the previous grit. The final sanding with 320 or 400 should leave no visible sanding lines. Skipping the intermediate grits will result in sanding lines from the coarse grit being left in the wood.

Once the final shaping of each piece of the puzzle has been accomplished, sand each piece beginning with 150, or if the surface is very rough, 80 or 100. Use silicon carbide paper because of its special cutting, non-clogging action, or cloth-back aluminum oxide paper, but

don't use stiff or brittle back paper. To sand the puzzle bottom, glue a sheet of sandpaper to a flat surface (I use a piece of particle board which I lean up in the corner when not in use). Slide the puzzle back and forth over the paper until the bottom is flat, even and well sanded. I use three grits: 150, 220, 320.

When the final sanding to 320 grit (or even 400) is finished, put the puzzle back together. Study the changes which have occurred from the original, and from the translation to three dimensions. Hold a light (preferably a clamp light or a spot light) to one side, and create dramatic shadows. Each piece of the puzzle sculpture can be seen individually, or it may be viewed as part of the whole. Study the pieces, study the whole, study the spaces left when you take one part away. This created void is called negative space.

One piece in its own space displaces that space, forming lines and shapes around itself. These spaces formed by the central mass are equally as important as the wood piece itself. The object we create cuts the space, like a sound breaking silence. An object may have a momentous effect if it "does or says something" in creating this new space. With each object, a statement is made.

Does the piece or, perhaps more importantly,

Above right: *Carving and shaping a common cut-out wood puzzle produces stunning effects, such as the play of light on the surface, and helps in the understanding of mass and shadows.*

Above: North Wind, *relief carving by folk artist Mary Shelley.*
Opposite: *Jean Arp,* Two Heads, *1929. Painted wood relief, 47¼" x 39¼" (120 cm x 100 cm). Collection, The Museum of Modern Art, New York. Purchase.*

the experience of what the piece does to the space say something? I believe the simplest, purest forms say the most.

Consider this. The space around us exists like silence at night. For the most part, we are unaware of the space, or lack of noise. When we place an object or sound within the space, we suddenly become aware of it in a different way. Think of not only what goes on within the piece being made but also what goes on outside of and because of the piece.

The principles learned in the carving of this puzzle may be used in countless other projects or works, from traditional relief carving to abstract sculpture.

Above: *Dan Dustin, Bowl of Spoon, 1985. Mountain laurel root burl, 8" (20 cm). Collection, Lancelot Braithwaite III.*
Left: *Melvin Lindquist, spoons of cherry burl, 1973.*

DESIGNING AND CARVING A SPOON

The spoon is an age-old utensil, one of the first implements invented by man. It combines two elements: the bowl whose form echoes the cupped hands or natural concave shape of a shell and the handle whose natural precursor is a stick or poke. These two elements combined produce unique utility and make the spoon an intriguing sculptural study. Variations in the form of each element and their inter-relationship allow widely varying design possibilities within the basic requirements of the piece.

Traditionally, spoons have been made out of naturally occurring wood formations that already have the basic spoon shape. A spoon may be split out of a branch or flitch of a log. Early spoonmakers usually split their wood out of twisted branches and did minimal carving on the bowl and handle. The use of a solid uniform block of wood in this exercise provides the beginning student with the opportunity to learn and practice several valuable techniques of sculpture and workmanship including template making, cutting techniques and the use of simple clamping devices.

Designing the Spoon

In this exercise, we start with a piece of dimension lumber, preferably pine, basswood, butternut or mahogany cut to the specific dimensions of 1³/₄″ x 1³/₄″ x 10″. I like to use this block as a template to lay out practice rectangles on a sheet of graph paper. Make several drawings of spoons within the rectangles. Choose one of these designs. On a large piece of drawing paper, trace three rectangles from the spoon blank: two signifying the top view and side view of the spoon, and the third one to become a three-dimensional drawing of the block and the spoon within. Draw in the top view and side view of the spoon, and draw the side and top view of the spoon on the three-dimensional rectangular block drawing. This will help you to visualize the spoon within the block of wood. You can make a three-dimensional rendering of the spoon to help to get a feeling of the shape of the object. Next, using children's modelling clay, make a model of the spoon.

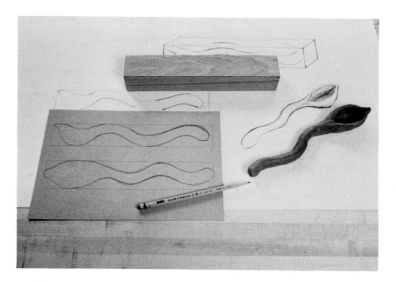

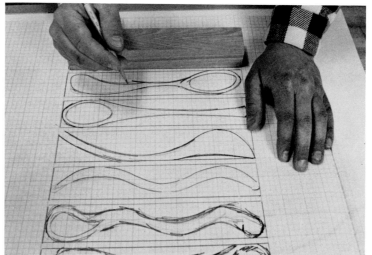

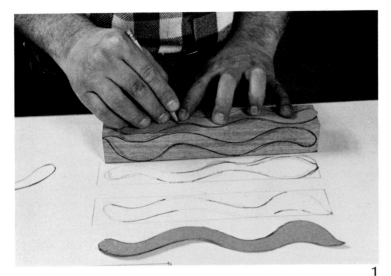

1

3

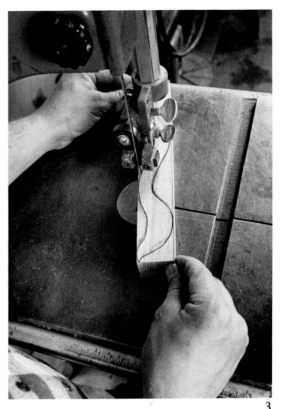

2

Template-Making and Transferring

A template is an accurate pattern of a form used in transferring a design or shape to another surface.

Draw two rectangular blocks on a piece of thin cardboard. Redraw the spoon top and side views. With a pair of scissors, cut out the cardboard forms which are the templates. Place the side and top view templates on the block one at a time and transfer the spoon onto the block.

Rough-cutting with the Band Saw

The band saw may be used to take the work out of cutting. It requires skill and practice. If not yet proficient with the band saw, the student should use the coping saw for this step. See instruction on coping saw use in the "3-D Puzzle from Block" section.

Caution: It is important to be proficient in band saw use before attempting this kind of cutting on your own. See the section on general safety rules for power tool use in Chapter 5.

Set the band saw to 1/2" above the height of the spoon blank. This is low enough to provide for good control, yet high enough to allow the pencil lines to be clearly seen. Cut the side view

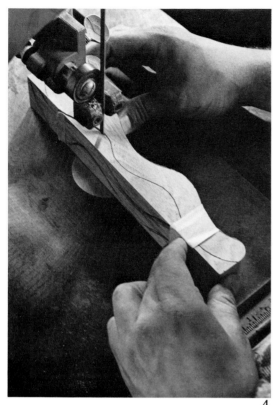

5

4

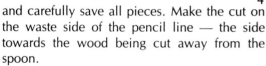

6

and carefully save all pieces. Make the cut on the waste side of the pencil line — the side towards the wood being cut away from the spoon.

The end cut is made by turning the block and sawing around the curve as far as possible. Turn the saw off and back the wood out of the blade. Then saw in the opposite direction to complete the cut.

Once the side view spoon form has been cut from the block, reassemble the block, putting all pieces in their original positions, and tape the block back together with masking tape. Then cut the block from the top view, liberating the spoon form from within.

Marking and Carving the Bowl of the Spoon; Shaping the Handle

The shape of the inner bowl of the spoon is pencilled in on the spoon blank. Refer back to the drawings and the clay model. Clamp the spoon in the vise while doing the bowl, but be very careful not to put too much pressure on the spoon or it will crack. Begin by using a small gouge and make several plunge cuts into the bowl with the chisel, cutting with the grain

1

3

4

2

rather than against it, causing the chips to lift up and out of the bowl. Clean up and round out the interior of the bowl with a small spoon gouge.

Do the back of the spoon bowl with a straight flat chisel using a paring motion. The stem or shaft of the spoon is formed with a Surform or other rasp. The spoon is held in the vise with the outer waste piece acting as a clamping device. The rest of the spoon handle may be shaped with rasps or by using a drum sander attached to the drill press.

Sanding the Spoon
Begin sanding the shaft of the spoon using a cloth-backed aluminum oxide paper. Tear the paper into long strips 1/2" to 3/4" wide. By wrapping the strip around the shaft and sanding in the

5

6

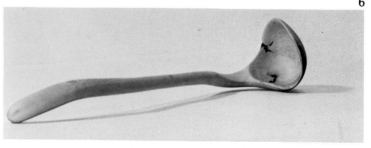

same manner as buffing shoes with a rag, the final forming and smoothing may be achieved.

Sanding the bowl exterior of the spoon is done by holding the spoon in the hand while shaping and smoothing with sandpaper held in the other hand. The interior sanding of the bowl is the most difficult, and it is done by working the sandpaper into the form with the thumb or a small dowel, achieving a uniformity.

With each of these processes, the sanding begins with a coarse grit, usually 80 to 100, changing grades to 150, 200, 320, and in cases of dense non-porous wood, 400 grit. Each successive grit removes the sanding scratches from the previous grit until no scratches are visible.

Wood responds to firm but gentle coaxing. Rough forcing results in bruised wood. Sand gently, let the grit do the work, work with patience, develop a rhythm in your work, and you will achieve the results you desire.

Above right: *Dan Dustin,* Mountain Laurel Ladle, *1980. Root with bark inclusions, 12" (30 cm) long. Collection, Norman Stevens.*
Right: *Dan Dustin,* Personal Eating Spoon, *1984. Mountain laurel with burl, 7" (18 cm) long.*

CARVING A SMALL BOWL BY HAND

The bowl is one of the simplest of all forms, yet one of the most difficult to carve because of the strict symmetry which demands control and discipline. Within the bowl lie nearly all sculptural carving principles. The simple bowl has three parts: a body or outside (exterior form), the bowl hollow or inside (interior form), and the rim, lip or top edge. The three distinct aspects and their interplay provide for infinite variation.

To begin, prepare a pine or other softwood block (see section on "Preparing the Board") 6" x 6" x 2" thick. Be sure the edges are square and that the block is of clear wood (straight, consistent grain with no knotholes or defects). Find center, then glue and clamp a waste block to the bottom center of the block.

The waste block is attached merely for the convenience of easily holding the carving in a vise. This is a common sculptural practice, although many sculptors use a "sculptor's screw" — a long screw which penetrates the carving bench and up into the carving block. The point is to be able to work freely with both hands and the screw or waste block makes this possible. The use of the waste block is preferred for pieces in which you don't want a hole — such as a bowl. The screw works well for sculpture which will be mounted afterwards.

The center of the block is found by drawing

*Carving a Bowl
by Hand*

1

2

3

4

5

6

diagonal intersecting lines from corner to corner. Using a compass with a pencil point, scribe a circle on the top of the block just shy of the maximum diameter the block will allow. Next make another circle $1/2''$ in from the first circle. These circles represent the wall thickness of the bowl. The lines are useful in defining limits.

Once the two main circles have been drawn, begin carving down into the bowl with a small gouge, making a petal-like design. Starting with the first cut, work in one direction either clockwise or counterclockwise. If the wood is soft enough, hand-push the chisel. If it is too hard, or the carving begins to hurt the palm, strike the chisel with the mallet in short decisive blows.

Be careful not to go too deep into the center. It may be prudent to drill a $1/4''$ hole to within $1/2''$ of the bottom of the bowl to act as a depth gauge.

Each pass of chiseling or gouging around the bowl will widen the diameter. Attempt to carve in a manner that does not rip or tear the wood. If the wood is ripping or tearing excessively, check the sharpness of the chisel. It may need sharpening again. Use the chisel as a lever to lift

out the chips. Push or strike the gouge into the wood while prying at the same time. Keep the cuts radiating out from the center. Make final "sweep" cuts from rim to bottom center of bowl. Use a wider chisel, perhaps a spoon gouge, to make smooth finish cuts.

The carving of the interior before removing the excess wood on the exterior is purposeful. The bulk of the wood in block form has greater stability and makes the carving of the interior easier. Likewise the block can be clamped in the bench vise, rather than using just the waste block which is designed more for finishing work.

To carve the exterior, turn the block upside down on a piece of scrap plywood and mark the shape. Find the center of the square and make a circle representing the outside diameter of the bowl with a compass. Make concentric rings around the waste block on the back side which will act as a guide for carving. Reposition the block properly over the square on the scrap plywood, and clamp to the bench. Gradually begin chiseling off the corners, being careful not to split the grain, then begin shaping and rounding

the bowl exterior. The exterior may also be rough shaped by sawing with a coping saw or band saw.

After the rough exterior conical shape has been achieved, chisels may be used to shape the bowl to its final form. Then the exterior may be rasped and sanded for a smooth finish, or the gouge cuts may be left for a textured finish.

If you choose to leave the gouge cuts as a finish, whether they are "chip marks" or long even cuts, lightly sand with 320 or 400 grit to smooth out and finish. This finish sanding breaks over the edges of the cuts, blending and softening, providing a more desirable visual and tactile surface.

Now that the exterior form and shape are complete, clamp the bowl in the vise by the waste block as pictured and finish the interior. Use calipers to check wall consistency. Open the calipers to the widest or thickest part of the bowl, then gradually bring the entire inner surface to the desired thickness. Use rifflers to shape the interior concave after chiseling. Then sand, beginning with 60 grit, and continue by following this progression: 80, 100, 150, 200,

320 grit. Use a quarter of a sheet of sandpaper at a time, backing it up with a foam rubber pad to aid in sanding as well as to protect the hand.

Once the interior and exterior surfaces are finished, you may deal with the rim. The rim is perhaps the most important aspect of the bowl, for it either separates the inside from the outside, becoming an entity unto itself, or it may tie the two together by providing a smooth, subtle transition.

If you want the rim to be noticed, invert the bowl and flat sand it on the sandpaper board (see "3-D Puzzle from a Block" section). Relieve the rim of all gouge marks and nicks until it is smooth.

Study the bowl in this stage. Bring it into the space where you live and look at it before going any farther. Begin to make decisions based on your observations. Do you like its shape? Do you like the rim? Should it be changed? What would you change?

Take as long as you need — five minutes, a day, a week — to decide what direction in which you wish to proceed. Finalize and resolve those decisions by doing. Round over the lip

with light sanding, or use a rasp to work the edges, followed by sanding.

After all of the sanding is finished, place the bowl upside down, on a blanket to avoid damaging it. Using a flat chisel placed end-grain to the waste block, strike the chisel with a mallet, breaking loose the waste block. If the block does not come free at first, change the chisel to the other end, making sure it is end-grain. Gradually, alternating ends, the block will come loose. Chisel off excess splinters and glue, keeping the original flat bottom surface intact, parallel with the bowl lip.

Sand the bottom by moving back and forth along the sanding board until the bottom is finished. Be very careful to keep the bottom sanded parallel to the top, or it will tip the bowl, throwing it to one side or another. You may wish to round over the edges of the bottom to achieve a more pleasing appearance. The bowl may be left natural, or finished as discussed in the chapter on finishing.

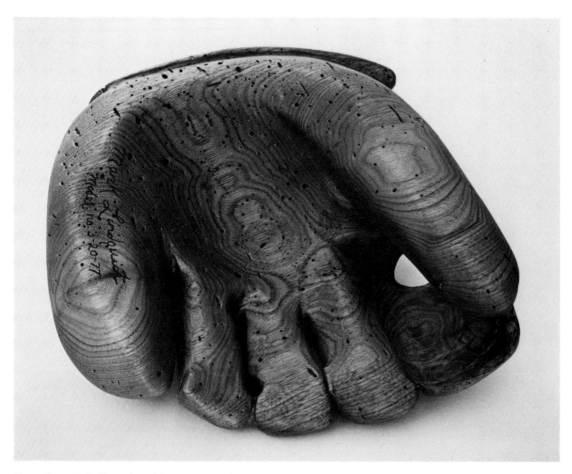

Opposite: *Michelle Holzapful,* Knitting Basket #1, *1985. Elm burl, spalted maple, walnut, ebony, 18" x 16" x 18" (46 cm x 41 cm x 46 cm). Collection, Janine Linden. Michelle Holzapful creates a trompe l'oeil piece using turning and carving techniques.*
Above: *Author,* Pro-Model Mitt, *1977. Butternut, life-size.*
Right: *Albert Lindquist,* The Harpist, *late 1920s. Basswood, 12" (30 cm) high. Using the techniques described in this chapter, an infinite variety of forms may be achieved. The same basic techniques used by the author to sculpt the Pro-Model Mitt were used by Albert Lindquist (author's great uncle) to carve* The Harpist.

CHAPTER 8 Using the Band Saw to Create Sculpture

CREATING SAWN FORMS — CARVING WITH THE BAND SAW

The band saw is an extremely versatile tool. Its typical uses are seen in the areas of cutting flat work such as circles for turning blanks, curved parts for furniture or simply as a convenient "rough saw" for sizing lumber. The most unique feature of the band saw is the thin blade which makes a very narrow cut allowing for the shaping of wood unlike any other tool.

The band saw may be used, in addition to its traditional uses, to carve and texture wood in creating sculpture. Because of the nature of the tool and the process, a different feeling is achieved due both to the spontaneity with which the cut may be made and the continuous nature of the cut. Unlike carving with chisels or the die grinder, where small portions are removed from the mass one by one, whole sections of material, perhaps important in themselves, are removed rather than destroyed by carving.

The possibilities for curvilinear statements are endless. The cut itself becomes a statement, exposing rhythmic compound curves and angles. This process, however, poses a new problem. The cut must be carefully preplanned and studied because each cut represents a major commitment. Spontaneous cutting demands that the sculptor know the tool and the results that it will yield well enough to anticipate the ever-changing combinations of effects. Band saw carving allows for a serendipitous development of the

Opposite: *Hugh Townley, Mirror at Ollantaitambo, 1980. Mahogany cut with band saw, 49" x 51" (124 cm x 130 cm). Courtesy the artist.*

1

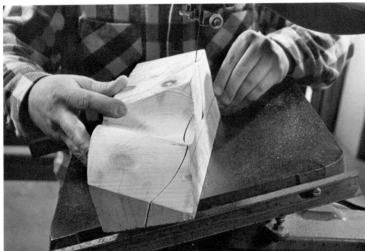

2

3

4

sculpture, since holding the sawn pieces together and passing the saw through them often yields unusual and unexpected forms.

In the following exercise — creating a free-form sculpture with the band saw — a simple block (a pine 4″ x 4″ x 10″) is used as a practice piece. Waste wood should be used to practice with as the initial results with the band saw are unpredictable until familiarity is acquired.

Caution: Observe all power tool safety rules. (See Basic Shop Safety Rules at start of Chapter 5.) Learn proper technique from an instructor before attempting this kind of cutting on your own. It is important when making curvilinear cuts to use a 1/4″ skip tooth blade. Very sharp curves may be achieved, but be careful not to push or twist the blade too much or it will become damaged or kinked.

Should the blade become kinked or wedged, do not try to pull the piece out of the blade, as that action will pull the band off the wheels. Turn the saw off, unplug it, and then carefully pull the piece out. If the blade is pinched, sometimes it helps to take off the saw guards and rotate the wheels counterclockwise while holding the piece (this reverses the direction of the movement of the blade.) If it is still pinched, insert a screwdriver, old chisel or wedge at the beginning of the saw cut to relieve the pressure on the blade.

If the blade has a kink after you take the wood out, start over with a new blade since a kinked blade can be very dangerous.

Begin by making an initial curved cut in the

block, and then turn the block and make another cut. After initial cuts are made, the piece may be turned and areas shaved off by passing the wood through the saw in a serpentine pattern of movement. The blade may be used to texture the wood by making slight, consecutive cuts. It is interesting to experiment with the possibilities of form achieved by the curvilinear patterns of compound cuts, textures created by the kerf of a cut and/or the purposeful decoration of the piece by making close cuts with the band saw. After having achieved the final form by successive passes on the band saw, the form may be worked additionally by hand-sanding lightly, and the saw cuts may be cleaned up, using a Merit Abrasives flap wheel.

The sawn form may be displayed as a free form sculpture or remounted in the original block from which it was cut. Wood sculptor Hugh Townley creates numerous sculptures and wall hangings using the band saw carving technique.

Top left: *Hugh Townley,* The Shout, *1965. Various woods assembled with dowels and glue, 31" x 41" x 13" (79 cm x 104 cm x 33 cm). Courtesy the artist.*
Top right: *Giles Gilson,* Colored Water, *1977. Mobile, laminated wood, 30" x 46" (76 x 117 cm). Collection, Gary Baher.*

THE BAND SAW BOX

The band saw box described in this chapter (variations on which I have been making for several years) is a sculptural container formed from a solid block of wood. It is cut apart, and the pieces are rejoined in their original relationships after the removal of the core which occupies the containing space of the box. The basic concept is adapted from experiments done by my father during the sixties. Art Carpenter has been making band saw boxes since the 1950s, and has influenced many current box makers.

I've arrived at this method based upon a machinist's or patternmaker's technique of building a jig or "block." The "Cloud Box" form is very rounded containing complicated curves which, as all woodworkers know, create many difficulties in clamping while gluing. Rather than using specially made jigs or clamping devices which would conform to the curve, I've developed this system. A minimal amount of precise cutting defines the outer form and inner parts of the box and the waste material becomes a ready-made clamping device. Therefore, in this system, it is essential to use the utmost accuracy in measuring, laying out, transferring, marking, cutting, sanding and assembling to achieve perfect results.

The band saw box method is a sophisticated technical process of joinery requiring machine-like precision work similar to that of the patternmaker while achieving a seemingly natural, flowing, organic form. These steps involve a wide variety of techniques, skills and tools, all of which have numerous applications in wood sculpture. Each unfolding step in the series influences the next and often inspires new ideas for sculpture and the development of ever more sophisticated techniques. The band saw box exercise serves to introduce the sculptor to the intricacies of craftsmanship and invites the craftsman to discover the endless possibilities of form.

Opposite: Cloud Box, 1978. Stacked laminated walnut, bird's-eye maple, birch veneer, walnut veneer.

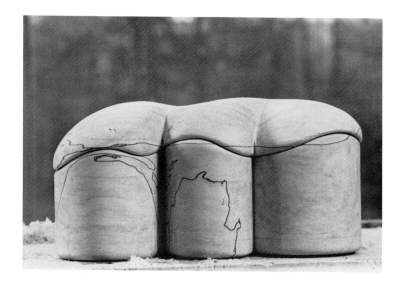

Selecting the Wood for the Band Saw Box

A band saw box may be made from a variety of woods. The block may be cut from a log with the band saw, cut out directly with the chainsaw or built up by laminating several layers of wood (see previous section on Stacked Lamination). Since the construction of the box is relatively pure in concept, I prefer to make the box out of a solid block, preferably of spalted wood (see section on Harvesting Spalted Wood). Spalted wood lends itself well to the band saw box because it is relatively easy to work and produces spectacular results, particularly when the zone lines and grain patterns match up through a proper cutting apart and reassembling of the box. The lines are almost always predominant over the glue joints and act as a camouflage. However, a block of adequate size of any kind of wood may be used as long as the wood has been properly dried to prevent cracking. Be sure not to exceed the maximum opening height of the band saw in the height or depth of the block.

In the box illustrated in the step-by-step sequence that follows, I have used a block of spalted wood approximately $6^{1}/_{2}$" x $6^{1}/_{2}$" x 14", cut with a chain saw from a sugar maple log. Before cutting a block of spalted wood, it's important to evaluate the markings of zone lines in order to determine where they will be located in the finished piece. The proper cut will unfold wonderful zone line patterns; the wrong cut may simply exclude any patterns at all.

The block is sized and squared as illustrated in the section on "Preparing the Board." Then

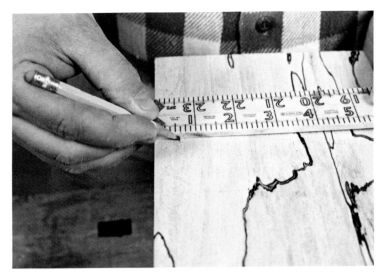

determine the top and bottom of the box. It's important to look the block over very carefully for any checks or potential cracks. With the "Cloud Box" design, often cracks or checks or defects in the wood can be cut out simply by designing around them. I try to position the best markings toward the front or face of the box with the focal point (the most interesting patterns) on the top or lid of the box. Once this orientation is established, the construction of the box follows a very orderly and precise sequence of steps.

The Making of a Band Saw Box
● Step 1. Layout and Marking

Make two lines on the block indicating the cuts for the box bottom and the box top. I use a system for marking used by many furniture-makers and patternmakers which is using the fingers and the pencil to form a "human compass" or divider. Positioning the pencil at an exact point determined by the ruler, a straight line of fair accuracy may be achieved by tensing the muscles of the hand (thereby assuring a consistent measurement) and sliding the whole hand along the surface of the board that is parallel to the line which is being scribed (essentially transferred).

This technique enables a relatively quick and accurate line rendering or marking and is of course infinitely adjustable.

Next make a curved line which indicates the cut for the box top. In creating a "Cloud Box," I base the line on a natural form echoing that of a gentle mountainous landscape or cloudlike formation. The ups and downs of the line are essential to the functioning of the box as they help to seat the lid to the box, creating a "cushion" for the lid. The line is drawn in free-form or may be transferred from a template (see sections on designing and template-making in "Designing and Carving a Spoon").

● Step 2. Cutting the Top and Bottom

Caution: It is very important to be fully competent in the use of the band saw and to use proper hand positioning when making cuts. (See Basic Shop Safety Rules at start of Chapter 5.) Avoid any unnecessary risk, taking care to reposition hands at every convenience out of the blade's path. To achieve accurate results the band saw must be in proper "tune." Each cut must be started and completed without stopping.

Now, cut the box bottom on the band saw (which of course is very carefully and accurately squared prior to cutting, using a new or very sharp blade — 1/4" skip tooth). The maximum opening height of my band saw guide is 6 1/2", so I have been very careful to not exceed that dimension in sizing the block. It's important to make a consistent and careful cut (I do it freehand) and sometimes a rip-fence is advisable in this step to insure accuracy.

The bottom wall thickness is a strong 1/2". This first cut is made well to the waste side of the line. (The waste side refers to the wood which will not be used. Since a saw kerf, the thickness of the cut, is normally wider than the line, we refer to the line as having two sides, the good side and the waste side. Cuts are generally made on the waste side, leaving a trace of the line on the wood that is intended for use.) The waste side, in this case, refers to the area above the box bottom. Cut accurately to leave a very clear line on the box bottom. This line will serve as a guide to sand to.

Next, cut the top, following the line carefully, as accurately as the saw will allow, now attempting to split the line rather than cutting on one side of it. This cut is extremely critical since it forms the union of the top and the bottom. It must be a continuous and smooth uninterrupted cut. It is better to deviate from the line, in this case, than to stop and correct, leaving a gap. When sawing the curves, the block must be rotated dramatically to accommodate the arcs of the cut. Because it is the nature of the tool, the band has a tendency to twist and sort of snap back when you change directions for a new cut. There is, however, a limit to how far you can push the blade. Push too far in a twist and the blade will simply overheat and break at the weld.

• Step 3. Sanding the Box Bottom

Now that the bottom has been removed from the central bulk or mass (which will be the body of the box), it is sanded. There are several methods of sanding, and it is important to use the method which is most accurate and safest given the level of expertise and skill of the worker. Since the side which is being sanded will be the finished inside bottom of the box it must be finish-sanded to 320 grit. This surface may be hand-planed or hand-sanded. For ease of sand-

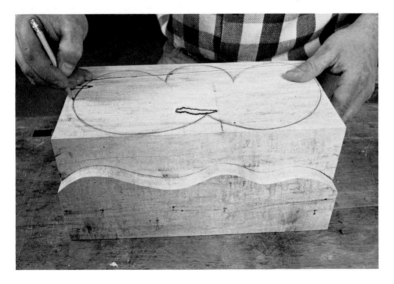

ing and expediency, I use a combination disc and belt sander. This method requires utmost skill, confidence and experience and should not be used by beginners.

I do the rough sanding on the disc, being very careful to keep my fingers out of the way, and intermediate sanding on the belt, also being very careful to keep hands and fingers out of the way. There's a sort of clamping pressure that I've developed in my fingers and fingertips which grasps, manipulates and controls the wood. But it requires always complete attentiveness and caution and utmost control.

The same steps are repeated for the body mass, although it is not necessary to finish-sand, since it will be lap-sanded next. Lap sanding is used to "true" the bottom of the body. Using a spray disc adhesive, successive grits (150 and 220) are applied to a flat surface and the box is stroked back and forth over the sandpaper. This assures a uniformly flat surface.

The underside of the box lid and the top of the box body are rough-sanded. I use an oscillating spindle sander. An alternative to the drum sander is the foam pad dowel. Refrigerator insulating tubing, which is 1/2" thick foam rubber, is slipped over a dowel slightly larger than the inside diameter of the tubing, and different grits of sandpaper are wrapped around and taped. Final finishing of these surfaces is not done at this stage.

● Step 4. Designing and Template Making

The bottom, the body, and the top of the box are now stacked to reform the original block. The actual shape of the exterior form (from a top view) is determined and finalized, again based upon the markings and grain patterns and, of course, a pre-conceived notion of the form.

It is important, at this stage, to be aware of checks, potential cracks, irregularities and faults which the box form is designed to avoid. If the wood is perfect from the start, the box form may be designed on paper and simply applied to the wood. Designing directly off the wood surface, utilizing the visible information, offers distinct advantages, however, over "blind" interpretation.

When the form has been finalized and penciled in on the top of the box top, it may be transmitted to template form using tracing paper overlay. The wall thickness is penciled in on the

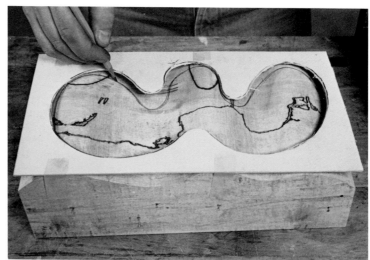

paper, allowing for a minimum of ¹/₂". The tracing paper is then laid over and taped to light cardboard, and the inner wall line is cut out leaving a negative template.

Now removing the lid of the box, the template is accurately taped to the top of the box body, and the inner line which represents the inside of the inner wall of the box interior is transferred from the template.

● **Step 5. Cutting Out the Center**

The template is removed and a carpenter's framing square laid parallel to the right hand block surface is used to mark a line signifying the band saw entry point into the box interior.

Making sure that the band saw is accurately square, running properly and very sharp, the cut is initiated. The object of this cut is to remove the interior bulk of the block leaving a cavity which will ultimately serve as the containing space of the box. It is vital that the cut be an accurate continuous single loop without flaw. There are no second chances or opportunities to correct mistakes. It is important to stay as close as possible to or on the line; if anything, allow the blade to wander inwards toward the center of the box rather than toward the exterior. A complete manipulation of the block in back and forth movements requires careful control and frequent repositioning of the hands. The final cut should allow the blade to end up in the initial or original kerf, achieving a tapered "feathering." Once the blade is in its original kerf slot, it is essential to turn off the saw, waiting until the blade stops, and then carefully back

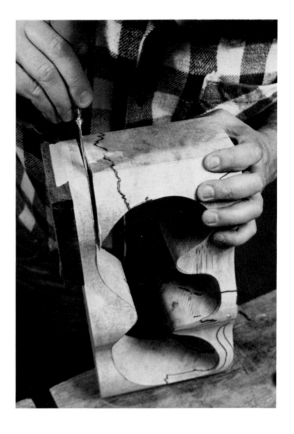

Above: Raining Cloud Box, 1979. Stacked laminated walnut, Plexiglas and spalted white birch, 6" x 10" x 11" (15 cm x 25 cm x 28 cm). Collection, Robert Sedestrom.

out of the wood through the original entry cut.

● **Step 6. Gluing**

The next step is to remove the inner cut portion of the box and to rejoin the box body by gluing it at the band saw entry point. Since the interior portion which was removed will be used in another step in the construction of the box and must be preserved, it it necessary to make a clamping jig for the interior of the box to insure a tight joint. The portion of the center core which was adjacent to the joint is used as a template to mark a glue block which will be cut for use as a clamping device.

It is important to prepare for all steps in clamping, doing a "dry run" prior to gluing. I attach a clamp pad or block, which is simply a wood block taped to the outer surface, to prevent damage from clamping pressure. Be sure to open clamps to proper size and clamp without glue to make sure it comes together properly. Feeling confident that you're prepared, apply the glue into the joint with an old kitchen knife, spreading it evenly on both surfaces. A glue block placed on a concave surface tends to "walk around." I place a piece of sandpaper

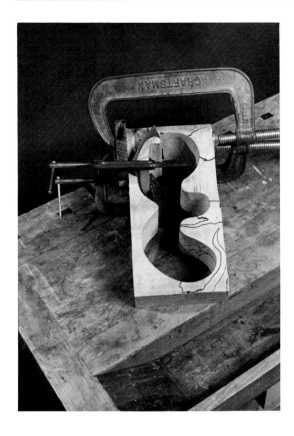

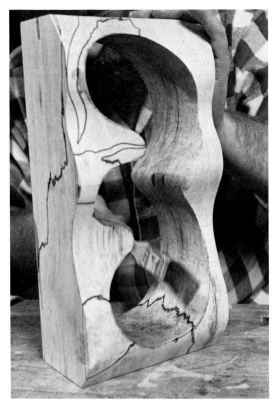

folded in half grit-side out between the box interior and the glue block to prevent slippage. It's important to apply adequate pressure, being very careful, however, to avoid cracking the box.

● Step 7. Finishing the Box Body Interior

Once the glue has dried (it is important to allow adequate drying time, approximately 4–5 hours with Titebond Glue), the clamps may be released, gradually easing off pressure in sequential order.

The interior of the box body is now sanded using the oscillating spindle sander or the foam pad dowel sanding method as described in Step 3 previously. Since there are many curves and very little space to get one's hand into, conventional hand sanding is very difficult. The dowel sanding method works very well, and is used for finish-sanding the interior. It is important to finish-sand thoroughly at this point when the box is open from both top and bottom because once the bottom is applied, there will be very limited access, and sanding will suddenly become very difficult.

After a thorough inspection, checking for sanding marks, apply a finish coat to the interior surface with straight polyurethane finish. This is brushed on thoroughly (particularly on the end-grain) and then wiped dry with a soft cotton rag such as an old T-shirt. The finish serves to seal the end-grain, to prevent checking and also to aid in the finishing of the interior and in the step which requires a glue resist when clamping the bottom of the box.

The beauty of reassembling the box in block form is that it is a self-jigging clamping device. The disadvantage in this one instance of clamping the box bottom is that the hollow space is no longer accessible and makes glue clean-up impossible.

● Step 8. Positioning and Preparing the Box Bottom

In a matter of a few minutes, the interior finish will have dried. Reposition the box bottom and tape it to the box with masking tape. Apply finish to the inside bottom of the box and allow to dry. Next, reposition the top and turn the box bottom side up. Using the template which was cut out in Step 4, scribe the line which represents the box interior. Then, freehand, sketch in

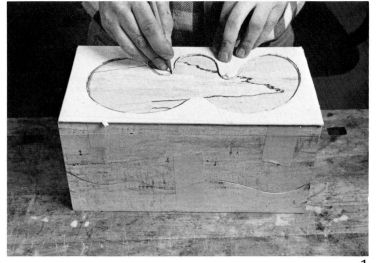

1

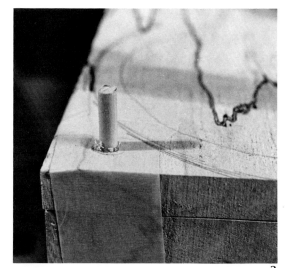

3

2

4

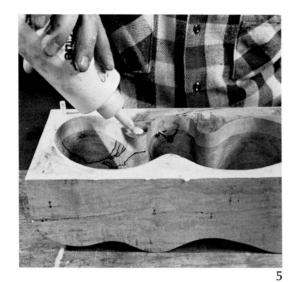

5

6

a new line indicating the box exterior. Using a ¹/₄″ drill in the drill press, set the depth for approximately ¹/₂″ penetration into the waste area (the four corners outside of the box proper) and drill four holes and peg home pre-sized ¹/₄″ dowels into each. The dowel end which penetrates the block should fit snugly but be loose enough to easily disassemble. Cut the tape and again remove the box bottom.

● **Step 9. Gluing and Glue Resist**

Potters use a technique called "wax resist." The areas of a pot that are intended to remain unglazed are waxed. During firing, the glaze that has been applied to the pot does not adhere to the waxed areas, and the wax burns off. Using this technique as a potter inspired me to apply it, in principle, to gluing in woodworking.

Tape the inside bottom edge of the interior of the box with ³/₄″ masking tape, being very careful to keep the edge of the tape flush with the bottom of the block. Apply a very slight amount of glue to the bottom of the block, enough so that the bottom will adequately glue, but not so much as will squeeze out into the box interior. Reposition the top and place the box bottom side up. Seat the bottom using the dowels to indicate the box bottom's precise position. Apply pressure and some rubber mallet persuasion to assure adequate seating. Now open the box and apply a fingertip amount of pastewax in the crack. Place the top back on the box and clamp the whole block back together with as many clamps as the area will allow.

7

8

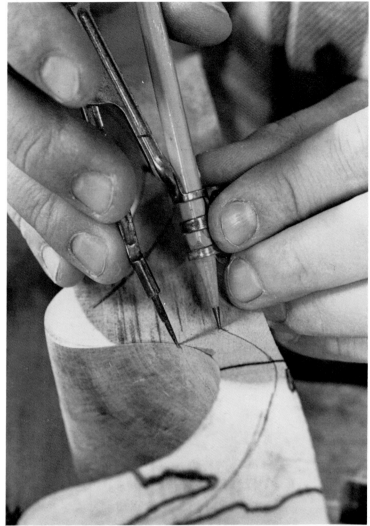

1

3

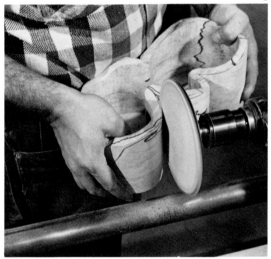

4

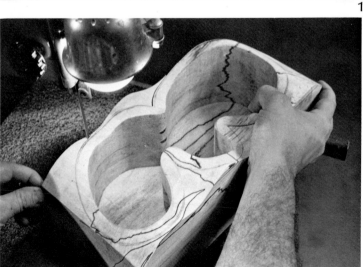

2

● Step 10. Cutting the Box Exterior

Once the clamps have been removed from the box, use a compass set at approximately ¹/₂″ to transfer a line parallel to the interior of the box to the top of the box body. It's vital to maintain a consistent and accurate line to establish a uniform wall thickness.

Next, cut out the extraneous wood, being careful to cut accurately on the waste side of the line. It is important when changing direction never to pull the piece out of the band saw in an attempt to back up or back out of a cut because this action will dislodge the blade from its track. Rather, turn off the saw, wait until the blade stops, and then pull the piece out and start a fresh cut. It's important when making a connecting cut to maintain complete control and accu-

5

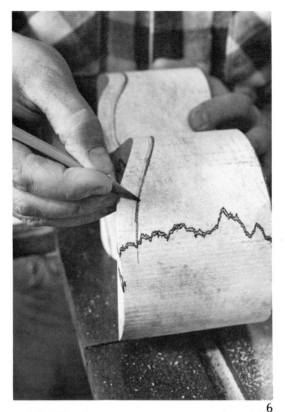

6

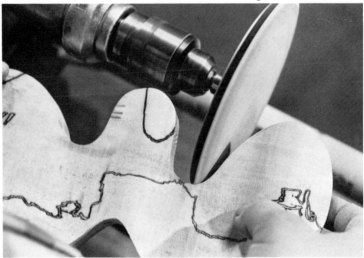

7

racy at the point of the cut.

● Step 11. Sanding the Box Body Exterior

Initial rough sanding of the box body exterior is done on the 12″ diameter disc sander. This is especially convenient because a table which is mounted at a right angle to the disc provides a steady rest for the box. Use a fairly heavy grit (50 grit) for disc sanding since a great deal of shaping is done in this process while also removing the band saw kerf marks. There are many areas of the box body which cannot be reached, but the rough sanding is greatly reduced using this method. After the rough sanding of the exterior walls by disc sander is done, I make a quick pass on the bottom of the box.

Foam Back Sanding I chuck the DA sanding pad (see the section on "Foam Back Sanding") in the drill press chuck of my Shopsmith (a drill press will do, or for that matter, a simple washing machine motor will, too) and rough-sand the areas that could not be reached with the large 12″ disc sander. I've found that with a little practice this is an extremely accurate and efficient method for getting into the contours. I go through the various grits: 80, 150, 220, 320, to finish-sand the box exterior. Hand sanding is an alternative to this method.

1

2

3

4

5

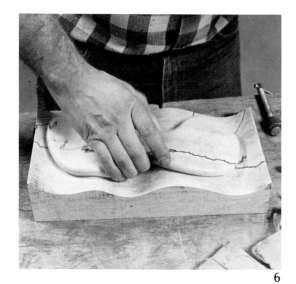

6

7

• Step 12. Cutting, Sanding and Attaching the Lid Positioner

The lid positioner of the box top is marked and cut from the top of the inner core (which was removed from the box body) using the "human compass" method. The band saw cut is made on the waste side of the line.

Use the same foam back system sanding disc to finish-sand the bottom and edges of the lid positioner. Break over all the edges of the lid positioner achieving a smooth, undulating form.

Next, reposition the lid positioner in place on the box lid which is upside down on a flat surface, and place the box body in position on top. Trace a line indicating the box exterior onto the box lid, and carefully remove the box body so as not to disturb the position of the lid positioner. Note how the spalt lines in the lid and the lid positioner in the photograph match up.

Holding the lid positioner to prevent it from moving, scribe with pencil where the positioner is, indicating the area to be sanded on the box lid (shown in chalk in the photograph). That area is then sanded with the foam back sanding method.

Next, the lid positioner is glued to the lid. Apply a very minimal amount of glue to prevent the glue from oozing out between the finished edges of the crevice. With the lid positioned bottom side up on the bench, place the lid positioner on the lid in the approximate area where it will seat when glued. This is easily recognized by the grain or spalt marks in the wood as well as by the natural positioning created by the un-

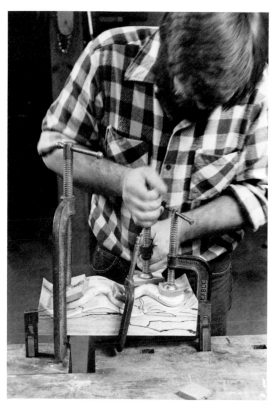

8

dulating band saw cut. Again place the band saw box body on the overturned lid and line up the grain and the spalted line patterns, and then carefully remove the box body from the lid. Then using homosote clamp pads and C-clamps, clamp the lid positioner to the lid.

• Step 13. Finish-sanding the Box Body

Being done for the most part with using the box as a form for positioning and marking, fin-

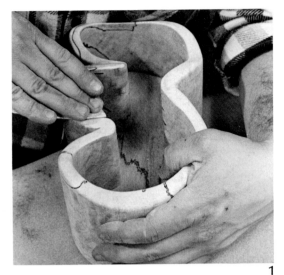

1

2

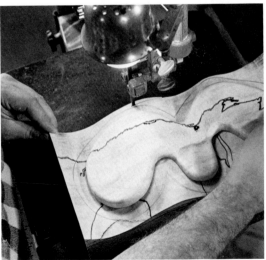

3

4

ish-sand the lip of the box body and the rest of the box body to 320 using the foam back method, and then finally, touch up by hand sanding.

● **Step 14. Cutting Out and Shaping the Top**

Once the lid positioner has been glued to the top of the box, the box top is placed bottom side up, and the box body is repositioned (upside down) on top for marking purposes. Mark the lid approximately a half a pencil width away from the box. The half pencil width is determined by marking with the pencil rather than the point against the box. This excess allows for a slight overhang.

Next cut out the box top leaving a liberal distance (approximately 1/8") on the waste side for sanding purposes. Tilt the angle of the saw table to approximately 45° and trim off excess wood following the basic contours of the lid. Now clamp the top in the bench vise and begin rough-shaping the top with a hand-held high speed die grinder. This shaping can also be done with chisels, files and rasps; however, I prefer the die grinder since it is the quickest and most direct method. I try to achieve a sense of flowing movement in the form of the top, a rhythm that puts the box top in harmony with the body.

Reposition the box lid on the box body several times checking the progress of the carving. Once you are satisfied with the form, use the foam back sanding process for finishing, and then do final finishing of the lip of the lid by hand.

5

6

Above: Spalted Maple Cloud Box, *1978. 6″ x 6″ x
12″ (15 cm x 15 cm x 30 cm).*

Band Saw Box with Drawers

The band saw joinery technique illustrated through the making of the "Cloud Box" can be applied in many different ways for furniture making and sculpture. For instance, the box may become a hollow form in the buildup of a sculpture, or the body of a large chest of drawers — the possibilities are unlimited. The band saw box is a puzzle, which may be kept simple or elaborated upon. A natural elaboration on the "Cloud Box" is the addition of drawers. The following sequence on the "Cloud Box with Drawers" will illustrate how the band saw technique may be modified.

Opposite: Cloud Box with Drawers. *Spalted maple with padauk drawer buttons, 6" x 6" x 12" (15 cm x 15 cm x 30 cm).*
Above: *Michael Graham, Side Design, 1977. 11" x 5" x 4" (28 cm x 13 cm x 10 cm). Courtesy the artist.*

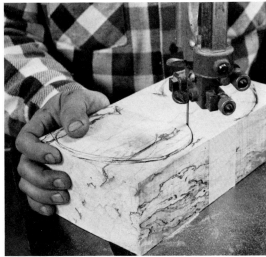

● Preparing the Block

The "Cloud Box with Drawers" is essentially two boxes, an upper box which is a short version of the "Cloud Box" previously illustrated, and a lower section which contains the drawers and also provides the bottom for the upper box. When the two are finally put together, the effect is that of one box with drawers, but the making is done in two sections.

Using the techniques described in Chapter 6, "Preparing Stock for Use", prepare a solid block 6" x 6" x 12" or two 3" x 6" x 12" laminated blocks. The block or blocks must be carefully surfaced and precisely square, as precision will be required in making all cuts for the box.

● Marking the Box

In the previous section on making the "Cloud Box," I illustrated the use of the template system for determining the form and division. That method is recommended for creating the box with drawers also. Throughout this sequence, however, I will create the design directly on the block to show how that is done. This method takes less time, but the results are more uncertain for the inexperienced woodworker.

Mark a curved, flowing line for the lid around the top of the single block or the laminated block which you have designated for the upper box. If you are working with one solid block, mark a straight line around the block to divide it lengthwise into two rectangular blocks. Next, draw intersecting perpendicular lines through the center of the drawer section front. Now mark the drawers, centering them on the hori-

zontal line as illustrated. The drawers must be laid out so as not to interfere with the curves of the outer walls of the box or with each other.

● **Making the First Cuts**

Using the cutting techniques described in Step 2 of "The Making of a Band Saw Box," cut the box top. If you are working with a solid block, cut the upper box from the drawer section along the line drawn in the previous step.

● **Cutting the Upper Box**

The upper section is made in the same way as the "Cloud Box" without drawers. Follow Steps 5–7 and 10. Rather than using the "machinist's jig" method for determining the form that was demonstrated in "The Making of a Band Saw Box," I have drawn the outer form of the box freehand. This is a shortcut method which may be used when designing new forms. Tape the top to the body; then mark the outer form of the box. Next saw the form according to the instructions in Step 10. Scribe or transfer-mark the inner wall, and saw out the inner section, following cutting directions in Step 5. Glue the body back together at the entry cut as in Step 6. Finish as in Step 7.

● **Marking the Lower Back**

Stack the lower and upper sections together using the waste from the upper box to line them up. Mark the inside wall on the top of the drawer section. Remove the waste piece, then trace the outer form keeping the upper box in place according to the inside wall line.

● **Marking the Drawers**

Square up lines from the edges of the drawn-

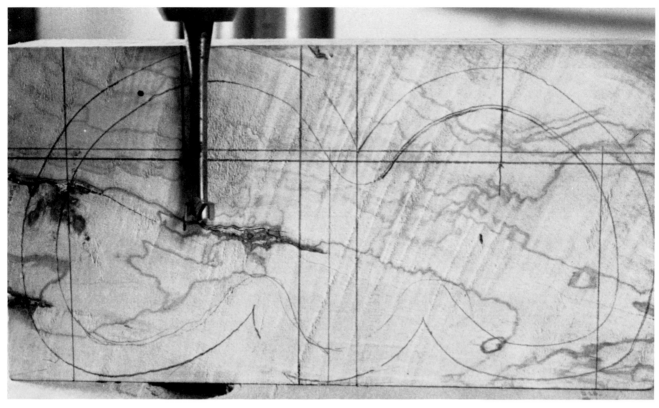

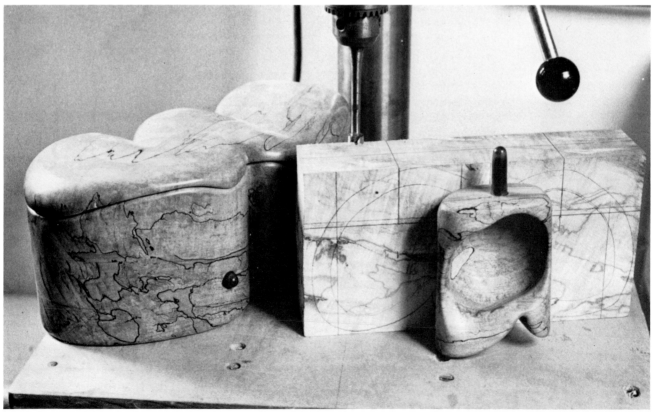

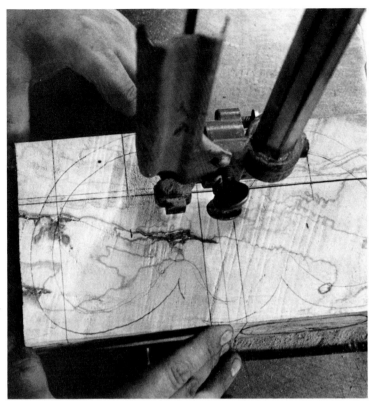

in drawer fronts across the top of the drawer section of the box. Determine the back of the drawers by where the inner wall line intersects with the squared up drawer lines. Mark a line at this point parallel to the back of the block. This will form the box back.

● **Drilling the Push Pin Holes**

In order to open the drawers, an interesting mechanical device is used: a "push pin" drawer opener. A 1/2" dowel (preferably made of a hard exotic wood) extends from the drawer back through the box back. These pins should be located dead center in the back of each drawer. I prefer to have the pin extend through the drawer back exposing the end-grain of the dowel in the drawer inside. Mark and drill 1/2" holes for the push pins as illustrated.

● **Sawing the Drawer Section of the Box**

Once the push pin holes have been drilled, the body back can be sawn. Saw on the waste side of the lines using band sawing technique described in "The Making of the Band Saw Box" Step 2. Accuracy is critical.

*Band Saw Box
with Drawers*

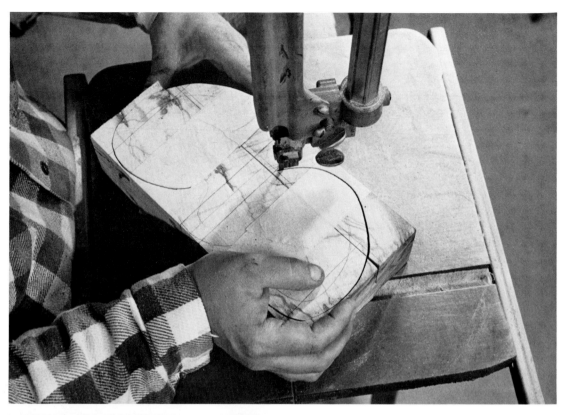

After sawing and removing the body back, turn the block on edge, and saw the drawers as illustrated. Now tape the entire lower block back together; then saw the outer form which will correspond to the pre-sawn upper form.

● **Putting the Box Together**

Glue the lower section together where the band saw entered to remove the drawers as in Step 6 of "The Making of a Band Saw Box." Follow the directions in Steps 12–14: cut, sand and attach the lid positioner; glue the upper and lower sections together (Step 9); cut, sand and shape the top. Carve or band-saw the drawers out. Prepare and insert the pins, and sand, finish and assemble the box.

Opposite above: *Michael Graham, Arc, 1979. Curly koa wood, 14" x 4" x 4" (36 cm x 10 cm x 10 cm). Courtesy the artist.*
Opposite left: *Michael Graham, Spiral Pipe Form, 1980. Walnut, 48" x 24" x 24" (122 cm x 61 cm x 61 cm). Drawers closed. See also p. 131. Irving Lipton Collection, Los Angeles.*
Opposite right: *Espenet, band saw box, 1970, teak, 9" x 9" x 16" (23 cm x 23 cm x 41 cm).*

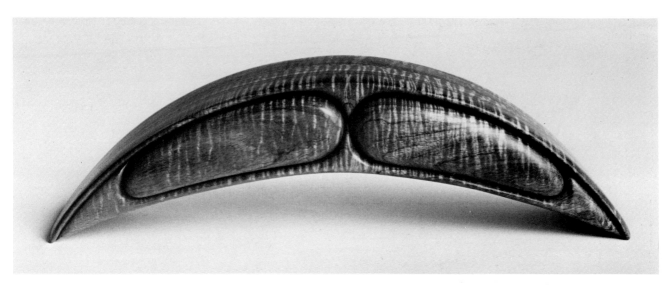

Above: Spalted Maple Cloud Box, 1974. 6″ x 6″ x 12″ (15 cm x 15 cm x 30 cm). Collection, Mr. & Mrs. Paul Alpert.
Left: Cloud Box, 1979, stacked laminated ash, walnut veneer and spalted white birch, 6½″ x 6″ x 11¼″ (17 cm x 15 cm x 29 cm). Private collection.
Opposite: Michael Graham, Spiral Pipe Form, 1980. Walnut, 48″ x 24″ x 24″ (122 cm x 61 cm x 61 cm). Irving Lipton Collection, Los Angeles.

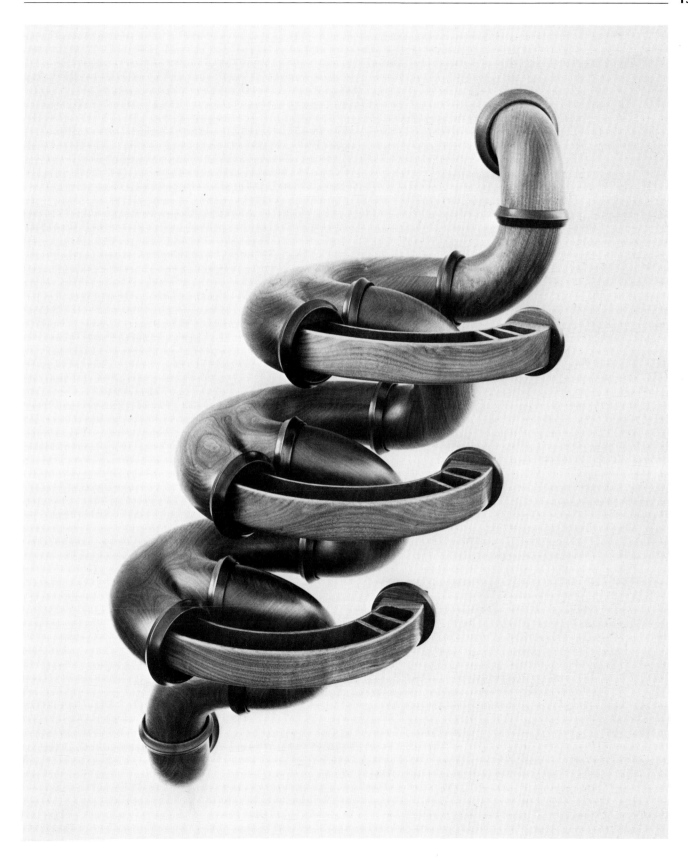

CHAPTER **9**

Finishing

RAISING THE GRAIN

Machining and sanding damage the outermost layer of cells of the surfaces of wood. Sanding also pushes the cells over and causes them to lie flat, producing a seemingly smooth surface, like grass after being rolled with a lawn roller. If left this way, however, these cell fragments may eventually raise up, making the surface of the wood rough. The first step in finishing after sanding, therefore, is to raise the grain.

Wetting the wood with a warm damp rag makes the cell fragments stand up. The wood is then allowed to dry, either naturally or by rotating it in front of a light bulb. The surface of the wood again becomes rough. A very light sanding with the final grit sandpaper will remove these damaged cells without disturbing the sanded surface.

FINISHES

Dry, sanded wood is like cloth in that it will absorb any moisture which comes in contact with its surface and will stain if the moisture has color in it. Wood is finished in order to protect the material and the prepared surface. Finish is also used to bring out the natural beauty hidden within the wood. Thus, two categories of finishes have been developed: those with the emphasis on protection — sealing finishes — and those with the emphasis on enhancing the wood — penetrating finishes.

Sealing finishes close up the surface of the wood and require little maintenance, whereas penetrating (oil) finishes are relatively "open" and require considerable attention. Regardless of what finish is applied, any finish is only as good as the finish sanding and preparation of the wood itself. All finishes bring out what is beneath, including scratches and sand marks.

Sealed finishes such as varnishes, lacquers, urethanes are usually applied by brush, allowed to dry, then lightly sanded and coated again, building up as thick a surface layer in this fashion as desired.

Penetrating finishes, oils such as linseed oil, tung oil, Watco Danish oil, etc. may be applied by brush or wiped on with a cloth. In any case, oil finishes must be wiped of excess oil after thoroughly soaking into the wood. If any oil is allowed to set up on the surface, it will become very tacky and nearly impossible to remove.

Note: Ventilation is required when using turpentine, polyurethane, lacquer, etc.

Finishing with Oil

In oiling, the oil penetrates deep into the pores (cells) of the wood (which are of course empty except for the residual moisture). The cells quickly accept the oil, filling up. The viscosity of the mixture determines the extent of penetration. A thick mixture of oil will not penetrate deeply because the surface layers of cells will quickly become clogged. Thin diluted mixtures will leak down into lower layers.

A simple demonstration illustrates the point. On one board place a spoonful of pure raw linseed oil or tung oil and quickly circle the spot where it rests. On another area of the board, place a spoonful of turpentine or driers (Japan driers or McCloskey's — a drier is a thinner which cuts or dilutes the thick base substance, speeding up drying time) and also quickly circle that spot. Notice that the drier area is a much larger circle and is much more quickly absorbed by the wood. The linseed or tung oil rests upon the surface, slowly working into the wood. The turpentine or drier will all but disappear. The oil loads the pores; the drier or thinner washes through them — thus the distinction between the two types of oil finishes: the wash as opposed to the fill.

Usually, the first application of oil is a wash to go down deep into the wood to prepare a foundation for successive applications. Normally I oil with light washes, adding successively heavier mixture coats until the applications begin to fill or load instead of washing. An old rule of thumb for oiling is once an hour for a day, once a day for a week, once a week for a month, once a month for a year, once a year for life. Of course, like the rules of thumb in drying, it does not take into account the types and densities of varying hardwoods.

Mixtures I most often use are tung oil and driers, and linseed oil with turpentine and polyurethane. Commercial finishes such as Watco oil or Waterlox are fine, especially in a pinch, but I prefer a more organic finish that I can control.

Certain woods are denser — rock maple is harder and denser than cherry or cherry burl, and cherry is much harder than white birch. The harder the wood, the more tight-grained and dense, and the thinner the mixtures needed for penetration. A thicker mixture will be necessary to fill the pores of open-grained wood.

Penetrating oil finishes fill the cells and perhaps even the cell walls of successive layers within the wood, producing reflective surfaces at varying depths within the wood. The wood absorbs and reflects light at these levels, glowing from within. The oil brings out the richness and warmth that were inherent in the wood.

Finishing with Sealing Finishes

Surface finishes reflect light directly off the surface, the finish being like that of a still lake or mirror. Glance at a finely finished surface of a table in the light at a low angle, and the wood is barely visible because of the glare or reflection off its surface.

The surface finish penetrates the wood only just below the surface where it sets up, dries and seals off the cells. The outer layer of cells are actually fully saturated, filled and permanently sealed by the finish. Subsequent layers will not penetrate beneath the initial coat but will rather build one upon another, forming a shell or coating surrounding the wood. Certain polyurethane finishes are available (as well as clear epoxy finishes) which enable the buildup of thicknesses up to 1/2" or more beyond the surface of the wood.

There are two advantages to this kind of finish. The surface of the wood is protected from injury by the finish itself. And the wood is completely sealed off from its environment, thus totally stabilizing it. Since no air or humidity can get into the cells there is little likelihood of any dimensional change in the material.

The problems with this kind of finish — particularly the heavy "goopy" finishes — are visual and perhaps philosophical. A built-up finish may protect the wood, but it also separates the viewer from direct contact with the wood itself. The wood is isolated behind an impenetrable barrier. We touch the finish itself, not the actual substance we long to feel. All built up surface finishes work this way.

In determining which finish is best for you, or for a specific piece, carefully weigh the advantages and disadvantages. Although an oil finish looks great — a rich lustrous glow emanating from within — it lacks the durability of a surface sealed finish. Water marks from the bottom of a glass will quickly penetrate the oil and raise up the grain of the wood below leaving a "water ring" on the surface. Drops of water will spot the wood. An oil finish must be given attention and care, continued oiling and maintenance. It will dry out and become bland and old looking. So finishes may be governed by life style. For the person who can oil and care for the wood, the rewards will be participation in the process and a close union with the material. For the busy person with little time or opportunity to care for the wood, an oil finish would become somewhat of a nuisance.

The "Fine Art" Finish

For non-utilitarian wood pieces which function as works of art, a finish is desirable which combines the visual qualities of the oil finish with the non-maintenance of a sealing finish. To this end, my father and I have developed what may be called the "fine art finish" — an oil finish base which brings out the color and depth in the wood, and a light surface seal which closes off the pores to evaporation and absorption.

In the fine art finish, oil is applied, at first a light wash, building successive layers of oil (tung or linseed) mixed in at least equal amounts with thinner or drier to penetrate deeply into the pores of the wood. Gradually the thinner or drier is decreased through successive applications (perhaps five) until the final coat is a hand-rubbed application of pure raw oil.

The oil is applied liberally and worked into the wood until it completely disappears. It is important to keep rubbing until all the oil disappears. The action of the hands working and kneading the oil causes the wood to heat up, opening its pores to receive maximum amounts of oil. The cells expand with heat, then contract with cooling. I believe the cell walls themselves take on oil when heated while hand-rubbing. During the cooling stage of hand-rubbing, the cells contract and push out excess oil, causing the wood to "bleed." So after several minutes, perhaps even hours, the surface may still push out oil. The oil may be simply rubbed back in, until no further "bleeding" occurs. Hand-rubbing is by far the best. The wood responds to touch.

After the final rubbing, the piece must sit for days, perhaps weeks, until it is time for the second stage: the sealing. The point in the "fine art finish" is to achieve a balance which displays the rich depth and beauty of the underlying wood texture but protects the surface.

In the mid-thirties to early forties, my father experimented with making jewelry out of plastic. He would saw and laminate thick sections of plastic together with plastic colors or dyes within the laminations. The result was rainbow colors transmitted to the outer surfaces, which if properly polished would gleam like jewels. In order to properly polish the plastic, its surface needed to be finish-sanded to a fine grit, with no sanding marks visible. Then it was "buffed" with

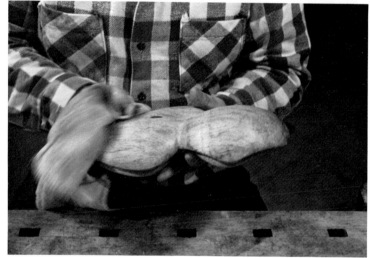

a polishing compound on a cotton buffing wheel which spun on a motor arbor shaft. The compounds available were in 6″ long bars and were a base substance such as animal fat or wax with a grit mixed in. The plastic would shine with continued buffings using successive grits.

One day, Melvin noticed that his wheel was clogged up with grit and was not working well. Normally, he would use a rough piece of wood to clean and clear the wheel, holding it against the wheel while it was spinning. This time, however, he picked up a smooth, finish-sanded scrap and tried cleaning the wheel. The wheel would not clear, but instead polished the wood. So he tried polishing smooth-sanded wood scraps with all the available compounds. He found that tripoli (a type of rouge or polishing compound) worked best, because the pigment was entirely compatible with the wood. Also, tripoli was very coarse, containing the heaviest grit for polishing, and worked well on the surface of the wood. Since then, Melvin has been polishing all of his pieces with tripoli, using a cotton buffing wheel. This then is the second stage in the "fine art finish" — buffing.

We have tried all different brands of tripoli and have found the tripoli offered by the Rockwell Company to be the best for woodworking finish applications. For small hand-held pieces up to one foot, a stationary buffing wheel is suitable, applying the tripoli to the wheel while it is in motion, and then pressing the work to the wheel. For larger pieces, a lamb's wool polishing bonnet on an auto body polisher works best.

The heat caused by friction causes the pores of the wood to open as it is polished, as in hand-rubbing with oil, and the surface cells receive the base material (wax, animal fat) of the tripoli. When it cools, it hardens, lightly sealing the surface and creating a smooth, even transparent finish with a sheen. The texture of the wood may be seen and felt, yet little moisture may enter in.

The fine art finish is a technique, rather than a formula, which may be varied for different situations. For instance, if a "quick" finish is required, or if oil would darken the wood too much (as in spalted wood), polyurethane finish or waterlox may be substituted for oil. The urethane is applied by brush or wiped on, and the piece wiped dry. The process uses three rags: one for applying, the second for wiping excess, the third for soft buffing dry. If one coat seals adequately, the buffing may begin as soon as it is dry and hardened (best to wait twenty-four hours or overnight). The sealing step of the "fine art finish" may also be varied, for example using paste wax or other compounds instead of tripoli, or using a cotton buffing cloth to polish by hand.

The "fine art finish" is a light, pure, simple, honest finish which is meant for finishes of art work rather than functional craft. The finish will water spot or mark, scratch and dent easily, but at least maintains the beauty of the oil finish without the necessity of constant maintenance. Merely rubbing or buffing with a soft cloth will bring up the shine. The piece may also be re-oiled right through the tripoli finish when necessary (however, dissolving it, necessitating beginning the buffing process anew).

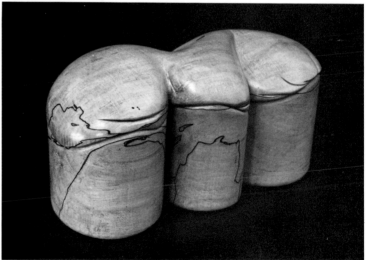

PART III Harvesting and Sculpting Wood with the Chain Saw

CHAPTER 10

The Chain Saw

Many woodworkers and sculptors now harvest and cut up their own wood using the chain saw, thus extending their control of materials back to the selection of the tree. Naturally, woodworkers have experimented with and developed other uses for the tool. In carving, the chain saw can be an incredible time-saver, accomplishing hours of handsawing or chiseling within a few minutes.

The chain saw can be surprisingly delicate. It can make light carving cuts, plane a surface or clean up rough spots quickly and accurately. The chain saw can also be surprisingly crude. It can accidentally gouge through the side of a carved bowl from unexpected kickback and ruin hours of work in a quick slip. Use of the chain saw requires understanding and experience, skill and caution and diligent maintenance.

Caution: Although the power of the chain saw makes it look easy, cutting trees with it is extremely demanding and dangerous. Many serious accidents occur because a machine that was designed for the professional is taken too lightly by weekend yard workers and wood hobbyists. Physical strength, alertness of mind and body, seriousness of purpose, concentration, skill and knowledge are all essential for the safe operation of the chain saw. Do not just buy a chain saw, read the instruction book and start cutting. First get professional instruction.

THE SAW AND ITS MAINTENANCE

The Chain

The chain saw "chain" is simply a series of chisels or gouges put together to make a loop of small blades. Each chisel makes its cut, then goes around to clear the chip, become lubricated and cool off. In succession, each chisel chips away at the wood until the cut is made. With speed and power behind the chain, a very fast and precise cut can be achieved.

The kind of chain, and its sharpness, largely determine the effectiveness of the saw. Most chain saws come equipped with the old-fashioned Oregon chain that has been used for years. It works well but doesn't give the quality cut essential to my work. The standard Oregon chain is literally rounded, so the tooth is like a gouge, while the low-profile chain teeth are like chisels, which make a cleaner, planed cut. The Oregon low-profile has extra chip rakers called anti-kickback rakers that indeed live up to their name. They keep the saw from bucking and allow seemingly impossible cuts like straight-in plunge cuts and waving smooth planer cuts.

● **Sharpening**

Ancient Japanese master carpenters sharpened their chisels between cuts: one cut and they sharpened the blade. Optimal sharpness allows the blade to be pushed through the wood

with much less force, but even more importantly, these craftsmen were concerned with the quality of the cut. They wanted to have the new, first-time feeling with each cut. I remember as a child thinking that if I was extremely careful with my chisel, it would stay sharp and not need sharpening. I could never understand why my father had to sharpen his tools so often, especially when he too was careful with them. Finally one day I got curious and used one of his chisels, and I was amazed at the difference in ease and cleanness of cut when using that newly sharpened blade.

Sharpening is the toughest job to master in maintaining the chain saw, but once you've got the feel for it, it becomes routine. The low-profile chain must be sharpened differently from the standard Oregon chain. The file is tipped downward 10° to accommodate the tooth angle, rather than being held perpendicular to the tooth. I sharpen after every several cuts, mainly because it's easier to keep the blade sharp than it is to push a slow-cutting saw around.

The trick to filing is to duplicate the manufacturer's angle or the one which you have set. It's easy to make a cut in an already existing path. After a while the angle comes naturally, and the speed may come if you need to sharpen quickly.

Before starting to sharpen, make sure the chainsaw switch is in the off position. The chain should be loose enough to slide around easily for quick movement. Then make a couple of quick passes at each tooth at the correct speed to allow the file to clear the metal from its teeth and still cut. The angle that I use is based on the manufacturer's recommendation but can be varied to suit different cutting problems. Work as many teeth as possible until the saw housing is in the way, then move the chain along. I clear the file between sets of sharpening because it clogs up with metal particles. I knock the handle on the workbench (reseating the file while loosening the particles) and then wipe it on my pant leg. You can use a rag followed by a brass brush. A clean file works better and will last much longer.

You can't expect a file to last too long though. Metal against metal wears quickly. At best expect about twenty filings from a file before it begins to drag. Files are relatively inexpensive. I'd rather spend the extra money to always have

a good file than end up with a less than sharp saw.

Maintaining the level of the rakers (the extra metal parts directly in front of each tooth) is an important part of sharpening. The rakers clear the sawdust out of the way for the cut of the tooth, and they also set the level of the cut of each tooth. As the tooth gets filed back farther away from the raker, its cutting height changes because it is on an angle sloping back toward the saw. So as the tooth decreases in size, the raker must be filed down in order to expose the cutting surface of the tooth. You can buy a fancy little metal gauge to measure the raker height, but I simply file about three flat file passes down per ten or so sharpenings.

I like a good amount of tooth exposed for the cut, so I initially drop the rakers down below the specified level and then maintain that difference. More exposed tooth means more cut, quicker cutting, but more strain on the motor. Since I perform many operations with the same saw, I sharpen the blade like a combination blade to avoid changing chains for each different cut. With this system, I can hollow out the inside of the burl bowl, cut off logs, rip flitches

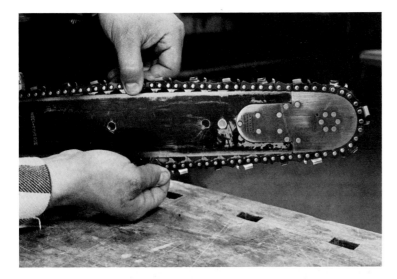

or plane boards — all with the same chain. The key is to keep an extremely sharp chain with low rakers and to keep the saw in good running order. High rpm with lots of power make for a great cut. A properly sharpened chain will produce a nice cut at any rpm.

● **Setting the Tension**

Once the chain is sharpened, I set the tension. This is accomplished with the take-up screw near the bar which controls the little pin that moves the bar forward and backward. Keep the grit and greasy sawdust accumulation out of this area to avoid getting it in the clutch. This would cause the chain, sprocket and bar to wear.

Everyone, including the manufacturer who is not always right, has a different idea about proper tension. When hollowing out a bowl, I leave the chain a little loose because it heats very fast and, if tight, will stretch an undue amount. For planing, the chain should be taut. I like a fairly tight chain when crosscutting logs, for a nice straight cut. Loose means that the chain sags a little bit underneath so that light shows between the bar and tips of the sprocket runners. Taut: the chain shows light between the bar and the teeth. Tight: no space between the chain and the bar, tightened just to the point that they touch.

When tightening the bar, put the bar on a surface and push down, or lift it up with your hand until the play is taken out. When cutting, the bar vibrates and will slip upwards. Adjusting

Above, from top: *Loose. Taut. Tight.*

it in the beginning will keep the chain from be-ing loosened excessively through successive cuts. It's normal for a chain to loosen as the heat and vibration cause it to stretch.

The Saw
It is important to maintain all the parts of the chain saw if you want the saw to run properly and cut well.

● The Bar
Although a hard tip bar is alright, I like the sprocket nose bar and normally prefer the six-teen-inch length for versatility and control. The sprocket nose rolls a little more smoothly with-out heating up so much on the end. The sprocket nose needs lubricating so the bearings won't wear out.

It's important to flip and file the bar occasion-ally so that it wears evenly on both sides.

● The Motor
Good maintenance is very important to keep the motor running well. I prefer the electronic ignition saws so that I don't have to fool with points, and I change the spark plug periodically whether it needs it or not. There's nothing worse than being out in the woods and having the saw

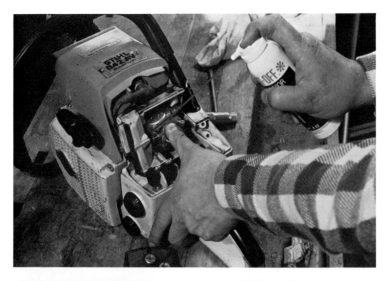

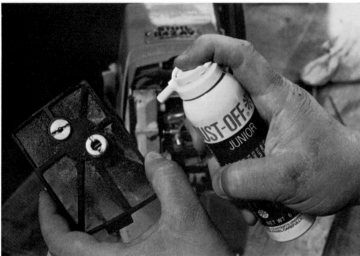

refuse to start because of a bad spark plug. Occasional cleaning of the plug gives you an opportunity to check how efficiently the motor is burning fuel.

● **The Fuel**

It's important to follow manufacturer's directions about the correct fuel mixture and cleaning the motor. The air filter is the most important part to keep clean. If the filter is clogged, the carburetor does not get enough air, and the engine will not rev up all the way. The motor loads down, performance drops, and with the carburetor gasping for air, it works harder, clogging up the filter with more fine powder. The dust will eventually get into the carburetor and clog the fuel line. Keep the filter clean, and the machine will sing.

Sharpening, lubricating and cleaning are about as far as I go in chain saw maintenance. If anything major goes wrong, I take the saw to a good, reliable mechanic and let him handle the problem.

CHAIN SAW HAZARDS

Following is a list of the nine major chain saw hazards and how to avoid or compensate for them.

1. *Starting:* When starting the chain saw, the operator controls the throttle with one hand. The other hand pulls on the recoil starting rope which tends to throw the saw off-balance. The bar can swing around and hit a nearby object or person or the operator's leg. To avoid this problem, hold the saw securely on a board or the level ground with a foot in the trigger guard, holding the saw to the board or ground.

2. *Noise:* Wear ear protectors. Loss of hearing (industrial deafness) can result from repeated use without ear protection.

3. *Chips:* Wear eye protectors — not just glasses, because chips can come in from the sides.

4. *Danger from the Bar:* Do not swing the saw quickly in any direction, or operate near people. Make sure everyone is well back from an imaginary arc drawn by the saw bar.

5. *Kickback:* Most chain saw accidents are caused by kickback. Allowing that portion of the bar which is above the center point of the tip to come into contact with the surface being cut can cause the chain to dig into the wood and get caught. The bar receives the momentum from the chain. The result is a violent snapping back of the bar toward the operator's upper body. It often occurs when cutting brush or by accidentally hitting a log with the tip of the bar. To avoid this deadly situation, always cut under controlled conditions. Carefully position the wood to be cut so the bar will not accidentally catch in it or a nearby log. Know exactly where the tip of the bar is at all times.

6. Pinched Bar: Unless the log to be cut is carefully positioned, the edges of the cut may lean in on the blade, pinching the bar with such pressure that it is impossible to pull out. Prop the log securely before cutting, or put a wooden wedge in the cut shortly after beginning.

7. Dirt: Cutting through dirt will dull the chain. Clean the log before cutting by removing bark and brush. Prop up the log so you avoid cutting into the ground. You can also cut most of the way through in as many places as desired, then roll the log over and complete the cuts from the other side.

8. Metal in the Tree: A chain can be totally ruined by running into an imbedded metal object within a tree. Spikes, nails, barbed wire and other metal objects may be found deep within large trees, totally hidden from sight because the tree has enveloped them completely. Once I found a horseshoe in the crotch section of a tree, probably hung there and forgotten. Nails and big spikes are the most commonly found metal. When the chain hits them, the saw shakes and bounces, and several teeth are destroyed.

A metal detector is handy for indicating approximate location of metal within a tree. Without a metal detector, I rely on experience and intuition to tell me when a tree or log is likely to contain metal. Large trees by the side of the road, at the edge of a field or in a yard are apt to contain metal. You can never be sure when you will run into metal, so it is wise to anticipate the feel of the chain saw tooth hitting metal and to develop the quick reflexes needed to stop cutting immediately.

9. Dull Blades and Improperly Maintained Saw: A dull chain and an untuned saw will cause extra starting efforts, the use of your strength instead of the saw's, "horsing" of the bar through the wood — all of which result in

Above: *Sometimes a healed over formation on a tree will indicate metal within. Saw gently until feeling the first "tick," then split down through the cut with wedges. Often the split will pull out or expose the metal.*

fatigue and frustration, increasing the likelihood of accident. Always keep your saw in top condition for efficient and safe use.

BASIC CUTTING TECHNIQUES

The conventional method of using a chain saw is the way in which it was designed to work most effectively: the standard crosscut. The saw passes through the log with optimum efficiency and cuts it in two. I've never seen the manufacturers warn against unconventional uses of the chain saw. Perhaps it never occurred to them that anyone would be creative enough, or brash enough, to consider other applications. The chain saw has one thing going for it that discourages creativity — *intimidation*. I have been intimidated by the chain saw from the first time I saw one in use, realizing that with one mistake the machine can inflict serious injury in an instant. The main requirement for using a chain saw is respect for the tool. It doesn't hurt to run tingling shivers up and down your spine once in a while thinking about the danger.

I used to have a great fear that the chain would fly off in mid-cut and get me by the throat. One day the chain did come off, but what a disappointment: having lost its drive and momentum, it merely jumped off the bar and lay limp. Once the chain is through the drive sprocket cycle it has no power. The time to worry about the chain is when it is racing around the bar, open and exposed to the body. No quick hand movements. No swinging around. Everything must be deliberate and carefully controlled.

If the chain is sharp, and the saw is in tune, it will do all the work. Many people think that horsing the saw will get it through the piece more quickly. Horsing is any up and down jerking motion of the saw. The most efficient, accurate way to saw is to let the saw pass through almost by its own weight. A good saw properly sharpened and tuned will cut well.

Crosscutting
Although a simple procedure, making a good crosscut requires skill and control. Begin the cut perpendicular to the log, aiming the bar so that the finished cut will be at right angles to the length of the log. Any deviation from the per-

pendicular plane will produce waste. The kerf of the chain saw is about one-half inch, but there is much more wood lost due to the sideways motion of the cutting and the minor inaccuracies of the "by-eye" cut than by the kerf. In making a crosscut, I rev the motor once, touching the log, and simply guide the saw with very little down pressure through to the end of the cut. When sectioning a small log, I cut seven-eighths of the way through for each section along the length of the log and then turn to the other side and cut to meet each previous cut, until all the pieces are free. These final cuts are made with the tip of the bar (below the center point) as though simply snipping off each piece.

Ripping

Ripping is about the most difficult cut the saw can make. Cutting the log lengthwise is very hard because the saw must cut with the grain rather than against it. In crosscutting, the saw is slicing across the cells. The rip cut slices with them, encountering the material in its strongest structural form. The wood resists this cut much more.

Ripping may be achieved by approaching the log in three ways. One is to stand the log on end, and cut down through it with the length of the blade perpendicular to the grain. The saw will work its way down through the wood at a certain rate depending upon the hardness of the wood and the power and condition of the saw. The chips, an indication of the saw's performance, will be broken and mixed with sawdust powder as the chain grinds away at the wood. This method works for ripping, but I've found it to be very inaccurate, since the bar tends to wander.

Another approach is sawing from the top through the width of the log as it is lying down lengthwise. Now the length of the bar is parallel to the grain. The chips are long and stringy with very little powder. This angle of cutting is the best for me since it delivers the cleanest cut. The saw works less hard, and it is very easy to control the accuracy of the cut. I use this method when cutting short blocks for turning and make them exactly the length of the bar. If the log length is greater than the bar length, but less than twice its length, I sometimes make a cut in one end, and finish from the other end. Unless the chain is very sharp and you are good at matching up cuts by eye, this method will be less accurate than the end-on approach.

Approaching the log from the end as it lies on the ground, and allowing the front of the bar to lead the rest of the saw through the length of the log makes an extended cut of any length possible. In this third approach, the blade forms a 45° angle with the axis of the log, halfway between the positions of the blade in the other two methods. This angle of approach is used with an Alaskan Mill (see Chapter 11) attached to the bar to make very accurate planks.

CHAPTER 11 Harvesting Wood with the Chain Saw

HARVESTING SPALTED WOOD

My family moved east from California when I was five. My father continued working for General Electric, established his shop in our home in Schenectady, New York, and bought some land in the Adirondacks. This land contributed much to the development of our way of working with wood: getting the wood the way we did, becoming familiar with the forest and the tools of the logger. From the land we learned about the life of wood and the complexities that lie within. Most important, there on our land, we found our first pieces of spalted wood.

The way we got our wood in the early days, the 1950s, was mostly fun. Mel would get the chain saw and the oil and the axe together, and we'd go trudging out into the deep woods of the Adirondacks. We'd head back looking for wood to be used for turning and for firewood. It was great going through the woods.

Mel would cut down big dying diseased trees to make room for the young ones. He always lectured me about that and told me never to cut down a tree that I wouldn't use. Even in the depths of the forest we would trim the branches from a fallen giant and pile the brush neatly by its side. Soon the tree would transform into a huge snaking tube lying on the forest floor. When we came back the next year, it would be covered with leaves and look like a long hump in the ground where the earth might have heaved during an earthquake.

The best part of all of our wood-getting trips was letting the imagination run wild, thinking about the forms that were created and witnessing the effect our presence and our actions made in the woods. We were always careful to leave the woods cleaner than when we had arrived. After cutting and stacking wood, we would carry some back to camp with us, leaving the rest for future trips. This was a time of patient observation for my father and a time of rigorous training for me. He watched the wood and the leaves and the wind, while I watched him and what we did in the woods. It was a special time.

My father's land was very wet. I used to kid him by saying that he had bought swamp land, and he would laugh, saying that some day I would come to appreciate it.

Then one day, when we were cutting the base of a tree, an old white birch, I saw a sudden flash, a gleam in my father's eyes. I'll never forget that look. It was a look of surprise, wonder, excitement, and greed, the look of having discovered gold right before his eyes. Curious black lines darted all over the face of the cut. By the light filtering through the steam rising off the leaves and the smoke from the chain saw, I saw the most beautiful wood ever created. I felt I was a part of something momentous and of real value.

Mel sent me back to camp to get the shovel, and I dug and dug around the base of the tree to expose the roots so that we could saw farther into the stump without dulling the chain by cutting dirt. I smiled while making several trips back to get all of the wood. I finally understood

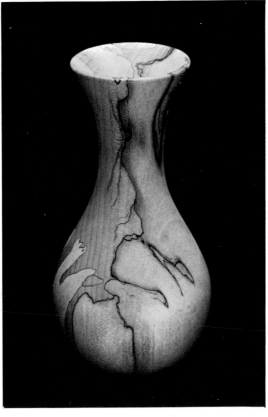

what my father was always talking about. It was fun. It was good to go out into the woods and find treasure. This wasn't work. It was excitement and adventure.

Finding Spalted Wood

Finding spalted wood is really very simple once you know what to look for. Throughout the north, there are fallen or dead standing trees in varying stages of decay which may contain spalting. Maples are the best because they take longer to spalt and so retain hardness. Birches are often disappointing, since the bark may be intact while the inside has rotted to mush. Regardless of the species of tree, there are several signs to look for that indicate that spalting is likely. However, even with years of experience, you won't know for sure until you cut into it.

The first sign to look for is the type of land where the tree grew. Trees are more likely to spalt in a swampy or wet region. The next clue is the soil that the tree is resting on. It should be rich dark earth, mossy or covered with rotting leaves. Even in a generally dry area, if a tree falls in a hollow surrounded by rotting leaves or by a brook on mossy ground, it may spalt. The third sign to look for is mushrooms or fungus. If the side of a tree, or the end of a previously felled tree, is covered with mushrooms, spalting may lie within. However, mushrooms on the side may indicate that the tree is too rotten. The fourth sign to look for is actual spalting on outer layers of the wood under the bark or where the bark has come off of the tree.

Another indication that the wood is in the right stage for spalting is that, although in a moist environment, it appears fairly dry. Wood that appears very wet is probably too green to spalt, still containing most of its bound water.

If the log looks old and rotten, strike it with an axe and listen to the sound. Good hard wood will ring. A "thunk" means the wood is probably rotten. Wood at the proper stage of decay for

Left: *Melvin Lindquist,* Spalted Birch Vase, *1968. 5" (13 cm) high. This vase is oriented so that the grain is vertical. This is called turning end-grain.*
Opposite top: *Melvin Lindquist,* Spalted Birch Vase, *1978. 8" (20 cm) high. This vase is oriented so that the grain is horizontal. This is called turning side-grain.*

spalting will make a sound something between a ring and a thunk.

Cutting the Spalted Log

Cutting spalted wood is like cutting gems. The object is to separate the log into sections that will yield well-formed pieces and reveal the most beautiful markings. The artisan, therefore, must visualize and position his creation within the log before even cutting it. Michelangelo believed that within the sculptor's material there are trapped forms, prisoners. It is the sculptor's task to liberate them by taking away the mass surrounding them. So it is with the spalted bowl, vase or other object that would be freed from the rotting log.

The first cut will be to expose the end-grain. Crosscut off about three inches from the end of the log that has been exposed to the weather. These three inches usually take out the end checks and the "mock spalting" that often occurs directly on the surface. Now, you can see the spalting, and begin predicting how it will appear throughout the log.

In addition to zone line formation, there are several other factors to consider before cutting up the spalted log. First is the use you intend to make of the wood, the type and scale of work you intend to do. Second are the limitations of your equipment, such as the height of the band saw opening (for ease of later cutting), perhaps the maximum capacity of a lathe or even the size of a jointer knife. It is important to know your own equipment and its limitations so you can make realistic decisions about scale. This need not prevent you from anticipating working with a larger scale in years to come when harvesting wood now. The third factor to consider is the location of the wood and the method to be used in transporting it.

Consider the length of the log. If it is long, the spalting may go in from one end for a short distance and then stop; the rest of the log will be just normal wood. Take an end-grain cut from the other end of the log. If spalting shows only on one end, start cutting in from the plain end every foot or so, depending on the size pieces you want, until spalting is reached. Use these plain chunks for firewood, or place them on end in the dirt there in the woods, cover them with leaves and leave them to spalt.

Having separated the spalted section of the log from the rest, cut it to desired lengths, carefully checking at each cut for changes in pattern that might influence the next cut. For turning blanks, you might cut 16" sections and then rip-cut pieces, staying away from the center or pith because it's sure to crack. Cut through any faults, cracks or spots that seem likely to check later. As you choose the spot to begin each rip cut, carefully observe both the end- and side-grain spalting as well as the defects in the wood. Try to place the best zone line formation on the surfaces of the potential bowl or other object.

Cutting the wood to usable size while harvesting is practical for transporting it, saves an extra step of chain sawing at a later time, allows the wood to dry more quickly than in log form and provides a ready supply of stock prepared for immediate use. However, if you have access to a cherry picker (log grapple truck) or other means of moving large logs, you can store the entire log and cut off sections as you use them.

Using the Large Chain Saw and the Alaskan Mill

If my observations of a large log indicate that it is probably sound and well spalted throughout, I may decide to cut it into large sections and/or slabs for future use in large-scale projects. Some sawmills are willing to cut up logs for individuals. Having the log cut at the mill, however, has two main drawbacks; transporting the log to the mill may be difficult and expensive, and maintaining control over the cutting of the log may be impossible. I prefer to bring the cutting equipment to the log and make careful, deliberate decisions about the wood.

In 1972 I bought a Homelite Super 1130G gear drive chain saw to use for cutting large pieces of wood. It has a five-foot bar with a helper handle and an Alaskan Mill attachment for milling stock to dimension. Working with the five-foot bar chain saw is exciting, but it is also extremely dangerous, requiring skill, strength, experience and alertness.

There are three main methods of cutting with the five-foot bar saw: freehand crosscutting, milling with the mill attachment and freehand ripping. The single-headed power saw, like the one I have, is much more versatile than the dual-engine models currently available.

The helper handle attached at the end of the bar makes it possible for another person to help with the handling of the five-foot bar. *The helper should be well-trained in chain saw use and safety and must be constantly alert while the saw is running because the exposed chain is very close to hands and body. The operator and helper must work out body language signals beforehand, since both hands must be on the tool at all times, and it is impossible to hear over the loud motor.*

The techniques and hazards for cutting with the large saw are the same as for an ordinary chain saw with added risk from the increased power, size of the blade and exposure of the helper. The ability of the operator and the helper to work together and respond to the saw and each other, and the seriousness with which they approach the work will help determine the degree of added risk. (See "Chain Saw Hazards" in Chapter 10.)

- **Crosscutting with the Large Chain Saw**

To ready the large spalted log for milling, the ends must first be crosscut off and the log crosscut into sections of the desired length. Crosscutting a three-foot diameter or larger log is difficult with a normal saw but relatively easy using the five-foot saw with the helper handle. Techniques and procedure for crosscutting are described in the "Crosscutting" section in the previous chapter on The Chain Saw.

- **Ripping with the Alaskan Mill**

The end-grain picture and figure must be carefully studied in order to decide which way the log will be turned before beginning the cuts. Entirely different surface marking will appear on the slabs depending on the orientation of the cuts. (See "Cutting the Spalted log.")

The first step in using the Alaskan Mill is to establish a flat upon which the rollers of the mill attachment can ride. I use an old ladder because it is wide and flat. I've drilled holes in it to receive nails that will anchor it to the outside of the log. It is necessary to wedge the ladder in several places, sighting and measuring to establish a flat surface parallel to the desired cutting plane.

1

2

3

4

5

When the ladder is securely fastened, the first cut can be made with the mill attached to the saw. This cut establishes the flat from which all subsequent cuts will be made; it also establishes the thickness of the first section of the log. Thickness may be varied in subsequent cuts if desired.

While using the Alaskan Mill, the operator and helper must both carefully watch and guide the rollers, being careful to keep them flat and in constant contact with the top surface (the ladder in the first cut). These guide rollers buck the saw against the log surface. Let the saw do the work, walking along with the saw's speed of cut, not forcing but following. Driving a wedge into the end of the cut when the cut is halfway through the log will prevent the log from pinching the bar.

● **Freehand Ripping with the Large Chain Saw**

In cases where it is inconvenient or too time-consuming to use the Alaskan Mill, or where accuracy is not critical because the sections will eventually be resawn prior to using, I sometimes rip-cut a large spalted log freehand. As in milling and in sectioning smaller logs for bowl blanks, the log must first be prepared by cross-cutting off each end and sectioning the desired lengths, then each section is studied to determine where the rip cuts will be made. Measure the log section for freehand cutting (sometimes a snap line acts as a guide). Normally, cutting through the pith will expose any rotten areas in the center of the tree. ***The freehand rip cut must be made with the same care and precautions as***

other cuts using the large chain saw. Be sure to discuss beforehand exactly how the cut will be made, and establish body language signals.

Storing Spalted Wood

After the wood has been cut and transported to the storage area, paint the ends of the blocks or planks with an inexpensive white glue and water solution, applied liberally, to keep the ends from drying too quickly. A green wood sealer of water-soluble wax may be used. For exceptional pieces, I have occasionally sealed with epoxy. This process can become costly, but certain pieces of spalted wood are so rare and incredibly beautiful that it is worth the expense. If having a record of the exposed zone line formation is important in determining future cuts, take a photo or make a sketch before coating the wood with glue or epoxy.

When applying the glue solution, I press a newspaper on the glued surface to avoid unnecessary mess when turning the log upside down to paint the other end. This also provides a good surface for recording the date, reference number and any other information.

HARVESTING BURLS

Finding Burls

Since proportionately few trees have burls, it is easy to walk through a forest and not see a single burl, even though several are there. A burl may be very high up in a tree or obscured by foliage. If the burl is smaller in diameter than the tree, it is visible from only one side; you may look straight at the tree and not see it. The multitude of trees in the forest makes a perfect camouflage for burls, and the inexperienced simply may not notice them.

There are a few clues to knowing where to look for burls. Although burls may grow in any terrain, usually the hilly, rocky, heavily wooded areas of mountainous regions yield the most. It seems that the rougher the terrain in a heavily wooded area, the greater likelihood of burl growth. When trees are gnarly and growing around rocks, they are more apt to grow burls. Often the rocks and ground in these areas grow lots of moss. An individual tree may give signs of burl formation that lead to the spotting of the burl, such as a gentle widening of the trunk where a burl grows on the other side or a gradual change in bark formation. If you find a burl, keep looking nearby — burls sometimes proliferate in certain areas.

But there are really no rules for finding burls. The way to hunt for them is to look carefully at each tree while walking slowly through the forest. After a while, you will be surprised at how far away through the trees you can spot them. A lot of ground can be covered by driving through a forested region, and many burls will be within viewing distance of the road.

Perhaps the most difficult problem in obtaining burls is getting permission to take them. I think the biggest and most well-formed burls grow either on government land or right in the front yard of sprawling estates or historical buildings, and are therefore not usually obtainable.

Once I found a cherry tree grove loaded with burls. The owner allowed me to cut the trees down (all of them) for his firewood supply, and I took the burls. Often I have traded small pieces of finished work for larger burls or lots of burls. Occasionally, an owner will accept money, but most often they will either give the burl freely, ask for a piece made from their tree or expect the firewood from the tree — any way, it is a lot of work and requires the additional skill of negotiation.

When I find a burl in the woods, I consider its quality, its distance from a usable road, cutting problems and what I am willing to pay or trade. Any woodworker who has harvested a big burl far from a road will undoubtedly remember the pain and difficulty of that deep-woods encounter. One way to ease the difficulty is to cut the burl in the fall and leave it in the woods until winter, then haul it out on a toboggan pulled by a snowmobile.

I like to hunt for burls in the fall, as they're easier to spot because the trees are shedding their leaves — it's also the nicest time to be working in the woods. After years of searching for, harvesting and loading burls the "old-fashioned way," I've begun to buy them from local loggers, who frequently find them, already have permission to take them and are equipped to fell them and pull them out. Town dumps are often surprising sources, as are tree-removal services and tree surgeons.

There are many new commercial sources for burls today, particularly on the West Coast. Manzanita, buckeye burl and redwood burl are available through various independent dealers who advertise regularly in popular woodworking magazines. Unfortunately, burlwood (particularly when green) is heavy and expensive to ship.

Cutting the Burl

A burl can be removed either by cutting it off the tree or cutting down the tree and then removing the section with the burl. If possible, I prefer the former because it eliminates dealing with the branches and other wood of a downed tree. Also, the tree normally lives on after the burl is removed, often becoming healthier. I never paint the cut, because the sealing of the cut causes the burled area to grow in upon the tree, reinfecting it. By leaving the saw cut alone, the burled area is allowed to dry up and die out. The edges of the tree will gradually grow around and over the wound.

When cutting the burl off the tree, it is important to have good footing either on the ground or on a secure ladder. Since the burl is often heavy, it is a good idea to either prepare a clear path for it to fall through, or rope it in a manner which will allow safe lowering after the cut. It is safest to rope the top of the ladder to the tree as well.

Cut the burl as close to the tree as possible, and as nearly parallel to its outside surface as the trunk of the tree will allow. Deep gouging cuts into the tree are pointless when the best use of the wood is achieved by a clean straight cut, leaving a neat area on the tree. You will always leave some good burled wood in the tree, but the only way to get it all is to cut down the tree.

When I cut a tree down to take the burl, I try to leave a foot or so of trunk on each end of the burl so that as the log dries, cracks and checks will not travel into the burl.

Harvesting a burl tree is more difficult than cutting a tree down for just one burl. First the tree must be studied to make the felling cut, then dropped in a place that is suitable for cutting the fallen tree up. Just as the spalted log must be carefully studied to determine the best cutting approach, so must the burled log.

Storing Burls

Drying and storing burls can be as uncomplicated as piling them outdoors or as sophisticated as packing them in layers of sawdust. When cut, green burls are very heavy, laden with bound water. Some woodturners prefer to use green burls. Burls turn most easily when wet but will warp and twist as they dry. Green burls may be stored under water over a period of time, which prolongs drying and eliminates cracking. Blanketing them in wet sawdust also retards cracking, promoting slow, even drying.

I prefer working dry, aged, mellow burls — checks and all. My philosophy of woodworking accepts the nature of the material, which is to expand and contract. I allow for the inclusion of checking within the design of the work, by either accepting the crack as it is or working it open to relieve its jaggedness. I like the spontaneity of working the dry burl, being able to finish the piece knowing it will move or shrink very little from its finished dimensions.

I usually leave burls uncovered outdoors, sitting directly on the ground for maximum exposure to the elements. Most begin staining and spalting, and I find the resulting colorations desirable. Yellow birch burls, for example, are relatively bland but become spectacular when colored or spalted.

It's a good idea to either mark the species and date of cutting on the burl or store specific kinds of burls in separate piles so that they will all dry together. Painting of the sawn surfaces will discourage checking but also prolongs drying. I'd rather let nature have its way. Since the grain is so twisty and gnarly, often the burls dry with few checks.

After exposing the burls to the weather for a year or two, I move them into an open-air shed, build a lean-to over the pile using corrugated transparent roofing or simply cover them with plastic. When the burls have sufficiently dried, they must be stored up off the ground, preferably away from sunlight. I pile them one on top of another in my barn. Due to their various unusual shapes, this storage is awkward and inefficient. I've built shelves and racks but haven't solved the problem yet.

Moving and Storing Large Burls

Moving burls, particularly the heavy ones, is often tricky and can be dangerous. I periodically hire a local logger to pick up burls for me and haul them to our burl yard which is in a constant state of change. As new green burls come in, older burls which have been outdoors must be dealt with, either cut up and used or stored. I try to be organized enough so that when the grapple operator is in the yard I can have him move pieces around to their next position for cutting. The old make way for the new.

A storage site is selected and waste block beams are placed on the ground. The burl is safety chained to the jaws, and the grapple operator lifts it off the truck bed for inspection. Since this may be the only opportunity to study the burl in its entirety, a careful study is made as hand signals indicate to the grapple operator in which direction to swivel the burl. Often I photograph the larger burls as a visual record for

purposes of later study, documentation and future reference. A good grapple operator can easily position a large burl accurately, but it's best to always think of safety first, keeping an eye out for problems, constantly thinking about quick reflexes in the event a piece should come loose.

I prop the burls higher on one end than another for ease of cutting. Normally the large burls, four to six feet in diameter, can be stored outdoors, uncovered for at least two years, but must be chocked on blocks for safety — to keep them from moving. The blocks also keep the burls off the ground which is better for drying and for observing and studying them.

Cutting the Large Burl

Often cutting large burls is perplexing and difficult. The rare giant burls are intimidating because of their massive bulk. After a year of drying and studying, I decide to cut a giant elm burl to make a large sculptural vessel form.

I begin by separating the best part of the burl from the log. Apprentice Michael Bruss operates the helper handle end of the five-foot bar chain saw as I begin the first freehand cut of the burl. The process is similar to freehand cutting of the spalted log but has been made easier in this case by propping up the burl at one end, allowing the saw to travel downhill. I wedge the burl in the kerf during mid-cut to keep the saw from binding. Once the cut is completed, the burl is pried and pushed off the log section. Gradually, the

burl gently eases forward and down off the blocks onto the ground in a vertical resting position. Using body weight and leverage, we separate the two halves and situate the large burl in position for work. Each section has potential for sculpture and may be further contemplated before the next step. Each successive cut unfolds new opportunities while simultaneously determining the outcome of the sculpture and the fate of the burl. Responsibility accompanies the use of materials on this scale. As each cut is made, the challenge increases. Awareness comes from investigation.

CHAPTER 12

Chain Saw Carved Vessels

When the wood sculptor sets out to create a piece based on an idea or visualization of the completed object, the means to this end are often unknown — solving the problems of technique is the hard part. Meeting this challenge, however, may become a step in a new direction, leading to new possibilities of sculpture. Gradually, techniques evolve — or personal adaptations of techniques — that aid in the making of the piece. The sculptor must learn to develop tools and "tricks" to create pieces faster and more accurately. The less time spent in manual labor, the more time may be spent thinking and seeing.

It is important while learning the following procedure for making the carved vessel to understand that this is not the only way to work. It is merely a method which gradually evolved through personal solutions to specific problems. Use these techniques to make your work. Better yet, understand the approach and principles of problem-solving and develop new approaches of your own.

Caution: Only those already competent in the use of the chain saw should attempt these techniques. Beginners must first learn the proper standard cutting methods before learning to carve with the chain saw. Instruction and supervision by a teacher is essential.

Opposite: Moon Over Crater Lake, 1979. *Chain saw carved sculptural vessel, maple burl, 26" (66 cm) long. Collection, Mrs. Robert Skinner.*

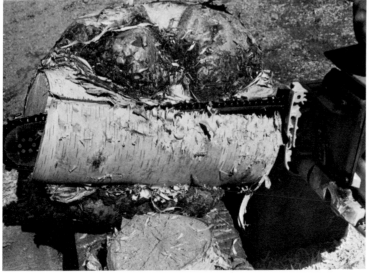

STUDYING THE BURL

In preparing to carve the burl vessel, studying the burl is of primary importance. I stand the burl on end, walk around it, turn it over, roll it around, turn it end over end, in an attempt to fully understand every aspect. Usually, I am concerned only with the burl and not with the section of tree trunk or limb to which it is attached. Therefore, I look for the best way to detach the burl from the trunk or limb. Usually, there is a bark inclusion where the burl and the limb come together which would eventually split apart once the carved bowl began to dry. It's important to spot this kind of problem prior to cutting.

I try to visualize the vessel in the burl before making any cuts. Usually, the burl will suggest its own shape or form by the way it grew. The outside of the burl is the outside of the bowl. The bottom of the bowl is usually the face of the burl that was outermost, parallel to the trunk or limb. The top of the bowl becomes what has grown in toward the tree. I look for possibilities, and attempt to work with an idea in mind. Sometimes, the burl will better suggest its form as the work progresses, and I will adapt and adjust my preconceptions.

PREPARING THE BURL FOR USE

Having studied the burl and having gained a feeling of confidence about it, I make the initial cuts, liberating the actual burl from the tree sec-

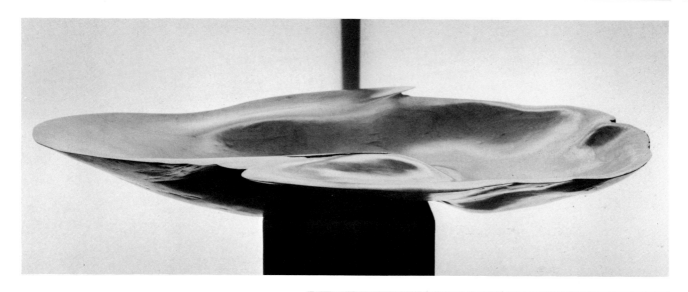

tion. Again I study the burl which is now trimmed down and looks more like the form of a vessel. I mentally establish the bottom of the vessel and decide which will become the flat upon which the bowl will rest. I then prop the bowl up on edge, wedging it with blocks (usually the waste cuts from the limb section) and make a chain saw cut which establishes the bowl bottom. Often, this flat surface ends up being parallel to the direction the tree grew and in the center of the outside of the burl. I'm careful not to remove too much burl as this cut almost always decides the size of the base of the bowl. It's critical to make a large enough flat so that the bowl will sit balanced, but not so large that the bowl will "sink" into the surface it rests on. A smaller base allows the bowl to rise, to appear to float.

Planing with the Chain Saw

After the cut to establish the flat, I "plane" the surface with the bar of the saw. To plane with the chain saw, hold the bar at a slight angle to the surface and pivot it across. This cutting action achieves a smooth, flat, consistent surface.

Attaching the Waste Block

After initial planing with the chain saw, I hand plane the bottom of the burl flat. Usually, I just buck the burl up against a large block and hand

Top: Flight of the Fish, *1978. Carved yellow birch burl, 28" x 40" x 8" (71 cm x 102 cm x 20 cm). Collection, Cornelis Tims.*

plane in the direction that works best until a smooth, uniform, flat surface is achieved.

After checking to be sure that the bowl will sit properly, I glue a square hardwood waste block to the flat surface. Since the block will be removed after the bowl is finished, a perfect glue joint is not required. It may be clamped, but I usually just weight the waste block with something heavy such as a cement block.

ROUGHING OUT

I remove the bark with a chisel (often a blunt tool like a dull screwdriver works best) and make a mark with chalk or charcoal to signify further wood waste, then mount the burl in a bench by means of the waste block. The carver's bench is a great tool for holding the burl but is not essential. The waste block enables the burl to be tightly held in a vise and therefore is the safest method for holding the burl while chain saw carving and finishing the bowl. Any clamping device (even a screw up through a board into the bottom of the waste block) will hold the burl for carving. It doesn't matter much what method of holding is used so long as the burl is held at the correct height for proper tool positioning, and is very secure.

With the burl secured on the carver's bench, I chain saw cut on the inside of my chalk marks to remove the waste wood. The burl is now "roughed" and is ready for the steps of carving which will further its development as a vessel.

This initial phase — the study, orientation and

roughing — determines to a great extent the fate of the burl. The eventual outcome is determined by our decisions and our work. The removal of each chip is final. Every cut must be carefully planned and deliberately carried out.

TECHNIQUES IN CHAIN SAW CARVING

In some applications, the chain saw can be used as an alternative to traditional sculpting methods using the mallet and chisel or adze. Although chain saw carving is dangerous, with practice and skill the sculptor may reduce much of the drudgery and time-consuming labor of carving. Not only will the chain saw remove bulk quickly, but it also can be used for surprisingly accurate detail work.

Sculptors who initially experimented with chain saw carving did most of their work with the bar fully extended as though it were a sword. When I first began, I also used the extended bar but eventually applied a concept gained from using drills and auto body grinders: the side handle.

The Side Handle
For the sculptor, the side handle is an important accessory to the chain saw. Most of the operations of chain saw carving may be done without the use of a side handle but are at best risky, because of the ever-present danger of kickback. The side handle is a tool handle similar to that found on an auto body sander. It is attached

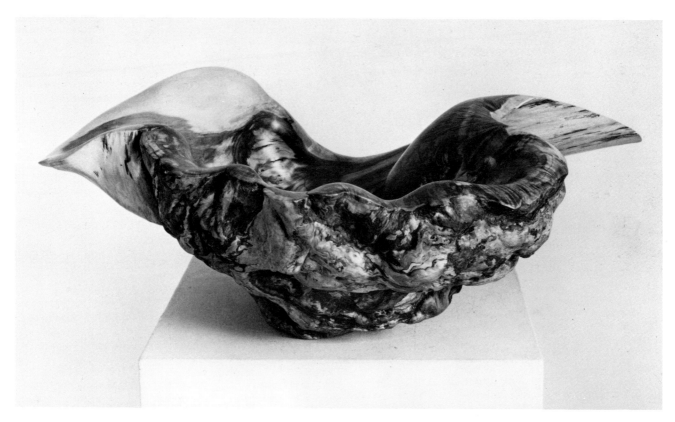

perpendicularly to the flat of the chain saw bar. Since I like to position the handle to best advantage for the amount of bar exposure necessary when carving, I drill and tap the bar at two-inch intervals along the length of the center line.

The side handle changes the balance of the entire saw, shifting the pivot point from the saw handle on the body much farther forward along the bar, decreasing the likelihood of kickback. The side handle allows accurate positioning and movement of the blade. Radial cuts, lateral movement, tilting of the bar and combinations of these positions can be more smoothly performed, increasing safety and precision.

Top: Flamingo Bowl, *1979. Red cedar burl, 20" x 12" x 32" (51 cm x 30 cm x 81 cm). Collection, Mr. Nathan Ancell.*

Tip Carving

Tip carving is potentially a very dangerous technique. But when mastered it proves infinitely more efficient and almost as accurate as any traditional method of carving. The tip or rounded end of the bar is used to remove interior mass from the form. Through experience, I have found the Oregon low-profile chain best for all chain saw carving. (See the section of "The Chain" in the Chapter 10 for a description and proper sharpening technique.)

I use two different methods of tip carving. *In any method, it is essential to realize that only the portion of the chain below the center point of the saw blade may be allowed to come into contact with the wood. Therefore, the saw must be held at an angle to the surface less than 45°. If the angle is increased, the portion of the blade beyond the center point may contact the surface of the wood and catch, causing devastating kickback.* (See "Chain Saw Hazards" in Chapter 10.) The use of a side handle will not only reduce the likelihood of kickback but also render kickback less dangerous when it does occur.

● **Kerf Cutting**

One method of chain saw tip carving is what I call kerf cutting. First secure the burl. I used to wedge and prop the burl on the ground and then rewedge and reprop as it worked loose. But holding the burl in a vise by means of a waste block, as previously described, is much more effective and safe.

With the prepared burl *securely* held at a convenient working height — usually very low permitting good posture and saving the back — bring the saw down into the wood at an angle *less than 45°* to the surface. As the cut progresses, pivot the saw blade into the wood creating an arcing cut. The left hand on the saw handle or side handle acts as the pivot point for the cut. The right hand moves up (pivoting the bar downward) and back. Pulling the saw blade back toward you through the wood as you make the cut establishes a consistent depth, and keeps the top part of the tip from coming into contact with the wood as it moves down and back through the cleared space. When the cut is complete, pull the saw carefully back up and out of the cut.

After the initial cut, there are two ways to continue this kerf cutting method of tip carving. One is to make consecutive identical cuts side by side, removing the entire interior bulk. The other is to make the cuts at half-inch or greater intervals; then knock the remaining wood out with a mallet, back of an axe or a similar blunt instrument.

- **Skating**

In the second method of tip carving, skating, the bar is moved from side to side in an arcing motion with the lower portion of the tip skating across the surface of the wood, removing bulk and shaping. This method removes the excess wood more slowly and is most useful for interior carving of shallow forms or where extremely precise shaping is required.

As in kerf cutting, the use of a side handle will increase safety and accuracy. And the burl should be securely held in a vise by the use of a waste block.

Hold the saw at an angle *less than 45°* to the surface of the wood. Lightly skim over the wood in a gentle sweeping action, just barely touching the surface with the chain saw. Gradually increase the downward pressure until achieving the desired amount of cutting while still maintaining a fluid movement. As the saw carves its way through the wood, creating a hollow, continually exert slight backward pressure on the bar to avoid the danger of kickback.

Using kerf cutting or skating techniques, I re-

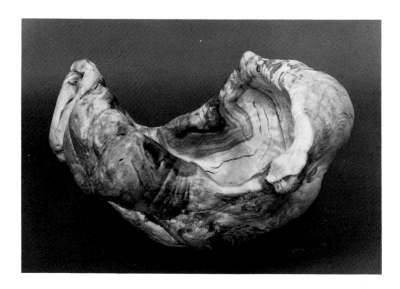

Above: Carved Maple Burl Sculptural Vessel, *1976. 12" (30 cm) long.*

move the interior bulk from the burl. I carefully measure and check the wall thickness for consistency. The final shaping is achieved by a finish cut with the bar of the saw. The finish cut is simply a finer, smoother rendition of the skating cut. With extremely light pressure, as though wiping, delicate final cuts are made. The rim of the bowl may be established and rough-cut using this method. It is important to smooth the surface as much as possible with the saw as all the ridges must eventually be leveled out. The final cut not only achieves the smoothness but also finalizes the consistency of wall thickness and the form of the vessel.

SHAPING AND SANDING THE BOWL

After carving the burl vessel with the chain saw, final shaping can begin. As in chain saw carving, an important aspect for safety and accuracy is the holding and positioning of the piece, preferably by the waste block in a vise.

Shaping and Smoothing with the Die Grinder

Although much has been accomplished with the chain saw, still more shaping is required to achieve the final form of the carved burl vessel. Traditionally, sculptors used mallet, chisel, rifflers and rasps. But, again, modern methods allow for new labor-saving tools. The high speed die grinder is a useful tool which aids in the speedy removal of material.

I use the die grinder to smooth out the rough

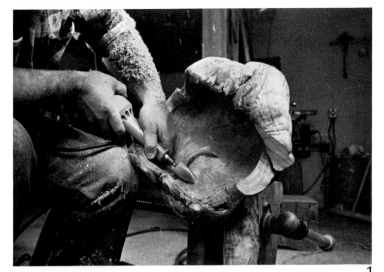

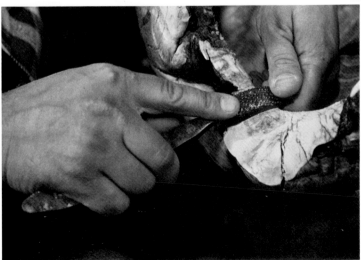

cut-marks left from the chain saw as well as to continue shaping the burl. The bullet-shaped ball mill works well for shaping the exterior lip of the bowl, which is usually the most difficult part to do. I prefer sitting down using my knees as support for my arms while holding and pivoting the die grinder. *It's important to have careful, firm control of the tool primarily because it is dangerous.* And also, the better the control, the more accurate the form, and the smoother the surface for less subsequent sanding.

The grinder is usually held with an overhand grip and works best with an arcing motion achieved by pivoting the wrist. Bracing the arms either close to the body or against the bowl helps in stability.

Using the Disc Sander

Once the final shaping has been accomplished with the grinder, the small 3" circular disc sander is used to smooth rough surfaces but also to continue refining the form. The final tuning up of each element may be accomplished with the disc. However the disc may not fit into every concave surface.

I hold the neck of the drill very low around the chuck with a firm but light grip so as not to get a friction burn (usually I wear a glove). The closer to the disc the drill is held, the more control. Again, it is important to brace the arm against the body or bowl to ensure stability, safety and accuracy. All parts of the bowl may be sanded with the disc through successive grits until it is ready for foam back sanding. The sand-

ing sequence is: 36, 50, 80, 120. Each successive grit removes the scratches from the last. During the use of 36 and 50 grit discs, all pecks, chips and tool marks must be dealt with since the lighter, finer grits 80 and 120 are not capable of removing trouble areas.

Final Shaping of the Edge

Although the disc works well in shaping the outer edge, additional hand tools may be employed. The Surform tool or sculptor's rasp allows for more precise control in sculpting an area. I like to fine tune an edge with a foam pad dowel.

Foam Back Sanding

After all shaping and rough sanding, the final finishing begins. Using the flexible back foam sanding pad chucked into an electric drill, I sand the entire surface of the bowl through each grit: 80, 150, 220, 320. If carefully done, foam

back sanding can entirely eliminate hand sanding, producing a perfect finish with no swirl marks or scratches.

FINISHING

After final sanding, the waste block is removed from the carved vessel. The bottom is next made flat by sanding with a belt sander or disc sander, then finish-sanded through successive grits using the foam back sanding pad. The burl is finished with several light coats of penetrating oils which are allowed to dry; then it is buffed with Tripoli. (See Chapter 9 on "Finishing.")

Above: Avalanche, *1977. Black birch burl, 16" x 8" (41 cm x 20 cm). Collection, Mr. & Mrs. James McRae.*

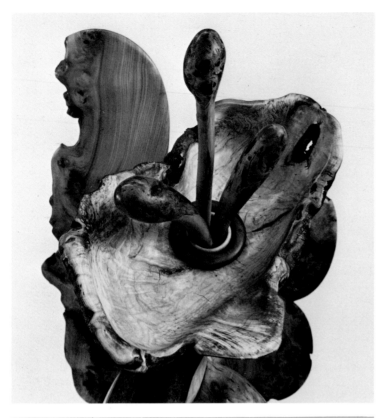

ABOUT FORM IN BURL SCULPTURE

The burl becomes a mirror of form and ideas. It reflects back what is put into it. It will take on the personality — the thought given it during the sculpting process. When thoughts are about modern organic sculpture such as that of Arp or Henry Moore, the burl becomes a statement — a vessel containing those ideas. When thoughts are about geometric forms and space-age ideas, the burl becomes sleek and smooth, honed and beveled, thin and light. When the thoughts are about nature, about the streams and forests, the hills and mountains, the ridges and valleys, the burl responds in kind and becomes a world in miniature. Looking at the vessel, one might be looking down from a hilltop into and across a valley and over to a ridge running along the opposite side.

Although the burl may become what we want it to, it has ideas of its own; it has a truth all its own. Make of it what you will, but see that your work is not contrived or gimmicky. The burl is noble and deserves treatment equal to its stature. The principles of organic form, of weight and mass, of rounded fullness speak most of what the burl is, of where it came from, of where it is going. Respect the wood by applying your understanding of form, in order to enhance, enliven, and bring out the best the wood has to offer.

Study form. Practice techniques on waste wood. Draw ideas before you make them. If in doubt on a certain piece, don't waste the wood, but rather make a study first. Make a model of a difficult area out of clay. Try to understand the direction first so that the execution of form is correct.

Once you have gained confidence and control, then push yourself to learn from the wood. When the wood presents a surprise in the form of a defect, don't be discouraged, but rather accept the problem as a challenge, an opportunity. Grow through the experience of sculpting the wood.

Look within to find your forms. Go past those that have already been done, and look for the forms that are uniquely your own. To begin, study the masters, but ultimately, become a master yourself.

Opposite above: *Author,* Forbidden Fruit Tree, *detail. Cherry burl, maple burl, elm burl, padauk. Collection, Greenville County Museum of Art, S.C.*
Opposite below: *Jon Brooks,* DeMeritt Chair, *1981. Spalted elmwood, 43" x 22" x 24" (109 cm x 56 cm x 61 cm). Collection, Peter DeMeritt.*
Above: *Henry Moore,* Reclining Figure, *1945–46. Elmwood, 75" (190 cm) long. Private collection.*
Right: *Henry Moore,* Two Forms, *1934. Pynkado wood, 11" x 17³/4" (28 cm x 45 cm) on irregular oak base, 21" x 12¹/2" (53 cm x 32 cm). Collection, The Museum of Modern Art, New York. Sir Michael Sadler Fund.*

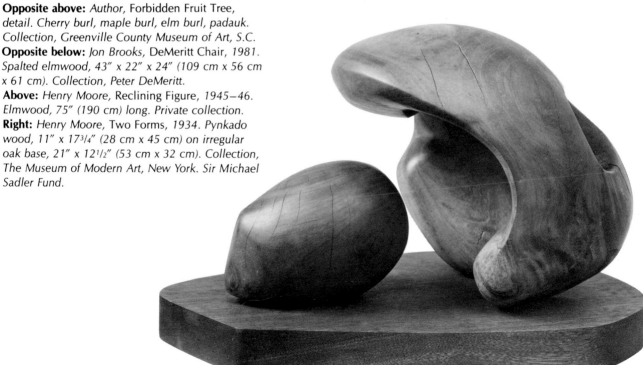

Top: *Isamu Noguchi,* Table for A. Conger Good-
year, *1939. Rosewood, 30" x 84" (76 cm x 213
cm). Collection New York Institute of Technology.*
Above: *Winslow Eaves,* Mahogany Abstract, *1972,
12" x 15" (30 cm x 38 cm). Collection, the artist.*
Left: *Brancusi,* Adam and Eve, *1916–21. Oak on
limestone base, 94¹/₄" (239 cm) high. Collection,
Solomon R. Guggenheim Museum, New York. Photograph: Robert E. Mates.*

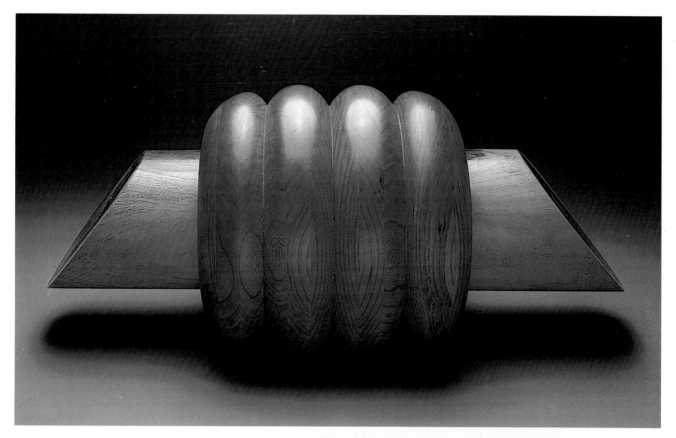

Above: Cylindrical #3, 1982. Black cherry, lignum vitae, 26" (66 cm) long, 12" (30 cm) diameter. Collection, Mr. & Mrs. Jack Pietri. Photograph: Paul Avis.
Right: Melvin Lindquist, Sung Vase, 1983. Spalted white birch, 16" (41 cm) high. Photograph: Paul Avis.

Above left: Three Easy Pieces, 1984. Walnut, tallest 10" (25 cm) high. Photograph: Paul Avis.
Above right: Mark and Melvin Lindquist, Ancient Lyrical Vase #1, 1984. Spalted maple, 26" (66 cm) high. Collection, Mr. & Mrs. Robert Stonehill. Photograph: Chuck Bosio.
Left: Winslow Eaves, Statement, 1960. Painted wood, 40" (102 cm) high. Collection, the author. Photograph: Paul Avis.

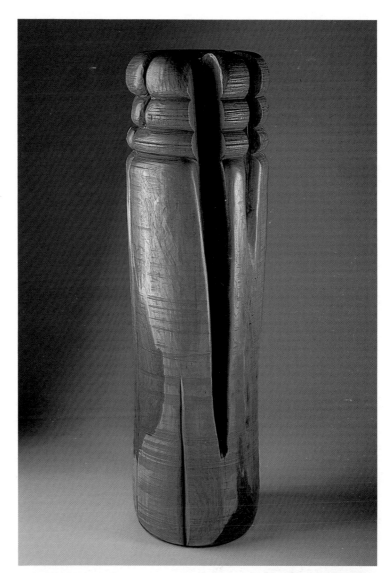

Above left: Monument to the Unknown Potter,
*1980. Birch burl, zebrawood, cherry burl, curly
oak, 36" (91 cm) high. Collection, Mr. & Mrs.
Richard Winneg. Photograph: Paul Avis.*
Above right: Will's Song, *1985-86. Walnut, 58"
(147 cm) high. Photograph: Paul Avis.*
Right: *Michael Graham, Breaking Weave (detail).
40" x 24" x 14" (102 cm x 61 cm x 36 cm).
Courtesy the artist.*

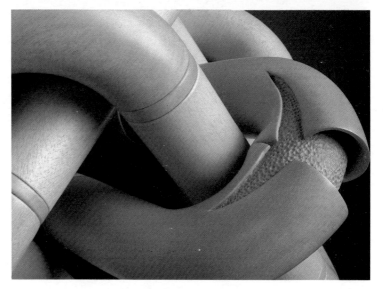

Opposite: Sculpture 1973-1983. *Elm burl, 24" (61 cm) diameter. Collection, Sol and Vida Roberts.*
Above: *Melvin Lindquist, natural top vase, 1983. Manzanita burl, 14" (36 cm) diameter. Photograph: Paul Avis.*
Right: *Melvin Lindquist, Geometric Series, Flat Top Vase, 1984. Buckeye burl, 16" (41 cm) diameter. Photograph: Paul Avis.*

Above left: Toutes Uncommon Bowl, *1980. Spalted yellow birch burl, 32" (81 cm) long. Collection, Duncan & Mary McGowan. Photograph: Bob Aude.*
Above right: Shogun, *1985-86. Black walnut, 67" (170 cm) high. Photograph: Paul Avis.*
Left: *Raoul Hague, Otsego Falls, 1976. Walnut, 65" (165 cm) high. Photograph: Bruce C. Jones. Courtesy Xavier Fourcade, Inc.*

Above left: *Melvin Lindquist, vase, 1978. Spalted maple, 12" (30 cm) high. Collection, Sam & Eleanor Rosenfeld. Photograph: Paul Avis.*
Above right: *Hugh Townley, Young Merlyn II. Mahogany, cherry, oak, walnut, maple, 33" (84 cm) high. Collection, Mr. & Mrs. John Fawcett. Courtesy the artist.*
Right: *Wendell Castle, Candy Dreams, 1985. Cherry, bubinga, 42" (107 cm) long. Photograph: Bruce Miller. Courtesy the artist.*

Above left: Broken-hearted Bowl #1, 1982. Mulberry burl, padauk, 14" x 8" (36 cm x 20 cm). Collection, Mr. & Mrs. Robert Stonehill. Photograph: Paul Avis.

Above right: Fruit Bowl, 1973. Spalted yellow birch, 12" (30 cm) diameter. Photograph: John Russell.

Left: Wendell Castle, Louis XV Chest with Hat and Scarf, 1979. 40" x 20" x 32" (102 cm x 51 cm x 81 cm). Photograph: George Kanper. Courtesy the artist.

PART IV

Woodturning

CHAPTER 13 Woodturning Tools

THE LATHE

I remember being intrigued by models of early lathes which my father made when I was young. The designs were so simple, I could easily understand their principle. The first lathe, probably invented by the ancient Egyptians, used a rope and a tree. Poles or stakes were driven into the ground to form upright supports. Spikes (primitive headstock and tailstock) were driven through holes in the upright stakes into the ends of the turning stock, which served as the shaft. One end of a rope was tied to a nearby tree limb. The other end of the rope, after being wound around the shaft several times, was pulled out in the opposite direction by a helper, bending the tree limb. As the helper let go of the rope, the tree limb would spring back, rotating the turning stock with power and consistency. The turner would cut with the tool on the "pull" stroke of the tree limb, and then wait for the helper to recock the limb for another whirl.

Another model my father made was a bow lathe, which was constructed in much the same fashion, utilizing the driven stake. It had a large bow-string wrapped around the turning stock. The bow would be pulled back and forth, and the turner would cut on the downward swing of the stroke.

Actually, the very first lathe was the potter's wheel. The simple potter's wheel has evolved through the primitive lathe and the treadle lathe to the most complicated of modern ornamental turning lathes.

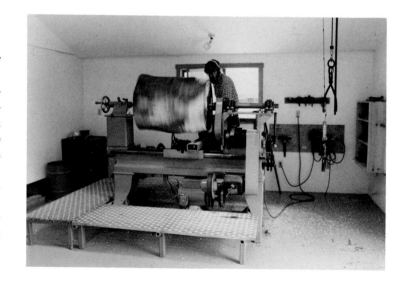

The wood lathe rotates wood around a horizontal axis at various speeds so that a hand-held tool supported by a tool rest can shape the wood by cutting and removing material. Instead of moving a chisel into a stationary piece of wood as in carving, the wood is rotated into a chisel which is stationary relative to the cut being made. This action produces a symmetrical circular form.

WOOD LATHE

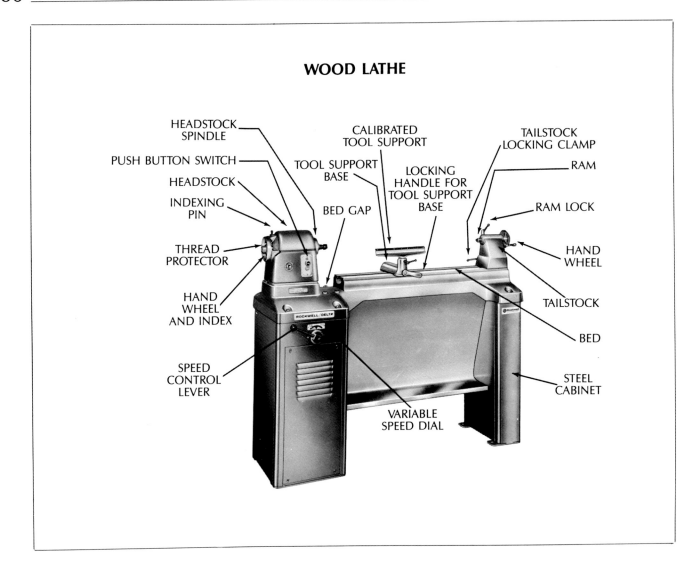

HEADSTOCK SPINDLE

PUSH BUTTON SWITCH

HEADSTOCK

INDEXING PIN

THREAD PROTECTOR

HAND WHEEL AND INDEX

SPEED CONTROL LEVER

CALIBRATED TOOL SUPPORT

TOOL SUPPORT BASE

LOCKING HANDLE FOR TOOL SUPPORT BASE

BED GAP

TAILSTOCK LOCKING CLAMP

RAM

RAM LOCK

HAND WHEEL

TAILSTOCK

BED

STEEL CABINET

VARIABLE SPEED DIAL

The main part of the lathe is the *headstock* which contains the rotating *spindle* which drives the piece of wood being turned. The spindle is a shaft which is threaded to accept a faceplate to which the wood has been screwed. The spindle is drilled through and has a tapered hole in the end to accept taper accessories. Some lathes come equipped with a pin which may be inserted into a hole in a plate attached to the spindle in the headstock. This *spindle lock* locks the shaft in position for tightening or loosening faceplates, and may be used to hold the piece still while working on it. An *on-off switch* is mounted near or in the headstock.

The *tailstock* is at the opposite end of the lathe from the headstock. It is used to center and clamp the turning stock. The tailstock slides to the headstock on the *lathe bed,* a set of bars or tubes which allow for adjustment and alignment of the tailstock. The tailstock can be positioned within a desired distance from the headstock and then locked in place with a locking clamp. A hand wheel moves the *tailstock spindle* or ram into the wood to apply clamping pressure. The ram contains a tapered hole which accepts morse taper accessories such as a tailstock center, which is a point around which the spinning wood revolves. Once in position, the ram is locked with a *ram lock.*

The *tool rest* slides on the lathe bed to be positioned for tool use when cutting. The turning tool is rested and pivoted upon the tool rest which can be adjusted for height, angle, and proximity to the turning blank.

The lathe sits on a *base* made of cast iron, or sheet metal in some cabinet models. The *motor* is mounted on the base or sometimes in the cabinet in lathes that have variable speed. Most common lathes have a 4 step *pulley system* of speed change.

The *inboard* side of the headstock is the side facing towards the tailstock. Most work is done inboard, between the center of the headstock and the center of the tailstock. The *outboard* side of the headstock is the side which faces the outside of the lathe. Larger pieces may be attached to the spindle on this end and turned with use of a free-standing *outboard tool rest.*

The size of the lathe is expressed in *swing* and *bed length.* The length of the bed is the maximum distance between the headstock spindle and the tailstock ram. Swing is the maximum diameter of a piece that may be turned, or twice the distance from the center of the spindle to the bed. A lathe with its spindle 6″ above the bed is said to have a 12″ diameter swing. Some lathes have a *bed gap* which is a space of the bed eliminated to allow for increased swing.

Choosing the Right Lathe

Because the lathe is a major piece of equipment and requires a substantial investment, choosing the right one is important. The main consideration when buying is capacity, since this determines the maximum size of work which can be produced. A beginning turner may make the mistake of buying a lathe of limited capacity that will be outgrown almost immediately or the opposite mistake of buying an extremely powerful, large capacity lathe that is intimidating and dangerous to learn on. It is best to start with a sturdy lathe of moderate capacity, 8″ to 14″ swing, and up to 4′ between centers. To allow for growth, get a lathe with a slightly larger capacity than you anticipate using.

The horsepower of the motor should be $1/2$ to $1 1/2$. A motor with less than $1/2$ horsepower is not strong enough to keep the lathe from slowing down or even stopping in the middle of some cuts. Turning a bowl should be done at a constant rate without interruptions, with a decisive cut, and this requires power. Certain lathe operations, such as blind boring, hollowing end-grain pieces, and turning large pieces to the lathe's capacity will require more power than spindle-turning, or turning vases and simple, smaller bowls.

Good design and engineering, quality materials and good workmanship are essential in a lathe. A lathe must be heavy and sturdy, especially for turning larger pieces.

Although added features are desirable, capacity and quality are far more important than extras such as an indexing head, a magnetic on-off safety switch or variable speed. These features add greatly to the price of a lathe without affecting the basic performance. Though I recommend variable speed, a good quality lathe with a pulley system of speed change will work very well.

Investigate different lathes that are currently available, such as General, Harrison, Myford,

Courtesy of Woodcraft Supply Corporation

Oliver, Powermatic, Rockwell and Shopsmith. Obtain the literature and make comparative analyses. If possible, attend workshops, classes or seminars on woodturning which provide a variety of lathes that you can try. After deciding on and purchasing a lathe, work with it to develop skill, confidence and knowledge.

As your understanding of woodturning, equipment and your own goals grow, so will your vision. Then you can decide whether or not you want a more powerful or specialized lathe. Before I got my patternmaker's and other large lathes, I used only the Shopsmith on which I had learned. Some of my best pieces were made on that machine. My father still uses his Model 10ER for smaller work. The important thing to remember is that good turnings do not necessar-

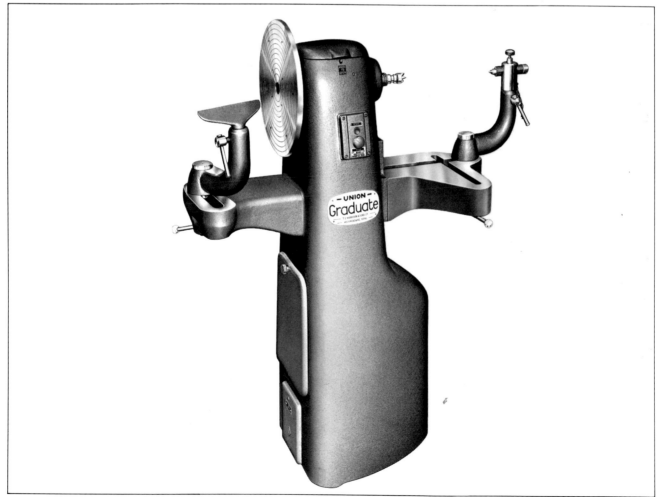

ily come from the best or newest lathes.

Rebuilding an old lathe is an excellent way to acquire a high quality lathe at a reasonable price, if you have the knowledge, patience and ability to work on machines. The services of a competent machinist are also a help. Old lathes are generally heavier, more substantial and made of higher quality materials than their counterparts today.

My longtime favorite is a patternmaker's lathe that is so old, it has no trademark. When I got it, it had long been neglected; our local machinist, Francis Mitchell, and I spent three years fixing it up and adapting it to my needs. This lathe is big and strong. It has a 30" inboard swing capacity, and faceplates up to 16" in diameter for an outboard swing capacity of up to eight feet. The speed of the lathe shaft is variable from about 50 to 3000 rpm. The speed of the motor remains constant and it never seems to heat up.

When I opened my Florida studio, I wanted to work pieces larger than the capacity of my patternmaker's lathe. I could not afford to buy a new lathe for each studio, so a local machine fabricator, Leonard Buxton, and I built a movable lathe. We created a "monster lathe" with a 40" inboard swing from an old machine lathe that had been sitting in a friend's barn for years. It took three days to clean it and then several months to design, modify and build the lathe and trailer.

The lathe has a speed range of 2 rpm to 3,000 rpm, and reverse. I'm able to turn almost anything inboard between centers manually or automatically. With the self-loading trailer, I can transport this massive machine with my van, then easily position and deposit it.

When I find a part of my lathe is not strong enough, I redesign it and have the local machinist make it. Often, a tool rest is not strong enough and needs to be replaced. Sometimes, the base can be replaced with something sturdier and a shaft diameter may be increased, perhaps also adding ball bearings. The heavier the base and other parts of the lathe, the less vibration will occur.

If a motor is not strong enough, it can be replaced. Power is necessary to provide for smooth, forceful cutting. It is very satisfying to watch the wood evolve into form under your hand. I've tried to approach lathe turning in a similar way to making pottery. I try to capture the spontaneity of the thrown vessel in the turned vessel, so that the piece forms with only a few passes. Actual turning time depends upon the size and nature of the material that is being turned, but the effective, smooth cut that provides for the feeling of spontaneity can only be achieved with the help of a powerful motor.

The motor must be mounted in such a way that it will not vibrate. The typical hanging motor arrangement is not good, since the motor can move and jump. The general rule for a good lathe set-up is to tighten everything down completely so that no movement or vibration exists.

It's best to become completely acquainted with your lathe, because someday, right in the middle of turning a very important piece, the machine will break down. That's the nature of machines. Having worked over and inspected every part of my lathe, I know its strengths and weaknesses. I have a supply of spare parts such as belts, bearings, pulleys and hard-to-get nuts or bolts, so I can replace parts without waiting. Often it is quicker, and sometimes even cheaper, to have a broken part machined locally, if a new part is not readily available.

I don't oil my lathes where I can wax. Oil attracts sawdust. Wax makes parts slide easily and will not gum up with fine sanding powder. I keep my lathe clean. Sawdust left all over the lathe will interfere with its smooth, safe operation. Some wood dust will even eat away at the paint. I don't second guess a lathe. When I hear an unfamiliar whine, I identify the problem right then. Unless it is something minor that can be attended to later, I fix it immediately. The most important thing to remember about taking care of the parts of a lathe is: **keep them tight and lubricated.**

Right: *Francis Mitchell, master machinist, milling lathe part.*

The Lathe

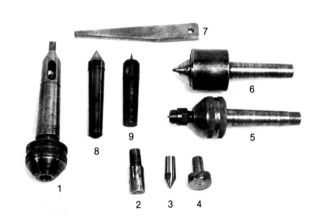

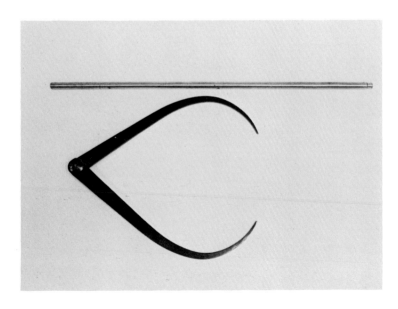

LATHE ACCESSORIES

The lathe is useless without the accessories which couple the wood to the machine.

Centers

One method of turning wood on the lathe is by holding it "between centers." The centers are accessories with morse tapered shafts placed into the tapered openings in the ends of the spindles. When forced into the spindle, the tapered end of the center locks and becomes securely fastened.

The *headstock center* is called a driver or spur center. The wood is driven into its point and spurs which, when the center is mounted in the headstock, become an extension of the spindle and drive the wood.

There are two kinds of *tailstock centers,* live and dead, which are attached to the tailstock ram in the same manner that the headstock center is attached to the spindle. Then the ram is tightened, forcing the tailstock center into the wood and putting pressure on the spur center, holding the wood securely between centers.

A *dead center* is stationary. The wood spins on it, requiring lubrication with oil or wax. A *live center,* a better means of holding the wood, rotates with the wood on ball bearings and does not require any lubrication. Some live centers have a tapered hole within the center itself to accept different heads, such as a cone center, a cup center, a flat center or a shaft center.

Headstock tapered accessories are released by a jolt from a *knock-out bar.* This is a separate accessory which slides through the hole of the lathe spindle. Tailstock tapered accessories are released as the tailstock ram is retracted into the tailstock to a pin which forces the taper out of the spindle.

Top: *Spur centers: 1. large #3 morse taper; 2. for Shopsmith (fits on a ⁵/₈" dia. shaft); 3. #2 morse taper.*
Middle: *1. Live center with taper adapter. Tapered hole in the live center receives inserts 2, 3, 4; 2. Shaft center insert; 3. Cone center insert; 4. Flat center insert; 5. Live center with cup center insert; 6. Live center (cone type); 7. Drift pin; 8. Dead center (cone type); 9. Dead center (cup type).*
Bottom: *Knock-out bar and calipers, a measuring tool.*

Lathes come with different size tapered holes in the spindles. A larger lathe may have a **#3** morse taper in the headstock, while a smaller one may have a **#2** morse taper. A *taper adapter sleeve* converts a **#2** taper to a **#3** taper. A *drift pin* separates the two tapers.

Faceplates

Faceplates are metal discs with threaded collars which correspond to the lathe spindle. They are fastened to the wood with screws for turning larger work. The term "faceplate turning" generally refers to bowl-making without using the tailstock. But I advocate the use of the tailstock for bowl turning as much as possible for the sake of safety. Holding a piece of wood between the faceplate and a center reduces the likelihood of the bowl coming off the lathe.

Faceplates are commercially available in various sizes for different size bowls and are usually made of cast iron. However, I prefer to have my own steel faceplates made by a machinist. Faceplates are available in right and left hand threads for inboard and outboard use. I discourage outboard turning because of the dangers involved. Most commercially available lathes are not geared slowly enough for larger turning. Larger turning requires special equipment and slower speeds.

I have had taper adapters made which enable me to interchange faceplates and accessories between lathes of different shaft sizes. I use a *spanner wrench* which fits into a hole on the adapter to loosen for removal. I have lathes with four different shaft sizes including the Shopsmiths which have a 5/8" spindle. The taper adapters enable me to use even the Shopsmith accessories on the largest lathes.

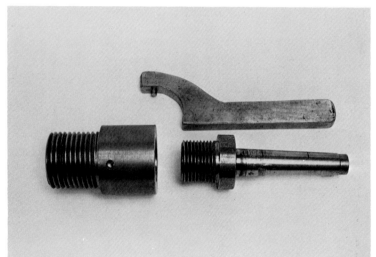

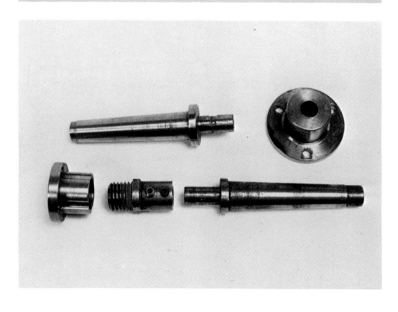

Top: *Faceplates.*
Middle: *Bottom left: adapter, 1 1/2" (8 threads per inch) to 2 1/4" (6 threads per inch). Bottom right: adapter, #3 morse taper to 1 1/2" (8 threads per inch). Top: spanner wrench.*
Bottom: *Bottom right: #3 morse taper to 5/8" dia. shaft (for Shopsmith accessories). Bottom middle: 5/8" dia. to 1" (8 threads per inch) (Shopsmith to Rockwell adapter). Bottom left: 1" (8 threads per inch) faceplate. Top, left to right: #3 morse taper to 5/8" dia. shaft (for Shopsmith accessories), 5/8" shaft dia. Shopsmith faceplate.*

Screw centers attach to the spindle of the headstock and are used for fastening work to the lathe by a center screw. They are useful for roughing work or for finishing small pieces quickly.

Chucks

A *drill chuck* may be used in the headstock or the tailstock. When used in the tailstock, work held by a faceplate in the headstock may be drilled by cranking the tailstock and advancing the drill into the revolving wood. A *chuck key* tightens and loosens the drill chuck. When the drill chuck is used in the headstock, any number of drill press accessories, such as buffing wheels, grinding wheels and drum sanders may also be used.

A *3-jaw chuck* screws onto the spindle and may be used for holding small pieces of stock or turned objects for finishing. Although primarily designed for metal, the 3-jaw chuck has many applications for the woodturner. A square chuck key tightens and loosens the 3 jaw chuck.

Tool Rests

Tool rests are available in different sizes and shapes. Standard tool rests, which come with most lathes, are designed for shearing techniques. For large heavy work using my carbide-tipped roughing tools, I have designed and built heavy-duty welded steel tool rests which absorb the shock better than the cast tool rests which often break under the stress of use with these tools.

A bowl rest (curved tool rest) is useful in turning compound curves and the inside of bowls. Right angle tool rests are handy for turning sides and faces without having to adjust the tool rest. Short tool rests are very useful for getting into hard to reach areas, and long tool rests are appreciated when turning long stretches or for spindle work.

Top: *Screw or stud centers.*
Middle: *Top: Jacobs chuck. Far right: 3 jaw chuck.*
Middle: 3-jaw chuck inserts.
Bottom: *Tool rests.*

TURNING TOOLS

Commercially Available Tools

Woodturning tools fall into two basic categories: scraping tools and shearing tools. Both are based on the forms of the carving chisel and gouge.

Scraping tools are used by beginners who have not yet developed shearing techniques and by experienced turners when turning a form or a part of a form that cannot be made through a shearing cut. Scrapers are flat, similar to carving chisels, and are beveled on only one side. They come with a straight edge, a pointed edge, a full rounded edge, a partial round or a skew edge. The scraper skew differs from turning skews used for shearing by having only the one bevel.

A scraping cut is made with the tool held at a right angle to the surface of the piece being turned. This is an efficient method of shaping wood through turning. However, a major disadvantage is that it tears the fibers of the wood, making considerable sanding necessary to produce a smooth surface.

Shearing tools include gouges of various sizes and depths (sweep) and skews which are beveled on both sides. A shearing cut slices cleanly through the wood rather than scraping shavings off. It is accomplished through the precise manipulation of a carefully sharpened gouge or skew held at a specific angle (relative to the angle at which the tool is sharpened) to the piece being turned. A properly executed shearing cut leaves a smooth surface requiring very little sanding.

Be careful not to overbuy turning tools. Most professional turners, although they may have many types and brands of turning tools, have only three or four favorites that they use consistently. A production turner may use only one or two tools to accomplish an entire piece.

A good basic set of tools for a beginner is a 1″ and a ¹/₂″ skew (beveled on both sides), a ¹/₂″ round-nose scraper, a ¹/₂″ gouge, a ¹/₄″ gouge and a parting tool. They should all be long-handled, good quality tools. The edge holding ability of the steel determines the quality of a tool. The tool should sharpen easily, hold a razor edge and be tempered correctly so it is not too brittle. To insure getting good tools, buy them from established companies with a good reputa-

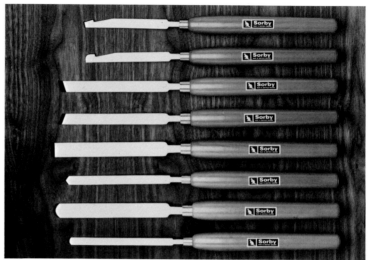

Courtesy of Woodcraft Supply Corporation

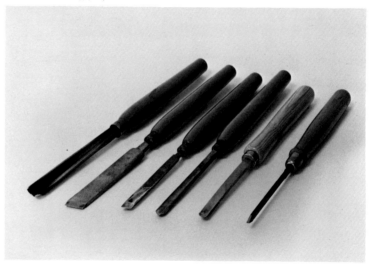

Top: *Scraping tools.*
Above: A good starter set.

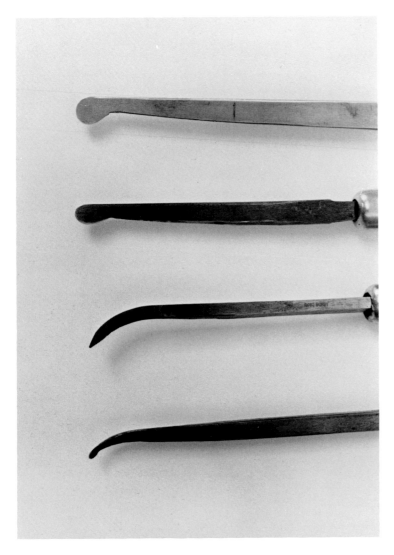

tion, such as these three English companies: Sorby, Henry Taylor Diamic Tools and Marples, all of whose products are available through fine tool catalogs. After learning to work with the tools you have, gradually add others as you need them.

User-Made Turning Tools

As you become more accomplished in wood-turning, you may wish to develop your own tools. Tools can be made to the exact length, weight, size and angle that works best for you. The simplest tools often work the best. An old file, ground and sharpened to a keen edge, will cut extremely well and endure heavy usage. It's important to douse the tool frequently while grinding since overheating will change the temper of the steel. Tool steel, drill rod, file stock or any high carbon steel will make good tools.

Sometimes a unique situation will develop in turning for which no commercial tool is suited. For instance, a sculpture I made called *Emerging Bowl* has a bowl within a bowl. None of the tools I had could be used to form the rim of the inner bowl, which is lower than the bowl sur-

Top left: *Old turning tools modified and re-sharpened to achieve unique cutting edges.*
Left: Emerging Bowl, 1982. *Spalted maple burl, 24" (61 cm) diameter.*
Top right: *Modified 1/4" skew.*
Opposite bottom: *Special carbide-tipped diamond point tool with a unique clamping device made by Melvin Lindquist in 1965.*

rounding it. I modified an existing 1/4" skew by heating it and bending it to the shape I needed. After I reground and resharpened it, it worked perfectly for its intended use.

Developing new techniques stimulates the creation of new tools. In the blind boring technique (see Chapter 18) used by my father for hollowing vases, a bent tool is required to finish-turn in hard to reach places. Melvin has developed several bent and curved tools which enable results not possible with conventional tools. His "snake tool" was made from an old square file, forged and bent, then ground and sharpened. Surprisingly, the snake tool does not catch or twist like most bent tools will.

I have a few tools designed and made by Jim Thompson of Greenville, South Carolina. He designed an ingenious tool holder at the end of the shaft for replacement and adjustment of a high speed steel cutting tool. The tool may be removed for sharpening or changing to another shaped tool and may also be pivoted to a desired angle for angled tool applications.

Tool steel turning tools are superior for many woodturning operations but require constant sharpening and attention.

Carbide-tipped Tools

When my father encountered the problem of tools getting dull quickly while turning spalted wood, he explored the possibility of carbide for the tips. He had first encountered silicon carbide alloys while working at General Electric in the late 1930s. Since all commercially available tools proved to be entirely inadequate, he and I were forced to make our own. We began developing our own carbide-tipped tools, silver-soldering the tips onto mild steel shanks that we had shaped to our needs. We eventually worked out a system for quickly and easily making a fine tool that can be produced in the simplest of shops. Since we began making our own tools, our turning time per piece with spalted wood and burls has been greatly reduced. We use high speed steel tools in our work and don't intend that carbide tools replace traditional tools but rather complement them. A sharp carbide tool does not have the keen edge of tool steel capable of a razor-sharp finish cut. But it will stay relatively sharp for a considerably longer time. In certain applications, such as roughing, part-

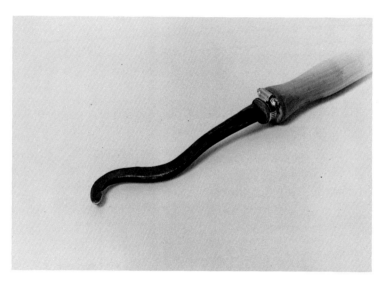

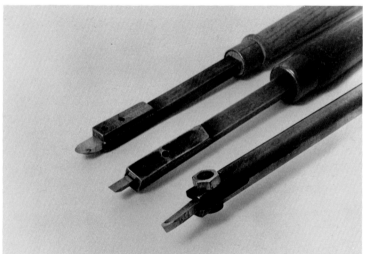

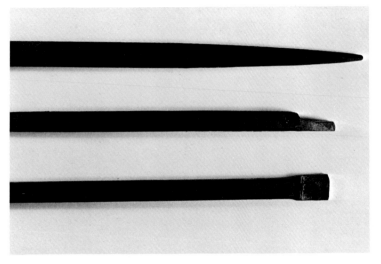

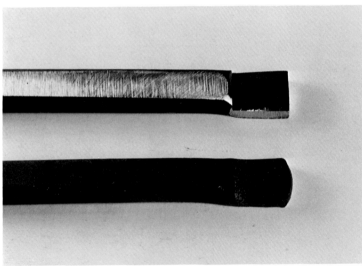

ing and cone separation, the carbide-tipped tool is unequalled in performance.

● **Making a Carbide-tipped Tool**

Carbide-tipped tools will outlast any tool you can buy, will take far more abuse and can be much more personal than store-bought tools. Making your own silicon carbide-tipped tools can be tricky if you don't have a background in welding and metal-working. However, they can be made in the shop by the following simple procedure.

Select a piece of cold rolled steel 1/2" square or bigger, approximately 12" long. Length and dimensions may vary from tool to tool, according to personal preference, but this is a good size with which to start.

Tang the end of the tool. The tang should be about 4" long and not quite to a point at its end. This takes practice, but with each hit of the hammer, the tang looks more and more the way it should if you're doing it correctly. An anvil and forge are ideal, but an oxyacetylene torch outfit and a good piece of steel to pound on will work as well. If these are not available, a tang can be cut and ground with a grinding wheel. Improvise with your own equipment, or go to a friend or a local garage or machine shop. If you can't make a tang, devise a method of making a handle which will accept a square shaft, or grind the corners to fit a round hole.

On the opposite (tool head) end, cut, file and/ or grind a step in the metal the depth of the carbide bit that you will use. The bottom must be perfectly flat. Try to keep the flat clean. The tip should sit flush with the end of the tool, and should hang over slightly on each side since it will be wider than the metal.

Most machine shop supply houses and catalogs have silicon carbide throwaway tips of varying sizes and shapes. They are usually available six to a package in rounds, triangles, squares and rectangles. Each shape corresponds to the shape of tool that you can make with it. Use the available carbide tip that comes closest to the desired tool shape, and modify it by grinding. Don't attempt to cut the tip or break it, because it will disintegrate, and if any large piece remains, it will probably have faults.

Top: *Top: tang. Middle: side view of step in tool head. Bottom: top view of step.*

Apply flux and solder to the bed. It's best to keep the tool in a vise and away from anything combustible. Heat the entire tool head a good orange hot using a reducing or normal flame at approximately 2000°. Apply a paste flux for use with silver solder. Heat the joint rapidly and uniformly, keeping the torch in constant motion. While the head is hot, apply a good portion of silver solder to the joint so that it fuses and covers the joint surfaces. While it is all orange hot, drop on an extra amount of flux. Don't worry about cleaning off flux residue, but be sure that no particles of foreign matter have entered the "pool" of solder. Next, using pliers, place the carbide on the tool where it belongs, simultaneously keeping everything hot. Heat the tip and the carbide together, and then position the carbide to fit the joint correctly with a screwdriver or other instrument of your choosing. Once the carbide is in position, continue heating, and apply an extra amount of solder to the back end of the carbide tip to fill the gap. Continue heating the entire tool head in a circular motion. Make sure the solder has penetrated all surfaces of the carbide where it touches the bed. Allow the whole tool to cool slowly and evenly; then remove the flux with warm water and soap.

The silver solder should be cadmium-free with approximately these proportions: 56% silver, 22% copper, 17% zinc, 5% tin. It should have a tensile strength of about 60,000 psi and a working temperature of 1250°–1500° F. The better the solder, the better your joint.

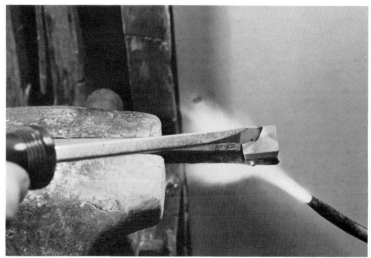

Only a thin film is needed to bond the carbide to the metal, but it must be entirely "sweated" without gaps or inclusions. After a few attempts, the process will become easier, and the joints will get better. The technique is worth learning and will prove invaluable in overall shop maintenance and repair. A local garage or machine shop can also do the soldering.

After soldering the tip to the tool, the tip must be ground. The best wheel for grinding silicon carbide is a diamond wheel, but its cost is usually prohibitive. A viable alternative is the green silicon carbide wheel. Montgomery Wards is one source of inexpensive 100 and 60 grit green wheels that have proven effective.

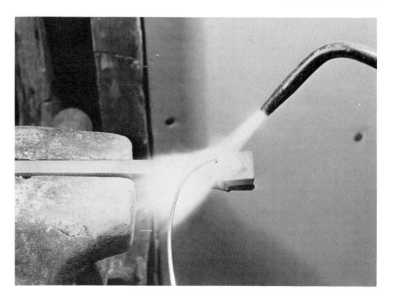

We do our grinding freehand, with the wheel spinning at 3600 rpm. Normally, we create an angle of about 15°–20°. The angle can't be too great or the carbide will not be sufficiently supported and might break off. Roughing should be done with the 60 grit, and finishing or honing with the 100 grit wheel. The smoother the edge, the longer the tool will last between sharpenings. A desirable sharpened surface will be uniformly smooth without breaks in the sharpened planes. Dip the tool frequently in water, as the tip will heat up and possibly melt the solder causing the tip to separate from the tool.

Probably the easiest and most rewarding part of making the tool is making the handle. A simple handle that fits your hands, and your eye, is all that's needed. Maple, ash, hickory or any good hardwood is suitable. Once the handle is turned, we drill the hole using the horizontal drill press, though a good hand drill will also work. We use an "adjustable ferrel" (which is actually a hose clamp), because it can be tightened when the wood shrinks and can be reused if the handle breaks or becomes obsolete. The ferrel should be applied before the hole is drilled to prevent the handle from splitting. The hole should be a gradually reduced series of consecutive drillings to make a tapered hole to match the tapered tang. For a good fit, heat the tang red hot, pierce it into the existing hole until it is nearly seated where it belongs. Remove the tang, allow it to cool, and reposition it in the hole, tightening the ferrel first, then tapping the end of the tool handle on a cement floor to drive

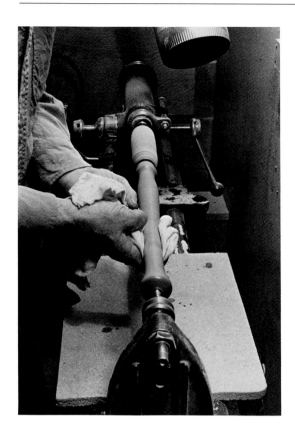

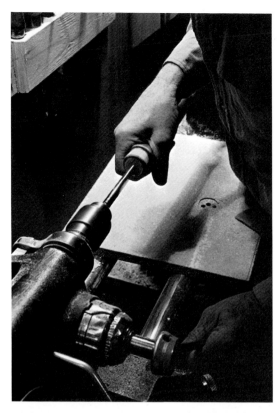

the tang farther in. Once it is seated properly, it is difficult to remove.

Using the carbide-tipped tool is different from using an ordinary tool, and it takes getting used to. It is used primarily for scraping. The tool has proven successful for us in outside diameter turning, normal faceplate turning, deep bowl turning and blind boring. If a new tool doesn't work at first, check the angles, and make sure you have sharpened it correctly. Also, make sure that you are holding it at the proper angle to the piece.

When I get used to a tool, I know its weight and balance to the extent that the tool becomes a very sensitive instrument. The surface often wears down in the place where I hold it, and it feels familiar and smooth, like the neck of an old violin. This polished surface is a record of the tool's history, and often the only record, as the finished bowls have long since been sold for the purchase of more tools, or the payment of taxes for the land that the shop is built on, or the groceries that sustain the family. It's only polish, but the kind you can see your reflection in. Perhaps that's what it's all about.

CHAPTER 14

Lathe Safety and Basic Woodturning

LATHE SAFETY

The lathe is and always has been the mystery machine in the shop. Often found in the corner piled up with books, tools and wood, it sits waiting for its next victim. Seemingly harmless because of the lack of exposed cutters, **the lathe is unmistakably one of the most dangerous of all the shop tools.** I frequently hear stories of people catching or pinching fingers between the wood, the tool and/or the tool rest. I've done it myself, splitting the bone of my left forefinger. Lathe accidents occur with regularity and, unfortunately, occasionally are fatal. It is sad and disappointing when you or someone you know has an accident. It is even more disheartening when the accident could have been prevented by following simple safety procedures. Accidents occur when we are not paying attention. Establishing routine safety procedures to the point where they become second nature will eliminate many accidents.

The dislodged flying object is the most dangerous of all lathe accidents. Several lathe companies have attempted to control the problem by installing a safety hood over the lathe, so that if the turning object becomes dislodged, it will be deflected by the shield. This is a good idea, but unhappily, the chips soon mar the surface and the plastic becomes clouded. I prefer a face shield, replacing the plastic regularly. The

shield will at least soften a blow as well as, in some instances, deflect a flying object. However, it should not be considered a sure defense against a direct hit. **Remaining out of the path of the bowl, especially when starting, and following the safety sequence listed at the end of this section will lessen the risk. Wear the face shield at all times, even when sanding. It might save your life.**

Owning a lathe is like owning a pet lion. It may seem to be tame, and a good friend, but when you do the wrong thing, or just when you think it's fine, it will turn on you. There is no such thing as a "domesticated lathe." Talking and thinking about accidents is discouraging but having them is worse. Follow safety procedures. Be in control of your tools. Don't attempt things you're not ready to do or are not totally capable of doing.

Do not force your tools to do what they are not designed to do. If your tool will not do what you want it to, then make a new tool, or buy one that is designed for that purpose.

Invent your own safety methods and procedures. Follow these systems like a check list.

Safety equipment is of extreme importance.

Wear a face mask. Get the best you can buy and keep it clean and well-fitting.

Wear a jacket or smock to keep the chips out. The day you reach around the back of your neck to get at those scratchy chips and catch the tool in the bowl, you will wish you had on more suitable clothing.

Wear good boots. Turners have a habit of laying tools down on tables. In a class I was teaching, a chisel rolled off the table and stuck into the exposed toes of a student wearing sandals.

Wear a tight fitting glove on the tool rest hand. When I split my finger, I believe that glove saved it for me. The glove will help to keep chips from burning your hand and gives added support. Be careful, however, about drawstrings and flapping material from an old worn-out glove.

If you clench your teeth when you turn, go to your dentist and have him make you a mouth guard similar to what boxers wear. Clenching can lead to TMJ syndrome which can cause untold problems throughout your system. The mask helps in this area as well. When chips hit your bare face it causes wincing. When you wince, you tense up.

Turn relaxed. If you are tense or nervous or have had too much coffee, leave the shop. Go chop wood or rake the yard or work on organization. Don't turn to work out your frustrations — go jogging or swimming for that. It is far better to leave the shop if your mood is not right. Many tools and pieces of special wood will be saved by doing this.

Keep a clean shop. I've gone into shops that were like a mud-dauber's nest. Chips, shavings everywhere. Tools scattered all over the benches, sawdust mixed in between. To get to the lathe I had to step over wood and motor parts. I knew one shop like that which eventually burned to the ground.

Be organized. I used to clean my shop but never organized it. Then I built a turning studio and began to think of my work as art rather than products, and my whole attitude and life began to change. I now regard my studio as a holy place — a temple where I go to perform my work — a place that I know I can do my best. I keep the walls uncluttered and white; I have fantastic lighting; and I am compulsive about cleaning. At night I don't worry about fire and when I come back in the morning, it's always a fresh new start. It's amazing what a clean and organized shop can do for your outlook.

Safety Sequence for Woodturning

☐ Make sure area is clear both underfoot and in the path of chips and the potentially dislodged spinning object.

☐ Make sure turning tools are sharp.

☐ Make sure lathe has been properly maintained. Check to be sure all nuts and bolts are tight, belts are tight and not frayed, bearings and moving parts are properly lubricated.

☐ Mount the wood properly. If using a faceplate, be sure that the screws are tight and that the faceplate is seated properly on the blank. If turning between centers, be sure the spur center and live center are properly seated.

☐ Tighten the tailstock spindle lock.

☐ Position the tool rest. Rotate the turning blank all the way around to check that it doesn't hit the tool rest.

☐ Put on face mask. A lightweight leather glove is recommended. Make sure sleeves are not loose.

☐ Assume proper starting stance, perpendicular to the lathe and out of the path of the spinning object.

☐ Check to see that the lathe is on slow speed.

☐ "Snap start" the lathe by snapping the switch on and quickly off. In the event that the lathe has been inadvertently left in the high speed position, this habit of snap starting could save your life. The purpose of snap starting is to be able to listen to and identify the speed at which the block is rotating. Learn to listen to the machine. If it starts making a different sound from usual while you are turning, turn it off and investigate.

☐ Turn lathe on and begin turning with cautious, light cuts. Gradually increase the cut as it becomes clear that everything is stable. Be sure to keep hands away from belts and other moving parts.

☐ When turning the lathe off temporarily to check the progress of the piece, also check to see that all mounting systems are still secure, and occasionally tighten the tailstock.

☐ When finished turning, set the lathe on slow speed.

BASIC WOODTURNING

To begin turning, it's more important to learn the workings of the lathe and skills of woodturning than it is to actually make something. I encourage students to use firewood or other scrap that is at least partially dry, preferably birch or maple, to practice the basic cutting techniques without having a finished product in mind. It is helpful to receive proper instruction from a qualified teacher when learning to turn. ***Follow all safety rules as listed in the previous section.***

Preparing to Turn

Select a round piece of scrapwood and cut off the ends parallel to each other and square to the sides of the wood. Find the centers of each end. Set the spur center in one end with a mallet and then mount the piece by replacing the spur center in the headstock and tightening the tailstock until the live center is forced into the wood. Position the tool rest parallel to the surface of the wood, a quarter-inch away from the outermost swing of the wood. This is determined by rotating the wood by hand, finding the point which is most out of center. The tool rest must be tightened securely and checked to be sure that the wood will not bang into it before the lathe may be started. Begin now to establish good safety habits. Check the lathe to make sure everything is tight, and that it is on slow speed. Make sure the floor space is clean and nothing is in the potential path of a flying bowl. Make sure tools are sharp. Tie hair back, button or roll up long sleeves, remove jewelry. Put on your face mask. Assume the correct stance — always perpendicular to the lathe, opposite the headstock, out of the path of the mounted block.

Shearing with the Gouge

A roughing gouge is used with an overhand grip to take off the high spots and to begin the initial forming of the wood. Before turning on the lathe, place the gouge on the tool rest against the wood as shown in the photograph, and by watching the position from a side view (the same angle from which the process has been photographed), lower the heel of the cutting surface to where it just barely catches as you rotate the block into the gouge by hand. When you have the right angle, you can cut the wood in the same way as with a carving gouge. Practice finding the right angle over and over again before turning the lathe on.

Once you have the confidence that you can achieve the correct cutting angle, you are ready to turn. "Snap start" the lathe from a position out of the path of the block, and then restart.

In the first stages of roughing out, the block is out of balance because it is out of round. De-

pending on the speed of the lathe and its sturdiness and the size of the block, the lathe will vibrate a certain amount. If it vibrates violently, do not attempt to turn the piece. Either recenter the piece so that it is less out of balance, cut it down in size, or discard it.

Begin making light shearing cuts, pulling the chisel from one end of the tool rest to the other and then pushing it back, keeping firm contact with the rest, taking off the high points of the imbalanced block. As you begin, the shavings will quickly mount up. Carefully clear the shavings as they obscure your view. Do not be concerned with the shavings at this point other than to remove them. Later, with practice, you can develop a method of cupping the hand in an overhand grip, forming a chute which will spray the shavings in any direction. Continue cutting, moving the gouge into the wood until you have made a cylinder.

The overhand grip is good for roughing out because it allows the hand to come in contact with the tool rest and slide along with the tool achieving a sturdy, clamping pressure. The underhand grip is for more delicate forming where the clamping pressure is not quite as necessary. It allows you to see the cut that's being made more easily than when the tool is covered up with the overhand grip.

The right hand grip of the tool handle is always an overhand grip, preferably close to the end of the tool for the most leverage. Whenever possible, particularly in roughing, try to brace the tool against your leg or side of your body for

5

6

added stability.

When shearing a curved surface, such as the outside of a bowl, the tool is rotated by the right hand and lifted up to achieve the correct cutting angle as the curve is being made. This cut is tricky for the beginner and requires patience and practice.

Practice roughing out and making smooth shearing cuts on the cylinder. Switch to a smaller gouge and hold the tool at one spot on the rest and push it into the block to study the cut that the tool makes on its own.

Practice with the gouge. Use several blocks, turning them down to 1/2" diameter. Mount and turn as many pieces of scrap wood as necessary to achieve competence and confidence with the tool.

The parting tool is used to make a separating cut and is pushed carefully straight into the wood — but not so far that the wood is cut through, as it would then separate entirely and fly off the lathe.

7

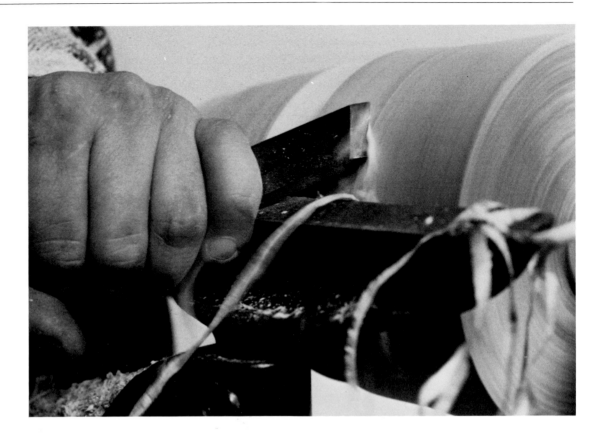

Making a Shearing Cut with the Skew

The skew is used to flatten and smooth surfaces in a similar way to a chisel. Again with the lathe off, position the skew as pictured with the tool resting on the tool rest and against the wood. Modify the angle of the tool until the cutting edge begins to grab as you rotate the wood by hand. If the skew does not make a nice, clean cut, stop and sharpen it with a sharpening stone. Practice attaining this angle, and then turn on the lathe (remembering all safety procedures) and practice making smoothing cuts until competency and confidence is achieved.

Facing Off the End-Grain of the Block

Reposition the tool rest as shown. Turn the skew over so that the point of the skew is facing in toward the center of the tailstock. Gradually pivot the skew down into the wood, peeling the shavings off cleanly. This process trues up the end of the block producing a uniformly flat surface. You may turn down to within 1/2" of the live center. Be careful not to go too far in towards the center or the piece may become dislodged.

Practice end-grain cutting with the gouge. Keeping the blank mounted between centers, reposition the tool rest for best cutting advantage into the end-grain of the block. In most turning, the best position for the tool rest is as close to parallel as possible to the surface being cut.

With a ¹/₂″ gouge, begin the cut by gradually easing the gouge into the wood at its outermost surface at the proper angle where the cutting just begins. Carefully turn the handle of the tool which will rotate the tool "up on edge," roughly parallel to the rotating surface. Make gradual sweeping cuts in toward the center making a smooth flowing hollow. Continue to practice hollowing between centers until competence and confidence are acquired.

The techniques for turning often seem difficult at first, but with discipline and practice, you will gain these skills. The key to understanding shearing techniques is developing a feeling for the cutting edge of the tool through repeated trial and error. When learning the techniques, do not attempt to make anything. Become familiar with the tools and what they will do; try to learn every cut a tool can make; then begin applying the techniques to simple forms. Start small, and see how the tool and your cutting affect the outcome of form. Make cylinders, spheres and cones — they are the basis of all turned forms. Once you have acquired these skills and achieved a level of consistent competency, you are ready to begin turning the smaller, simpler bowl and vase forms described in the following chapters.

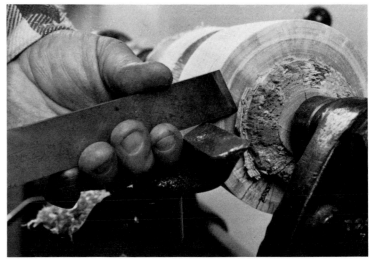

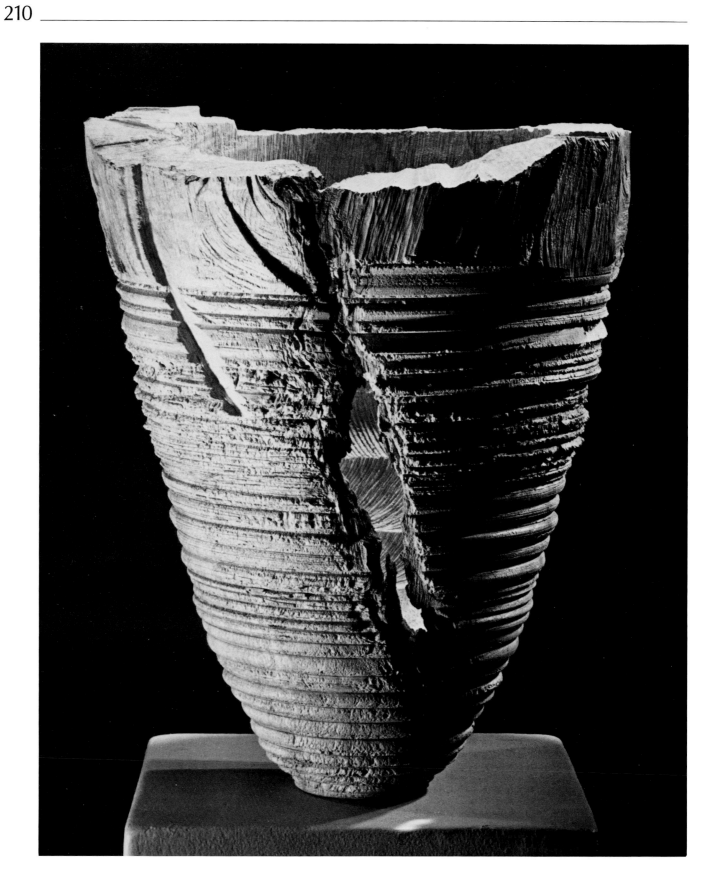

CHAPTER 15 The Development of the Work

Woodturning has undergone a tremendous revolution during the last twenty years. In the past, historical confines held the medium captive, bound by the chains of tradition, but key events and individuals have liberated woodturning to its present accepted craft/art status. Today, there is a fascination with woodturning as an art form. Much of the acceptance and understanding of current woodturnings has come from a specific evolution of form and thought which can be traced back to its origins.

Indians made bowls from burls, and the burl tureens of the early settlers and the Shakers are well known. Until the 1960s, most burl turnings, as well as native and exotic woodturnings, were strictly utilitarian. Woodturning by individuals was primarily a hobby. Junior and senior high schools included woodturning as a part of the industrial arts curriculum. Countless thousands of young Americans grew up with a cursory knowledge of the lathe and a personal experience of having made a walnut and maple stacked laminated bowl or a turned mahogany lamp. Many of these students went on to acquire lathes and made a hobby of woodturning.

PRESTINI: PIONEER

Very little in the way of serious, professional craft turning was done in America until the late 1930s when a Chicago Institute of Design professor became interested in the tool and unknowingly set a movement in motion.

An early proponent of Bauhaus principles in

Opposite: Ascending Bowl #5, 1982. Maple burl, 12³/4″ x 15³/4″ (32 cm x 40 cm). Collection, Mr. & Mrs. Richard Winneg.
Above: James Prestini, Cigarette Box, ca. 1936–41. Maple, 3⁵/16″ x 3¹/8″ (8 cm x 8 cm). Collection, The Metropolitan Museum of Art, New York. Gift of James Prestini, 1976.

the United States, James Prestini began turning perfect, controlled objects of wood which would have a profound effect on turning for decades to come. Prestini established this very significant precept: the turned wooden bowl could be created, viewed and appreciated as an art object. He made hundreds of his fine, intricate, thin-walled bowls, plates and other vessels, which were exhibited throughout the United States. His vision was extraordinary, for he was truly alone in his field. He established the basis for contemporary fine art woodturning, a foundation which is firm and secure.

In 1949, Edgar Kaufmann, Jr. of the Museum of Modern Art said, "This feat has been Prestini's, to suggest within the limits of simple craft the human pathos of art and the clean, bold certainties of science. He has made grand things that are not overwhelming, beautiful things that are not personal unveilings, and simple things that do not urge usefulness to excuse their simplicity. They are not precisely works of science or art, craft or convenience. Yet in their restraint and in their superb, direct assurance they touch our scope and potentialities, our limits and desires. It is this wide frame of reference that gives Prestini's bowls and platters their audience; art or not, craft or not, bowls or plain shapes, they speak directly and amply of our day to our day. Some other day will find a category for them; for the present, they remain Prestini's pure forms."

Kaufmann was prophetic in speaking of Prestini's "other day," for his works have become recognized nationally, and he has received critical acclaim for his artistry and contribution to woodturning and art as a whole.

Prestini himself acknowledges his unique position, as he declares in a current letter, "Handwork is very fashionable today. Though a lot of excellent work is being done, there is confusion by the participants and the public on the significance of handwork. There is more to handwork than making beautiful objects. Making involves the integration of craft and design for better understanding. Many good craftsmen know nothing about design. Being a craftsman doesn't automatically make you a good designer. Design is a highly developed intellectual skill. Optimally, the development of ideas through design gained from making things in three dimensions contributes to your total growth for better understanding."

Opposite above: *James Prestini, Jar, Cuban mahogany. Collection, The Metropolitan Museum of Art, New York. Gift of James Prestini, 1975.*
Opposite below: *James Prestini, Salad Set, Cuban and Honduras mahogany. Tray: 21⁷/₈" (56 cm) diameter. Small bowl: 6⁵/₁₆" (16 cm) diameter. Large bowl: 11³/₈" (29 cm) diameter. Collection, The Metropolitan Museum of Art, New York. Gift of James Prestini, 1975.*
Top: *David Ellsworth, cocobolo bowl, 1979, 16" diameter. Collection, the author.*
Middle: *Bob Stocksdale, paraking wood footed bowl, 1985, 3" × 7" (8 × 18cm).*
Bottom: *Rude Osolnik, laminated birch and walnut footed bowl, 1985, 11" x 11" x10" (28 cm x 28 cm x 25 cm).*

Above: *Ed Moulthrop, group of turned bowls, 1985. Left: sweet gum bowl, 25" (63 cm) diameter; middle: figured tulipwood, 30" x 47" (76 cm x 119 cm); right: pecan spheroid, 30" (76 cm) diameter.*

OTHERS WHO MADE THE MOVEMENT

In 1953, James Prestini stopped turning and continued work as a designer, teacher and sculptor, gaining international acclaim. During the 50s and 60s, several woodturners developed individually. Bob Stocksdale of Berkley, California, popularized woodturning by his consistent, professional approach to fine craftsmanship. Rude Osolnik of Berea, Kentucky, carried the folk traditions of production woodturning to new levels of expression and accessibility. He taught and produced countless thousands of turnings for sale to the public. Ed Moulthrop of Atlanta, Georgia, pioneered applications of engineering and chemical technology in the development of large scale architectural turnings. Melvin Lindquist also began his serious exploration of woodturning during this time. Among others, these woodturners worked steadily and quietly, gradually increasing the vocabulary and technology of woodturning, unknowingly laying more groundwork for a popular movement that would begin developing rapidly in the mid-70s.

During the late 60s and early 70s, when I began to pursue art and woodturning as a career, a few of my contemporaries were beginning to consider woodturning as a means to artistic expression. Stephen Hogbin took a design approach to woodturning and created monumental pieces, applying the principles and methods of the patternmaker.

In 1975, Dale Nish wrote *Creative Woodturning,* which has introduced contemporary ideas and methods into the teaching of woodturning and heightened interest nationwide. Nish's teaching at workshops all over the country, establishment of communications between woodturners and publication of three books documenting the movement have greatly contributed to the spread of information in the field. Beginning in 1976, Albert LeCoff brought key innovators together and conducted woodturning symposiums which made public the skills, philosophies and methods of the masters.

Among the important influences since 1975, David Ellsworth broke technical barriers with his perfection of the blind turning process. He continues to be the prominent master of the technique. With every technological and philo-

Top: *Dale Nish,* Wormy Ash Bowl, *Collection, the author.*
Above: *Stephen Hogbin,* Bowl, Walking Bowl Series, *1984, 8" x 12" x 4" (21 cm x 30 cm x 19 cm).*

sophical breakthrough, opportunities grow for woodturners. The movement escalates and gains momentum.

Prestini and others in the movement set the stage for a new level of personal expression in woodturning. They showed that the wooden vessel could be viewed as an object of value, interest and significance apart from its utility. Our collective attitude about the vessel has changed -- but not without the influence of Oriental art philosophy.

THE ORIENTAL APPROACH TO THE VESSEL

Throughout time, the bowl or vessel has fascinated people. Every aspect has been explored through the centuries by potters who daily made utilitarian vessels for ancient civilizations such as the Egyptian, the Greek and the American Indian. Vessels functioned as cooking pots, storage jars, water jars, eating bowls, apothecary jars, perfume jars, incense containers, etc.

Above: *Tea bowl, chi-chou ware, Sung dynasty. Collection, Museum of Fine Arts, Boston.*

These bowls were made by ordinary people who in those civilizations were artisans and craftsmen. The creation and use of the vessel was a vital and meaningful part of society. People relied upon vessels for their existence, but not merely as a means to an end; they invested the making and use of the vessel with ceremony, as an integral part of their lives.

The Japanese elevated the bowl to an even higher level — that of an art form. Within the tea ceremony, the tea bowl became a main focus, a physical symbol. The tea ceremony bowl has profound significance in their culture, symbolizing the seasons and harmony with nature. Whereas the vessels of other cultures had meaning and purpose, the Japanese elevated the bowl to new levels of spiritual and aesthetic significance. To the Japanese, the vessel had intellectual purpose as well as the traditional heritage of functionality. An art form was established which borrowed the best from both worlds: craft and art.

Each artist expressed his ideas in the vessels. Concern about form, surface and displacement became foremost. Within each of these areas, exciting and challenging advances were being made. No longer was it necessary to make a vessel perfect and pristine. Now the warped container was acceptable, symbolizing nature — human nature and the elements — earth, air, fire and water. Vessel making became newly ritualistic, each aspect from the wedging of the clay to the firing of the kiln having specific significance. Social, political, religious and economic concerns affected and inspired the makers and their audience. This was a new, and vital approach to the making of form — basic, primal and moving. The tea bowl came to symbolize various states of being such as poverty *(wabi)*, as well as various states of mind such as loneliness or solitude *(sabi)*. The vessel transcended its historical confines, becoming a form of sculpture.

The precedents set by Japanese folk potters, both ancient and modern, now directly influence our acceptance, understanding and appreciation of the "new wave" of woodturning in this country.

Top: *Don Reitz, Tea Bowl. Collection, the author.*
Above right: *Bowl, Chun ware, Sung dynasty. Collection, Museum of Fine Arts, Boston.*

MY SEARCH FOR DIRECTION

In every field of art, artists face the same ongoing problem within the creative process: finding direction, or gaining vision. There are those who copy the work of other artists, and there are those who are legitimately influenced by existing works, existing technologies, or prevailing schools of thought. But there are those artists who deviate from accepted norms, breaking away into uncharted territory, venturing on an exploration for personal expression that manifests itself in seemingly original forms and concepts. Although the work often *seems* mysteriously conceived, even, occasionally, to the artist, the elements of these forms and concepts inevitably derive from identifiable influences. This is the enigma of creativity, the evidence of the creative process with which artists have always struggled.

Henry James aptly wrote of this struggle: "We work in the dark, we do what we can, we give what we have. Our doubt is our passion and our passion is our task. The rest is the madness of art."

As students we learn by doing what our teachers do. But to pursue the work seriously, we must all eventually face the apparent surrounding darkness, follow our own direction, find our own way, or else settle for the stigma of mediocrity. Often the achievement of personal expression comes quickly after many years of study and practice — but perhaps it is the constant honing of skills and attitudes which enables the sudden revelation to germinate, then grow, nurtured by the confidence gained through hard work.

My search for self-expression through art began in childhood. As I grew up, the lathe became second nature to me. My father instructed me from an early age in turning wood, and we worked together regularly turning bowls and vases as well as many utilitarian items for the home.

My father's first turning was done in the late 1920s in a high school shop class. Throughout

Top: *Mark and Melvin Lindquist,* Black and White Eagle, Totem, ca. *1955–57.*
Above: *Melvin Lindquist, redwood wall-hung planters, ca. 1949–51.*

the years of his career with General Electric, first as a machine lathe operator, then as a first class machinist, and finally as a manager of quality control, he continued to pursue woodturning as a serious avocation. His first pieces were strictly utilitarian objects such as wall hung planters and collection plates for the local church. Eventually his interest grew in areas of aesthetics. He began turning vases in native and exotic woods such as zebrawood, rosewood and cocobolo. His work was smooth and regularly shaped. As his forms became more practiced and controlled, Melvin's interests became more technically oriented. He began challenging himself to create hollow forms and to seek solutions for seemingly impossible problems of woodturning. His approach to woodturning was that of the machinist, utilizing machine tool precision cutting with the flexibility and comparative looseness of the woodturner's lathe.

In college, I studied the formal disciplines of art: sculpture, drawing and painting. During my studies, one of my instructors drew my attention to ceramic sculptures. I was surprised to discover that Picasso and Noguchi, among many other painters and sculptors, were involved with ceramics. I became interested in learning about ceramics and pottery and soon abandoned my study of Gonzales, Arp, Moore, David Smith,

etc., to learn about other contemporary artisans. I studied the work of Peter Voulkos and Paul Soldner as well as others. Local potters Dave and Cathy Robinson were always generous about allowing me to come to their shops and watch, even to help out on occasion.

When I went to Pratt Institute in their MFA program, I continued to explore the areas of ceramic form, going to libraries and museums, familiarizing myself with other artists' work, learning about different approaches and techniques. I attended shows at Japan House and other New York City galleries. Gradually, I became convinced that the aesthetics of ancient

Top left: *Melvin Lindquist, redwood serving platter, ca. 1949–51, 14" (36 cm) diameter.*
Top right: *Author, Growth, 1968. Marble, 14" (36 cm) high.*

Top: *Author, four small pinch pots, clay, wood-fired with ash glaze, 1970.*
Above: *Darr Collins,* Tea Bowl, *1969. Collection, the author.*

and contemporary ceramics were somehow going to be expressed through my future work.

I left Pratt to expand my awareness and understanding of ceramic form through practical experience of the lifestyle, struggles and goals of a potter. In deciding to become an apprentice to potter Darr Collins, I wrestled with the inherent problems and commitment that apprenticeship requires. I'm glad I made that choice because of the skills that I learned and more importantly because of the experience I gained. Apprenticeships are very tricky — it's almost like becoming one of the family, sharing in all the hard work. At first, my teacher allowed me to do only the menial tasks, like starting the fires in the morning, cutting and carrying wood, sweeping, odd jobs and errands. To me, this was a privilege, just to gain exposure to the inner working of a studio. Gradually, he gave me harder and harder jobs and relied on me more and more with trust that I would accomplish what was expected.

From the beginning, we carried on a dialogue about form, about pots, about the lifestyle of the artisan. I borrowed books by well-known authors — Bernard Leach, Soetzu Yanagi, Susuki, and others — and pored through them constantly. Whenever a show catalogue came, I would study it carefully and draw the forms I liked. My teacher asked me questions about what I had read and put out certain pots he had made for me to draw.

Throughout these studies of ancient ceramics and tribal pottery, I began to notice that certain objects had much more meaning to me than others. I gravitated toward Shino, Oribe and Bizen ware. Although Hamada was the current recognized folk potter hero of Japan, I was much more influenced by Rosanjin, the lone wolf master who declined the honor of being a National Treasure, whose works had already been recognized by the Museum of Modern Art in New York City. Also, Tamba pottery — the rough Korean wood-fired folk pottery — impressed me with the honesty and directness of its earthy, textural quality.

The process we used to fire my teacher's pots was much like that of the folk potters. The approach was simple: late nights, up all hours into the morning, stoking the kiln with slab wood from the local lumber mill, watching the flames waft and fold in upon each other, enveloping the pots in a beautiful wildly orange flame. The ashes from the wood fell down upon the pots, melted, then fused to form ash glaze, like that of folk pottery. No amount of skill or craftsmanship or control could equal the results of this process — it was as if, at this point, the pots made themselves.

As I became less of an apprentice and more of an assistant, I learned that there was much more to the work than mere making. I saw my teacher spend much time just looking at what he made. All the while, as I made kick wheels from scratch, built the studio and kilns, much of the equipment, even living quarters, my teacher would not allow me to throw at the wheel. I could wedge clay, stack and help fire the kiln and do almost all the jobs in the shop, but I could not throw at the wheel. When I asked about it, he would tell me that in time those forms which I studied would manifest themselves, but that what was most difficult to master was discipline, and that I should go back to work. There was mystery to this relationship, mostly because learning about form is difficult. How does one explain how minor variances in volume, almost imperceptible to the eye, can affect the outcome of a work of art?

I was distressed when, standing by helpless, I would watch my teacher open the kiln and break every piece except the few he said belonged. These he put beside the few from other firings, and one day to my utter amazement he took down all but a few of those and, hammer in one hand, pot in the other, smashed them and let them fall to the ground. I wrestled with this idea during many sleepless nights. So much work, so much material, so much labor, only to be destroyed.

I would go back to the few on the shelf. As I looked, they seemed not very different from the broken ones. It irked me. I kept coming back, each time seeking some answer. Each time I came back, the small tea bowls quietly greeted me, each time speaking to me more. Eventually, the forms began to come clearer in my mind,

and I could see them simply by thinking about them.

One day, as if nothing had ever been unusual, the pieces seemed as though they had always existed, as though I'd known them all my life, as though they were part of everything else. Odd, however, was the change in me. I noticed very subtle things about the vessels. They had a kind of "life" to them, a fullness as though they'd just taken a deep breath. The colors, at first drab and dull, had a soothing, refreshing feeling, easy to look at. The shock came when suddenly I grew dissatisfied with my own pots and other belongings which I had always thought were special. They now seemed garish, inappropriate, almost gaudy. Eventually, I came to understand the secret. One special piece is worth more than a thousand of the lesser ones. In it is the ability to make change, to affect lives. As I watched the pot and the potter, I noticed each getting better. Eventually the potter began making fewer pots, and breaking fewer as well.

My teacher had different ideas about his pots. They were almost like people to him. This seemed so strange to me, how anyone could think of a pot with personality. Only later did I realize that they were his own traits which he had instilled into his work. These telltale reflections of himself, he confronted and learned from. This potter made his work out of a respect for materials and a drive to improve his skills, but there was a search or exploration apparent here also.

Above: *Kitaoji Rosanjin,* Jar, *1953. Wood-fired stoneware, 12³/₁₆" x 10¹/₂" (31 cm x 27 cm). Collection, The Museum of Modern Art, New York, gift of the Japan Society, Inc.*

As I learned about form, about the relationship of myself to my work and my new understandings, I became impatient at not being allowed to try out this knowledge on the wheel. I began working with the lathe I had in my own shop, and suddenly I had direction. It was as if I had found the key to a locked room. There were no questions about what to do, just problems which needed solutions. I knew what forms I wanted to make; I only needed to find the appropriate material and technology. These answers were surprisingly at my fingertips. I began to understand that the "survival skills" that my teacher always talked about were serious techniques which I possessed.

Translating Oriental Ceramic Ideals into the Medium of Wood

The look of ancient pottery was rough. The folk potters of Japan threw their pots in a few perfectly imperfect passes — the techniques gained only by years of hard work and practice — and accepted imperfections, celebrating them as providing the character in the piece. The thrown pot, natural and spontaneous, became the symbol of the way of life for that society.

I set out to make wood do what the pot did. I sought new ways to capture the essence, the spirit, the presence of the tea bowl and ceremony vessels. I used spalted wood and burl, much of which contained defects like bark inclusions, knots, holes and irregularities.

The zone lines on the surface of a spalted bowl turned to a pure and simple form became like the sgraffito found on many pots. The bark inclusions and other imperfections became like the imperfections of the thrown and fired pot

Opposite above: *Rosanjin, large bowl, 5¹/₂" x 21" (14 cm x 53 cm). Japan Society, New York. Gift of the artist, 1954.*
Opposite below: *Tea bowl, Sung 960-1279, 3¹/₂" x 7⁹/₁₆" (9 cm x 19 cm).*
Top: *Spalted wood tea bowl, 1970. 5" (13 cm) diameter.*
Middle: *Early spalted maple fruit bowl, 1972, 10" (25 cm) diameter. This fruit bowl was first turned, then buried for 6 months, dug up, washed off, returned and finished.*
Bottom: *Spalted beech bowl, 1972, 8" (20 cm) diameter.*

1

2

3

4

5

6

which were celebrated by the potter. The inclusions, holes and voids of these distressed woods created startling contrast to the smooth turned surfaces of the vessels, which owed their shapes to ancient vessels that I had carefully studied.

These first pieces which exploited the defects of wood were initially shocking and intimidating, even to me. At first, the vessels seemed ugly, coarse and rustic, but gradually began to grow on me. I could see that what I had set out to do — translate form and philosophy from one medium to another — had actually happened.

A new philosophy also emerged for the treatment of the lip of the bowl. Instead of allowing it to be a limiting factor, to interrupt the expressiveness of the surfaces of the inside and outside, I began to interfere with the continuum of the lip, allowing cracks or checks, knots or grain imperfections to make a statement on the rim of the bowl. At first, the effects were subtle: a minor dip, a break in the wood, a slight showing of imperfection. Gradually, with more confidence and more acceptance of the inevitable, the natural top bowl evolved.

At the same time, the turned and carved vessel was developed through turning, then carving a piece in patterns and rhythms. Two of the best of these early pieces are the *Carved Bowl with Ladle,* and the *Brancusi Cup* which combines the concepts of the natural top bowl and the turned and carved vessel.

The work grew out of functional objects. At

7

8

1: Hopi Basket Bowl, *1978. Spalted maple, 9" x 5" (23 cm x 13 cm).*

2: *Butternut knob bowl, 1971, 10" (25 cm) diameter.*

3: *Black birch root burl turned natural exterior bowl, 1971, 8" (20 cm) diameter.*

4: *Early forerunner of the natural top bowl, 1970, 9" (23 cm) diameter.*

5: *Spalted maple burl natural top bowl, 1974, 8" (20 cm) diameter.*

6: *Spalted elm burl natural top bowl, 1981, 14" x 16" (36 cm x 41 cm). Collection, The Arrowmont School of Arts and Crafts.*

7: *Turned and carved vessel with ladle. Spalted maple burl, 10" x 9" (25 cm x 23 cm). Collection, The Greenville County Museum of Art, South Carolina.*

8: Brancusi Cup, *1976. Spalted elm burl, cherry burl, soapstone inset, 8" (20 cm). Collection, The Metropolitan Museum of Art, New York.*

first, salad bowls or fruit bowls had those sorts of labels hung on them out of a sense of duty, preferring at that time not to totally strip away utilitarian connections. However, it was evident that the objects would not function in the way a "plain" bowl of uniform, sound material would. They would leak, deteriorate with use and change dramatically in character from the original "just completed" object. Eventually, I dropped my loyalty to utility, deferring instead to the greater and chief concern: communicating personal values and thinking through turned form. I began applying the principles of Oriental art to the tradition of woodturning. Gradually, the new bowls made of burl and spalted wood began to take on a life of their own.

As potters and crafts artists had a fascination with the Japanese ceramic ware, I had a similar fascination with the thinking of the Japanese artists whose work embodied the spirit of these principles. Suzuki writes: "Evidently, beauty does not necessarily spell perfection of form. This has been one of the favorite tricks of Japanese artists — to embody beauty in a form of imperfection or even ugliness. When this beauty of imperfection is accompanied by antiquity or primitive uncouthness, we have a glimpse of *sabi*, so prized by Japanese connoisseurs.

"Antiquity and primitiveness may not be an actuality. If an object of art suggests even superficially the feeling of an historic period, there is *sabi* in it. *Sabi* consists in a rustic unpretentious or archaic imperfection, apparent simplicity of effortlessness in execution, and richness in historical associations (which however may not always be present); and, lastly, it contains inexplicable elements that raise the object in question to the rank of an artistic production."

Above: *Turned and carved cherry burl covered jar with sphere nesting on top, 1975, 4" x 6" (10 cm x 15 cm).*
Left: The Full Bowl, *1981. Beech burl, padauk, 12" x 12" (30 cm x 30 cm). Collection, Paul Wolff and Rhea Schwartz.*

Above: The MacDowell Bowl, *1981. Spalted elm (from a sculptor's block stored at the MacDowell Colony, Peterborough, New Hampshire) made with chain saw turning techniques innovated by the author, 33" x 23" (84 cm x 58 cm). Collection, Dr. & Mrs. Alan Lubarr.*
Right: Evolutionary Bowl, *1982. Spalted maple, 18" (46 cm) high. Collection, Mr. & Mrs. Richard Winneg.*

Opposite: Obviated Bowl, 1984. Elm burl, 12" (30 cm) high. Sculpture incorporating the traditional bowl, the natural top bowl and the hollow blind-bored vase, turned from one piece.
Above: Broken-Hearted Bowl #1, 1982. Mulberry burl, padauk, 14" x 8" (36 cm x 20 cm). Collection, Mr. & Mrs. Robert Stonehill.
Right: Ascending Bowl #3, 1981. Walnut, 11½" x 8½" (29 cm x 22 cm) Collection, The National Museum of American Art, Smithsonian Institution, Washington, D.C.

Above: *Melvin Lindquist, Spalted birch hollow vase, 1984, 12" (30 cm).*

CHAPTER 16 Turning Spalted Wood

The examples of woodturning techniques in this chapter and the following ones set forth approaches which my father and I have used and developed over the years. These techniques assume the sculptor's point of view rather than that of a traditional woodturner. The techniques themselves are not vitally important to us, but rather the expression of form, aesthetic and philosophy that we have been able to achieve through them.

The sculptor should have a vision and seek the techniques as a means to fulfill it. It is valuable to learn techniques, but they should not determine the work. Learn techniques to gain skill in problem-solving and to establish a foundation from which to build your own direction and statement of form.

THE DEVELOPMENT OF TECHNIQUES FOR TURNING SPALTED WOOD

After our discovery of spalted wood on our land in the Adirondacks, my father and I began searching for more and were surprised at how much had been there all along without our noticing it. We discovered that the wood existed in varying stages of decay and noticed that the entirely rotten wood was riddled with zone lines that separated areas of vivid colors, even blues and greens. Since my father could only guess how the wood would work, we harvested wood in all stages of decay up to rotten. In the winter of that first year of gathering spalted wood, we

Above: *Melvin Lindquist, Spalted birch vase, 6"* *(15 cm).*

discovered many solid logs, much to our astonishment, that were full of zone lines, patterns and colors — unbelievably marked and much better than any that we had found during the summer. We carefully cut, hauled and stacked the pieces, only to find that with the spring thaw, the frozen wood turned to mush.

My father waited patiently several months for some of the wood to dry enough to turn. To start, he picked the hardest, least rotten pieces that contained just a few lines. It was wood that now we would reject as not having enough picture to bother with. These first pieces turned pretty much like good wood, still retaining most of the hardness of the birch.

The effect — the patterns and character — that the zone lines had on his turned shapes so excited my father that he used up the wood quickly. Then he was forced to begin turning wood in more advanced stages of decay. He soon discovered that the best marked pieces came from the wood that was in the intermediate to advanced stage. Unfortunately, he also encountered the terrible pecking and chipping produced in turning spalted wood. I was quickly discouraged by the amount of work necessary to create a smooth surface through sanding out the deep cavities in the surface. But my father had more patience and vision than I and would spend hours sanding for the reward of seeing the finished piece. At this time, I was interested in understanding woodturning techniques. As I could achieve very smooth surfaces using good dry cherry, oak, walnut and other native hardwoods, I continued working with these. My father continued working with exotic and native hardwoods, doing straightforward designs, but he also worked on coping with the new problems involved with turning spalted wood.

There were problems. The wood did not like being taken out of its environment. It checked. It took forever to dry. The end-grain ripping and tearing problem grew worse and worse.

A major problem was that the black lines within the spalting quickly dulled tools — the patience to sharpen them diminished. So my father began experimenting with the available tools, and, as discussed earlier, developed carbide-tipped tools. (See Chapter 13, "Carbide-tipped Tools," for a complete description.)

Carbide tips solved the immediate problem of dull tools, but the shape of the tool needed work. And beyond that, our entire turning approach needed to be changed. In turning spalted wood, there seemed to be no set pattern to follow — everything was different for each piece of wood. And even with the sharpest of tools and skillful turning, certain pieces in an advanced state of decay still pitted and chipped a quarter- to a half-inch deep.

At first, gouging sometimes knocked some pieces off the lathe because the tool would dig into a soft part of the wood and catch in a hard part. The gouge cut could also sometimes tear out great pieces from the wood. Scraping was only a little better. We needed a new approach to the old problem of torn end-grain. Like many solutions to technological problems, this one evolved slowly, but the basic process remained the same. The only reasonable solution to the problem of turning spalted wood turned out to be abrasive turning.

Our method began in experiments with "flap wheel" abrasives at a time when it was difficult even to get flap wheels because the manufacturer (Merit Abrasive Product, Inc.) was offering them only as an industrial product. John McLeod, a Vermont woodworker, suggested their use to my father. My father knew about flap wheels through General Electric but had not thought of applying them to the problems of turning spalted wood. A flap wheel is a wheel composed of numerous strips of sandpaper that extend from the center hub of the assembly which attaches to a high speed drill. When rotating, the strips conform to the shape of the object being sanded.

My father began by grinding the interior surface of a bowl — the biggest and most time-consuming problem — with a coarse-grit six-inch flap wheel driven by an electric drill. (The outside surface wasn't as bad because it was accessible and conformed naturally to sanding.) Using the flap wheel accessory, the inner surface of the bowl was sanded much more easily than by hand. The flap wheel, rotating in the opposite direction to the bowl, quickly and evenly sanded the interior, neatly removing the pecks and chips. It saved hours of work. This was a major first step in a whole chain of breakthroughs in the application of abrasive technology to turning spalted wood.

At this time (1969), I was studying metal sculpture in college. One day, while using my auto body grinder to polish a sculpture, the idea hit me. Why not use the body grinder on the bowl as it spun on the lathe? At first the idea of using such a large powerful tool to do such a small job was frightening, but I tried it. The room filled with dust almost immediately. I couldn't keep my eyes open. I turned off the lathe and was amazed to see, after the dust cleared, that what would have normally taken an hour or more of sanding had been accomplished in five minutes. A blower system, sucking the dust directly away from the spinning bowl, was an absolute necessity. I pursued the new technique and found that by carefully maneuvering the grinder with gentle back and forth passes, I could smooth the outside of the bowl with incredible control and accuracy, and even shape the bowl while grinding it. The tool and its application to wood were not new. But shaping with the auto body sander with the bowl spinning in the opposite direction was new to us.

Next, I got a smaller hand-held grinder — easier to control — to use with finer grits. I used it with 120 grit floor-sanding discs to prepare the outside of bowls. I also began using a small, flexible, rubber-backed sanding pad with locking discs to sand the interior of the bowl. Thus, abrading the spinning piece with power tools could now prepare the whole bowl for final finishing with hand-held sandpaper. It is an intermediate step, essentially a bridge between turning and sanding.

After several years of developing our techniques and talking to other turners who were also experimenting, we arrived at a theory that we now call "equilibrial abrasion." The shaft of a lathe turns clockwise. Most common rotating shop tools also turn clockwise. But if the shafts of two clockwise rotating tools are put together face to face, they rotate in opposite directions. We've found that two counter-rotating forces, with proper control and balance, can reach a state of equilibrium. We use abrasive discs on auto body sanders, rubber disc sanders and foam-pad disc sanders while the lathe is turning.

Above: Fine Woodworking Cover Bowl, *1978. Spalted maple, 10" x 4¹/₂" (25 cm x 11 cm). Collection, Alice & William Clark.*

Rather than holding the sandpaper still while the bowl turns, the spinning sandpaper works in the opposite direction against the spinning wood. The physics of the interaction aren't clear to me, but in practice there is a point — and it's not difficult to find — where the two rotational forces balance each other. The tool seems to hover over the work and the sanding dust pours away in a steady stream. The counter-rotational system partially overcomes the problem of end-grain tearing by providing a means to do the final shaping of the bowl without turning. Turning is still necessary to rough out the shape, and here the tearing must be continually fought. But after a certain point the grinder can take over. Carbide-tipped turning tools and equilibrial abrasion won't replace the traditional gouge and scraper, but they extend traditional techniques to deal effectively with the difficulties presented by spalted wood.

TURNING A SPALTED BOWL

I turn my bowls for reasons other than utilitarian function. My main purpose is to create a work that commands the space of a room, that lights

its environment. It is intended to display the beauty of nature and to reflect the harmony of humanity. The bowl is already full.

Making the spalted bowl requires complete and pure simplicity. The simpler the form, the more uncluttered the surface for the wood to display itself. Bowls with lots of curves and decorative lines cause the forms within the form to fight with each other and with the wood. Spalted wood is graphically oriented. To understand the art of making a spalted bowl, first understand the art of the ancient vessel. Study ancient Chinese and Japanese pottery vases, bowls and tea ceremony cups. Look at the work of Rosanjin. Investigate Tamba pottery. Study the masters and see simplicity at its best.

Turning a bowl of "plain" wood is difficult. Turning spalted wood adds another level of difficulty. Most spalted wood isn't like ordinary wood: the properties of the wood have changed, the cellular structure of the material has been altered and new rules must be applied where old ones fail. Using the abrasive method, turning spalted wood is transformed from a frustrating impossibility to a fascinating challenge.

I like to use wood that has dried for at least three years after harvesting. Occasionally, if the wood was already dry when harvested and feels okay after a year, I attempt to work with it then. But in turning the wood this soon, there is greater risk that it will crack or warp.

It is best to saw the blank so that the bowl lip faces the outside of the tree and the bottom of the bowl is toward the pith side of the wood.

This may seem extravagant, but it makes sense to have a bowl whose lip won't crack later. I have also made several bowls by turning end-grain up towards the lip and have had reasonable success. But the best way is to turn side-grain, so that the bottom of the bowl has side-grain, and the walls have end-grain. Usually, the most intricate markings are in the end-grain, so this is also an aesthetic advantage.

Cutting the Blank
The rough-cut block must be studied before making the bowl. First, determine the usable section of the blank by examining it for checks and cracks. I mark them with a dark charcoal pencil or piece of white chalk. It's important to envision a cylinder within the block and then imagine a bowl within the cylinder. Foreseeing the bowl within the block will enable you to determine if some cracks may be eliminated by turning if the bowl is oriented in a particular way. Draw lines on the block to indicate the unusable area, and band-saw it off. Now study the block again, and make a final decision on how the bowl will be oriented within it. Clamp the block in a vise, and hand-plane or power-plane the surface which has been chosen to be the bottom of the bowl. Be careful to keep that surface relatively parallel to the surface which has been chosen to be the top.

Finding the center of the block with a ruler, scribe a circle with a compass and saw the blank round on the band saw.

Mounting the Blank

Once the blank has been sawn round, I usually clamp it in the vise so it will not move while I measure and mark it. Carefully remeasure and re-mark the center of the blank, and then scribe a small circle a little larger than the outside diameter of the faceplate.

Next, carefully position the faceplate within that circle and mark points on the wood that indicate the screw holes. Remove the faceplate, counter-punch the screwholes and drill to the proper depth, using a 3/16" or 5/32" bit depending on the hardness of the wood. Reposition the faceplate within the circle, centering it carefully, and start the screws by hand turning them into the holes slightly. I use self-tapping sheet metal screws because their coarse thread holds well in the wood, and they can be used over and over again. Screw them in alternately, a little at a time, seating the faceplace properly onto the wood. You may screw them by hand or with a screwdriver bit in a hand-held power drill. Be sure that the faceplate is securely fastened to the wood, or it may vibrate loose and become dangerous. On the other hand, don't strip out the screws by overtightening. As the screws tighten down to their maximum point, they will squeak and screech. Let them squeak once or twice as they contact the faceplate and then stop and check to see if the faceplate is firmly seated.

The advantage of attaching the blank directly to the faceplate is that the method is simple and immediate. It has several disadvantages, however. One is that the screwholes must be

plugged once the bowl is completed. This problem, however, may be solved in a way that enhances the bowl. When plugged with spalted wood pegs, the screwholes add a decorative element to the bottom of the bowl, and reflect the process by which the bowl was made. A way to eliminate the screwhole problem is to eliminate that portion of the wood from the form, creating in effect a self-made wasteblock which is actually an integral part of the turning. This method diminishes the size of the piece which may be made from a given block.

Another disadvantage of direct faceplate attachment is that the faceplate is held only at the points of the screws into a block of wood that is relatively soft and may have weak areas. A glued wasteblock forms a bond with the softer spalted wood over its entire surface and is less likely to be wrenched loose. The faceplate is attached to the wasteblock, which is a uniform, hard piece of wood and unlikely to pull off.

Screwing the faceplate directly into the spalted wood blank also predetermines the minimum bottom thickness of the bowl, which also affects the thickness of the wall.

Attaching a Wasteblock

To use the wasteblock method of attachment, prepare a block of hardwood, preferably oak or maple, as illustrated in the section on carving a small bowl by hand. Daub glue on the wasteblock and on the bowl blank, and position the wasteblock in the approximate center of the bowl. Clamp the wasteblock to the blank with a C-clamp on each side, alternately increasing pressure until the glue oozes out and the wasteblock is securely clamped to the blank. It's important to allow the glue to dry for at least the time recommended by the manufacturer. I never turn a bowl sooner than twenty-four hours after the wasteblock has been glued. After the drying time, remove the clamps, find the center of the blank (not necessarily the center of the wasteblock), and screw the faceplate on as previously illustrated.

Important Note: Gluing the wood to a wasteblock with paper in between as many books suggest does not create a joint strong enough to withstand the stresses that occur in turning spalted wood. The blank may be unbalanced because of its varying density, and the turning tool is prone to catch where a soft spot meets a hard spot.

Rough Turning

Before beginning this procedure, a turner should have learned the safety procedures and techniques described in the Lathe Safety and Basic Turning chapter. Follow all safety procedures explicitly.

Mount the faceplate on the lathe. Move the tailstock, with a live center attached, up to the wood. Free faceplate turning is dangerous with spalted wood because of its varying density. Whenever possible, it is best to keep the bowl securely held between two centers. Since the faceplate is normally mounted on what becomes the bottom of the bowl, the bottom of the bowl will be at your left, next to the headstock, as you turn. With the lathe running at low speed, rough the outside of the blank to a fat version of the bowl you want to make. Use regular scraping tools, carbide-tipped scraping tools or a rough-out gouge as shown in the photos. Some spalted wood cuts like butter, some cuts hard, depending on the stage of decay. Often, advanced stage spalted wood seems to be

mush. It pecks and great chunks tear out of the surface leaving ugly pits and pockets behind. Even when turning with a sharp gouge, the pits are unavoidable. Don't despair, this is the nature of this material. Understand it, flow with it to achieve the desired end.

In roughing the bowl, try to apply the basic principle of a flowing curve to the form. Look for "dead spots" — breaks in the flow of the curve which interrupt the smooth path which the eye travels. Study the form as it is being turned. Try to work in front of a clean white surface so that the shape of the bowl can be observed easily while it is being made. Prop up a poster board or hang a cloth back out of the way as a backdrop. Learn to alternate your eye, looking first at the cut being made, then at the outer form being shaped by the cut. Eventually with practice, you may get to the point where you can watch and effect the form being made by observing that outer cut without watching the tool do it. The form becomes automatic. The roughing process can be an opportunity to practice arriving at form quickly.

Based upon your study of form, particularly ancient ceramic form, decide when the piece comes close to being "right." Switch to a finer gouge and begin making smoothing cuts. If you are using scraping tools, switch to a skew and scrape the bowl to a smooth form.

Reposition the tool rest and face-off the lip side of the bowl. I use a carbide-tipped square-nose tool and make plunge cuts in to the center. If you use a gouge, the tool rest must be posi-

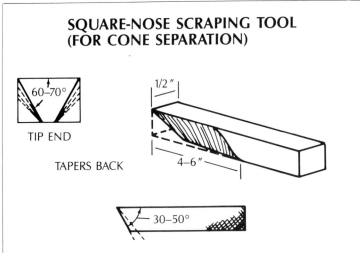

SQUARE-NOSE SCRAPING TOOL
(FOR CONE SEPARATION)

60–70°

TIP END

TAPERS BACK

1/2"

4–6"

30–50°

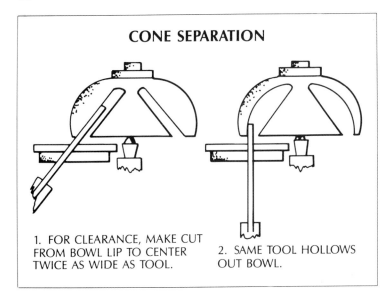

CONE SEPARATION

1. FOR CLEARANCE, MAKE CUT FROM BOWL LIP TO CENTER TWICE AS WIDE AS TOOL.

2. SAME TOOL HOLLOWS OUT BOWL.

tioned differently. The plunge cut with the carbide tool does the job quickly and neatly since it is cutting side-grain.

Separating the Cone

The outside of the bowl now looks more or less like what it will end up being. The inside is still a solid mass. I used to remove the inside of the bowl using traditional turning methods until my father taught me his cone separation technique. This trick removes an intact cone from the block of wood which may later be remounted and turned into another, smaller bowl. This method also keeps the bowl between centers longer. Practice and care are required to acquire the skill to perform this technique successfully.

To separate the cone, use a long, thick and strong square-nose carbide-tipped tool, or another homemade tool which may be made from a square shaped file or a 1/2" scraping tool. If you make the tool from a file, make the cutting edge on what was once the edge of the file, not the face, so the tool is rather thicker than it is wide. Grind the end to a short, sharp bevel (30° to 50°), and keep the corners sharp. Then add a long, sturdy handle for leverage. You may wish to grind a 1/2" scraping tool tapering the sides back similar to the one in the diagram, make a long handle for it and use it to practice the technique on waste wood practice blanks.

Start the cut at the inside of the bowl rim, and aim for a point well up from the bottom center of the bowl. The cut must be at least twice as wide as the tool, for clearance, and is made by a gradual pushing of the tool. The cuts must penetrate deeply enough to make a cone of the piece that normally would have been chips. Use the same tool to begin cleaning out the sides of the bowl.

Equilibrial Sanding of the Exterior

While the bowl is still held between centers (the cone is still connected, supporting the bowl with the pressure from the tailstock) begin sanding the exterior of the bowl with the equilibrial sanding method using a 6" auto body sander. *An important caution: Know well how to operate the grinder on a stationary surface before attempting to use it on the lathe, pitting the two forces against each other. It's very easy to catch the bowl (particularly in the abrading of the*

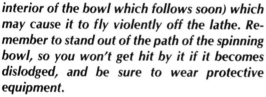

interior of the bowl which follows soon) which may cause it to fly violently off the lathe. Remember to stand out of the path of the spinning bowl, so you won't get hit by it if it becomes dislodged, and be sure to wear protective equipment.

Begin with a 60 grit silicon carbide floor sanding disc. Rest the grinder on your hip and use your weight to push it toward the bowl, moving from headstock to lip. Near the end of each pass, pull up the handle, turn your hand over on the handle, and reverse the direction to complete the sanding and shaping of the lip — all in one movement. The idea is to get motion and control going together, to think of the tool as an extension of the hand or, better, as a sensitive instrument. Paying attention to the sounds pays off. The right pitch will tell that the speeds are right. Ticking means the disc has a tear in it and will soon explode; click, click, click means there is a crack in the bowl; bump, bump, bump means there is a soft spot that the grinder is wearing away faster than the rest of the bowl.

Removing the Cone

After rough-sanding the exterior, take the bowl off the lathe and place it (faceplate still attached) on a pad on the concrete floor. Using a spoon gouge and mallet, strike the center of the cone — with the cutting edge of the chisel facing end-grain, not side-grain — making a good sharp whack. A few subsequent blows will pop the cone right out.

1

2

3

4

Once the bowl is remounted on the lathe, the inside must be cleaned up and finish-scraped to its final form prior to sanding the interior.

Sanding the Interior

Begin sanding the interior of the bowl using a high speed electric drill with a 3" locking 36 grit abrasive disc. Some pieces of wood will finish up more quickly if the initial sanding of the end-grain portions is done with the lathe turned off. Face the front of the bowl, and position the disc in the right side. This may seem wrong at first, but the wood sands much more quickly than it does on the left side.

Proper speed is the key to equilibrial abrasion techniques. If the bowl turns faster than the disc, the bowl will overpower the disc. The disc must spin up to twice as fast as the bowl (although not so fast that it burns the wood) in order to achieve equilibrium. There must be a balance of power and an overbalance of cutting action. In interior abrading, the disc should reach a flow, a floating movement, gliding back and forth from the bottom of the bowl to the lip, each pass grinding off a constant thickness of excess wood. Prepa-

5

6

ration sanding calls for knowledge and careful control. I use high speed (1,000–1,800 rpm), preferably two speed drills but not variable speed drills, since they can't take too much force. A cheap drill can't be used — it will quickly burn out. When you hit equilibrium, the tool will appear to be suspended, like a gyroscope, free to smoothly glide in any direction. This can occur only when the tool is properly cutting the wood. A good strong drill will really cut, and the bowl interior will quickly take shape. With practice, the bowl form can be precisely controlled and shaped by the equilibrial abrasion technique.

Finish-Sanding and Finishing the Bottom

Be sure the interior surface is sanded smooth, that the walls are consistent and the pecks are all eliminated. The outside and the inside may be hand-sanded. Cut a foam rubber backing pad to cool the sanding and cushion your hand. Work the sandpaper gently back and forth with not too much pressure through 150, 220 and 320 grit.

Once the finish-sanding has been completed, take the bowl off the lathe and clamp the faceplate in the bench vise to a make a final finish-sanding pass with the foam back sander. Sanding on the lathe leaves inevitable concentric sanding rings which may be removed with the foam back pad.

Next remove the faceplate and prepare to plug the holes. Drill the holes out on the drill press with a 1/2" Forstner bit to within 1/8" of the bottom of the screw hole. Cut plugs from a piece

7

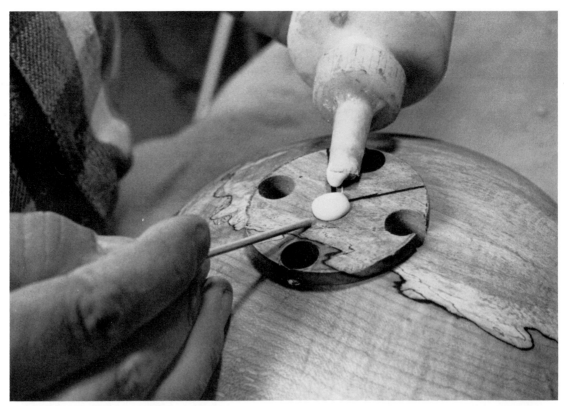

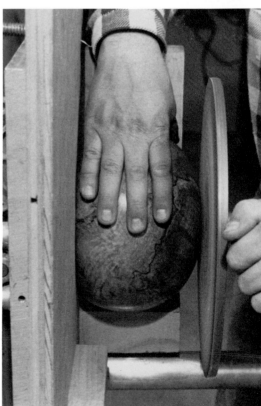

of spalted wood, preferably from waste from the wood the bowl blank was cut from. Use a $1/2''$ plug cutter in the drill press. Set the depth stop to the deepest point the cutter will allow, then drill several plugs. The prettiest plugs are made by positioning the zone lines through the middle of the plug. Turn the block on edge and rip the stock length-wise on the band saw. Tip the sawn piece and the plugs will fall out ready to use.

Position the bowl, bottom side up, on a blanket or pad spread out on the bench and daub a little glue in the center of the holes. Use a small dowel to spread the glue thoroughly in the holes. Spread more glue on the cut plugs by rolling them through the glue, then position them, orienting the grain the same as the grain direction of the bowl, and pound them home with a hammer or mallet. Wipe off excess glue with a damp rag, being careful not to get water on the side of the bowl or it will raise the grain, then cut or chisel off the excess plug sticking out of the holes.

The bowl bottom may be flattened by sanding it on the disc sander by hand-holding or by using a jig. When sanding by hand-holding, be certain the bottom is parallel to the top. The jig positions the bowl properly, assuring it will be sanded parallel. This attachment may be made to fit a drill press or a Shopsmith disc sander. As the disc rotates on *slow speed,* it is pressed into the bowl by moving the drill press arm. Sand the bottom until it is flat and flush with the point where the bottom ends and the bowl sides begin. Do not oversand because that will increase the diameter of the base, throwing the form off. This is the problem with many unsuccessful bowls.

Next mount a soft back foam pad in the stationary drill chuck and finish the bottom, breaking the edges over. Start with 150 grit and finish with 320 or 400.

An alternative method of finishing the bottom of the bowl is to turn it. First remove the faceplate and find the actual center of the bottom of the bowl. (Note that the bowl in the picture has been turned to include a waste portion equivalent to a wasteblock. This method works also when the screwholes left by a faceplate in the bottom of the bowl have been plugged.)

A special chucking pad, which is made from a metal rod, a wooden backing disc and a foam

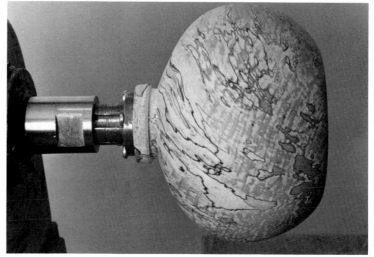

1

2

3

4

5

rubber pad, is held by the Jacobs chuck in the headstock.

The bowl is fitted over the pad (which has been made for this diameter bowl) and is held in place and self-centered with pressure from the live center in the tailstock. Now that the bowl is automatically recentered and held firmly in place, the bottom may be turned with a small gouge. A slight depression is made to relieve the bottom of the bowl from the actual sitting surface which is a flat from 1/8" to 1/2" wide.

Once the bottom has been hand-sanded on the lathe, the bowl may be removed, the center spindle cut off and the remaining portion finished.

You may sign the piece if you wish. There are several methods: woodburning, engraving with a vibrating electric signing tool or writing with ink.

Applying Finish

Finish the bowl with a fairly thick drying oil mixture (tung oil, driers and polyurethane) and apply until the wood won't take any more, then wipe off the excess. After the bowl is thoroughly dry (if you use Waterlox or urethane this may be overnight; if you use oil it may be several weeks) apply Tripoli to a cotton buffing wheel and buff the outside all around several times. Let the Tripoli polish the finish. Buff the inside with a bullet head bonnet. Hand buff the entire piece at length with a soft cotton cloth.

6

7

1

2

3

4

TURNING A LARGE SPALTED BOWL

Turning a large spalted bowl uses the same basic principles as turning a small spalted bowl but magnifies the problems and dangers, requiring experience, skill and modification of technique. The following sequence illustrates how I approach the large turning of spalted wood and should be attempted only by those with the proper large capacity equipment and the necessary experience.

While harvesting spalted wood and cutting it into blocks for transport and future turning, I sometimes come across a section of wood that is large enough, consistent enough and special enough to plan turning it into a large spalted bowl. If the block is too big for my band saw, I cut it round with the chain saw either in the field or later in my wood yard.

After studying the block, I plane it flat on top and bottom with the chain saw bar at the slight angle where the pivoting action of the bar on the surface creates a smooth planing effect. Then, envisioning the bowl within, I measure and mark with a square finding the center of the

5

6

7

8

block which will become the center of the bowl. I mark out with a compass or trammel points a circle in dark charcoal and then begin gradually cutting the blank. I make successive angled cuts with the chain saw until achieving a cylinder that is adequately round for turning.

I mount the faceplate to the blank in the same manner as the small spalted bowl; then mount the blank on the lathe and position the tool rest (rotating the blank all the way around once to make sure it clears the rest). *With the lathe on its slowest speed* (about 40-50 rpm), I turn it on and crank the tailstock ram with the live center into the rotating block. When turning a large mass, cranking the center in while the piece is spinning rather than before turning the lathe on helps to find a more accurate center.

On a large piece such as this, I prefer to use a carbide-tipped tool for roughing out instead of a gouge. I shape the outer form of the bowl with the square-nose carbide-tipped tool with a series of side plunge cuts. Increasing the lathe speed

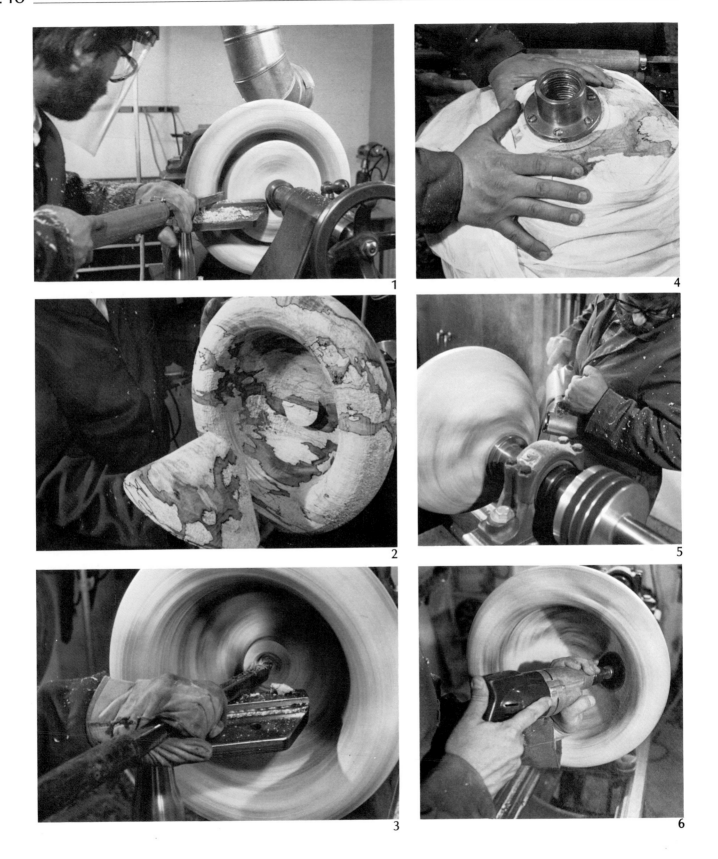

1

4

2

5

3

6

7

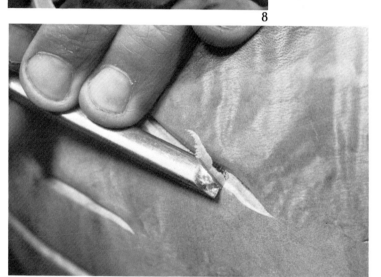

8

and using the same tool, I separate the cone. I am making a large, thick-walled vessel form, and do not hollow out as much behind the cone as I might in a smaller bowl. I give the cone a sharp whack to dislodge it.

Repositioning the tool rest, I finish-turn the bowl interior. Since the wood is relatively wet and some parts of it are even green, I leave the bowl in a thicker state than its final form is to be, and bag it within a plastic trash bag, leaving the side with the faceplate open to the air.

After a period of several weeks, I put the bowl into a paper bag to allow it to dry more quickly. After a few months, the bowl is ready to be re-turned.

I mount the bowl on the lathe and re-turn it with a gouge. Then the exterior is sanded with the body sander and the interior with a high speed drill. The inside and outside are hand-sanded with a foam backing pad.

During the drying process, the bowl developed some checks. I break over the edges of the checks with a small chisel and saw the cracks deeper so that they become more defined. Then

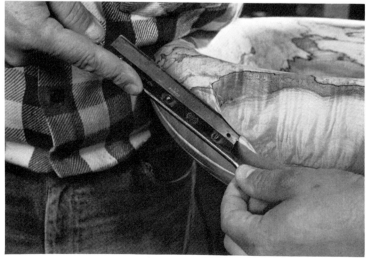

9

10

1

2

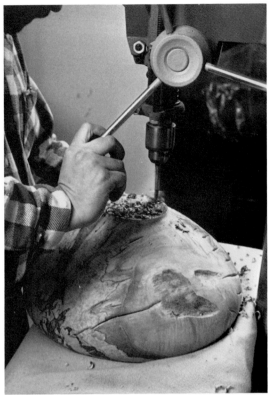

3

4

Turning a Large Spalted Bowl

I round them over by hand-sanding, accentuating them. I finish the edges of the sanded cracks with 320 grit on a foam back disc in a variable speed drill. Some woodturners fill cracks, but I prefer to celebrate rather than hide the nature of wood. Working the cracks offers interesting adjunct design possibilities.

I remove the faceplate, drill the screwholes with a 1/2" drill, set the pegs with glue, finish the bottom of the bowl first with the disc sander, then with the foam back sander, apply a hand-rubbed finish and buff with Tripoli.

Above: *Turned and carved bowl, spalted yellow birch burl, 1980. 28″ × 9″ (71 × 23 cm). Collection, Mr. and Mrs. Robert Stonehill.*

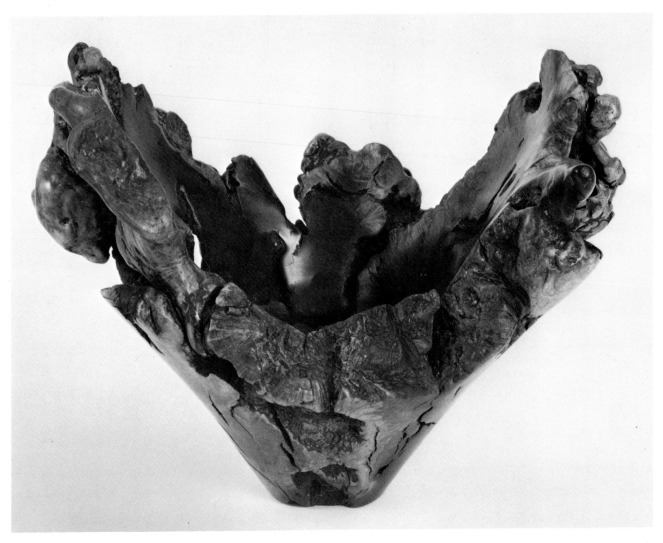

Above: *Mark and Melvin Lindquist, manzanita burl natural top/natural exterior bowl, 1984, 16" x 12" (41 cm x 30 cm). Collection, Mr. & Mrs. Mark W. Bates.*

CHAPTER **17**

Turning Burls

Sometimes I cut a big burl up into several sections to make turning blanks for smaller pieces. I cut the sections round with the band saw and stack them on a bench in the shop to be ready for turning. One day as I was looking at a stack of blanks I had just finished cutting, I noticed that one blank had a crack across the side that was facing me. I picked it up and found that the crack went all the way around. My first reaction was to think that the wood was no good — it was obviously unstable and would have to be discarded. But, I have always had a fondness for wood with faults and a willingness to change my preconceived idea of what a piece would become, so I went on to investigate.

This crack was obviously different from an ordinary drying check. I pulled on the two ends of the blank to see if it would come apart. Much to my surprise, it separated with the sound and sensation of opening a vacuum-packed jar of peanuts. The inside surfaces were astounding. In my hands were now two halves, positive and negative. The irregularities of the crack were not just surface lines but a landscape of moon-like craters, naturally formed by the way it grew. Thin, fibrous, barky material separated the two halves and peeled off easily. Undoubtedly, this was the natural barrier which prevented the two parts from fusing when they were growing. Instantly, I knew what the two pieces could become, and it was a simple matter of just "doing it" — putting the pieces back together and turning a single form, separating the pieces, turning out the inside of the bottom half making a bowl.

Turning Burls

When I was finished, I had a covered jar, the top recording one half of the natural fault, and the bottom recording a portion of the other half which became the rim and matched identically with the top. The top and bottom formed a perfect fit because the wood had grown that way and created its own irregular perfectly matched joint.

What I had thought was a crack was not really a crack, but a natural fault. A natural fault, with its hidden possibilities, can be recognized when it comes along only by a conscious observer who is responsive to the material and flexible in attitude. There are malformations, deformities, imperfections which become exposed during the process of turning the burl. The creative turner is constantly faced with decisions. Accepting or rejecting the imperfections of wood makes or breaks a piece.

When a potter consigns a pot to the kiln, there is an element of risk involved. The results of accident or serendipitous occurrence often add to the outcome of the piece and make it special. The same is true for the woodturner working with burl. Imperfections may be uncovered through the act of turning which enhance or enliven the form. Gradually, with experience, these happy accidents become less accidental. First, it is a question of seeing the results of the imperfections of wood and how they affect form. Second, it is anticipating the consequences of the relationships of form and material which lead to an intuitive control of the process.

The secret to turning burls is knowing how to orient the piece within the wood. Just as in turning spalted wood, the placement of the bowl within the burl affects the display of the wild and exotic grains and irregularities that contribute to the imagery within the bowl. But beyond the graphic implications of grain are the elemental aspects of burl form which greatly affect the outcome of the bowl. Within any given burl lies the possibility for a variety of forms. Over the years, my father and I have developed several approaches to incorporating the irregular aspects of burl growth into the bowl and vase forms. In the following sections are described some of our methods.

The following techniques require that you be very competent in the basic use of the lathe. Practice the cutting methods until you feel comfortable with them before attempting difficult projects. Forego projects that are too far beyond your current skill level. Most important is the unfailing observance of safety procedures. Follow the rules as described in the section on lathe safety. Remember to respect the equipment and yourself. Don't take unnecessary chances.

TURNING THE NATURAL TOP BOWL

Select a dry aged burl. If that is not available, you may use a green burl. Cut off the log ends if the burl was not removed from the log at harvesting.

After studying the burl, determine the orientation of the bowl within. The fullest part of the burl will become the mouth of the bowl. The opposite side becomes the bowl bottom. These two surfaces should be relatively parallel.

Turn the burl on its side (the cut log end) and tilt the band saw table so that the side of the burl which is the top of the bowl is relatively parallel to the band saw blade. Saw a flat to establish the surface that will become the bottom of the bowl (to which the faceplate will be mounted).

Measure the top to find the center of the burl, and mark the largest circle the burl will allow from its center to the cut ends with a compass and/or chalk.

Angle the band saw table and saw the blank. Invert the burl, clamp it in the vise, and attach the faceplate following the same procedure as in "Turning the Small Spalted Bowl."

Mount the blank, and rough-turn the exterior form with a roughing gouge. The success of the natural top bowl depends entirely upon its rim. It is critical to turn the burl without disturbing or interfering with the portion of its natural formation which becomes the lip of the bowl.

When nearing the lip portion of the bowl while roughing out, some areas of the rim will be higher than others (due to the unevenness of the burl exterior) leaving spaces or interruptions in the cut. Hold the gouge steady, and make the cut as though the wood were solid. Do not allow the tool to dip into the voids. There is a tendency for the tool to be pulled in and catch, resulting in damage to the rim. So be careful to keep a firm grip on the tool and to make a properly controlled cut.

1

3

2

The base of the natural top bowl should be small so that the sides flow upward gracefully and end in a perfectly natural resolution (which is the natural edge of the burl).

Use the auto body sander to make final shaping passes, particularly in the area of the top of the bowl which is the most difficult.

Reposition the tool rest and cut the cone from the center of the bowl. See "Cutting the Cone" in "Turning the Small Spalted Bowl." Remove the cone and finish-turn the interior of the bowl.

When making the interior finish cuts, particularly toward the rim, the bowl has a tendency to vibrate and may become dislodged from the faceplate. To minimize this vibration, I put the lathe at its slowest speed and with gloved left hand support and steady the bowl while making the cuts with the turning tool held firmly to my side under my arm. This is an advanced technique and should not be attempted by beginners. Often, a good solid burl will finish nicely without this technique, but it's helpful to be able to use this method when needed.

You may go back to the bowl exterior after the interior finish cuts have been completed and

4

5

make additional shaping cuts with the auto body sander.

Since the natural rim of the bowl is not regular and parallel to the bottom, it will be difficult to be sure of sanding the bottom flat in the correct plane after the faceplate is removed. Therefore I make a few turning cuts just above the faceplate with a point or small skew which indicate the plane that the bowl was turned on. Later, after removing the faceplate, I will sand to these lines, insuring that the bowl will sit level.

Take the bowl off the lathe and hold the faceplate in a vise. Finish the interior of the bowl with the foam back system. I use a wire brush on the outside lip of the bowl to remove grit and bark, then "whip" the natural edge with a 100 grit Merit Sand-o-flex accessory.

Remove the faceplate and plug the holes. Disc sand the bottom to the rings, and finish it with the stationary foam back. Or, instead of disc sanding the bottom, the bowl may be remounted and the bottom finish-turned as illustrated in "Turning the Small Spalted Bowl."

6

I use a thin mixture of tung oil, polyurethane and Japan driers for this piece. After several applications of finish, wipe off the excess, let dry thoroughly, then buff with Tripoli.

TURNING A LARGE BURL BOWL

In the following sequence, I turn a large cherry burl approximately 20" in height. Large burls make wonderful large bowls but are not for the beginner or even for the intermediate turner. As the bowl becomes larger, the problems increase exponentially. Large turning should only be attempted by accomplished and seasoned woodturners. The lathe must be big and heavy and powerful in order to bear the strains and stresses of turning large pieces. A large diameter shaft (2" to 3") is recommended. Everything must be heavy-duty, from the tailstock to the tool rest. The lathe must also be capable of turning at a slow speed. As the diameter of the wood increases, so does the surface feet per minute. So at 50 rpm a 16" diameter burl is travelling as fast as an 8" diameter burl at 100 rpm. Most commercially available lathes have low end speeds of 300-500 rpm which are far too fast when turning a large burl.

I study the burl from all different angles to understand its form. This cherry burl grew nearly all the way around the tree. As cherry has a tendency to crack, I try to orient the bowl side-grain rather than end-grain, as a side-grain crack may be dealt with by sanding, but a bad end-grain crack could conceivably jeopardize the structure of the bowl.

I use trammel points and white chalk to mark out the maximum diameter of a bowl which may be sawn. I cut off the remaining burl growth on the side with the chain saw. Often a large burl may hold several bowls within if you know how to cut it. After removing the smaller burl part which will become a natural exterior bowl (a bowl which is made in the shape that the burl grew and turned to disturb as little of the natural formation as possible), the rest of the burl is sawn round to make a larger blank for a natural top bowl.

To hold the large burl blank for mounting the faceplate, I invert it on a blanket draped over a small heavy-duty oil drum. I find the center, mount the faceplate directly to the burl and mount it on the lathe.

I chuck a 2¼" multi-spur bit in a Jacobs chuck on a #3 morse taper held in the tailstock ram in preparation for drilling a shallow hole to receive the live center.

Often the beginning stage of turning large burls is dangerous and requires special caution when turning the lathe on. I stand to the side well out of the path of the burl and jog the lathe up to speed. Jogging is a series of snap starts, allowing the mass to gradually reach its maximum rpm at the slowest speed of the lathe, which in this case is 50 rpm.

With the lathe at its slowest speed, I advance the tailstock ram forward and drill the shallow hole, establishing a flat surface to receive the live center.

Another method of mounting the burl, which provides for more accurate centering, is to first mount it between centers with a spur center in the headstock, adjusting both ends if necessary to find the most accurate center of each end. Then each end is turned flat to receive the faceplate and the live center. I prefer to mount the faceplate and then drill the tailstock end as previously described because it saves steps.

Next I secure the burl between centers using a specially made ball bearing cup center. I begin roughing the bowl with a large heavy-duty carbide-tipped tool. I shape the bowl to its final form using a series of tools and then sand the exterior with the auto body sander.

I use a special cone-cutting attachment to separate the interior cone from the bowl. This attachment is a custom made accessory which fits into the tool post and holds the cone-cutting tool for deep plunge cutting. This eliminates freehand plunge cutting which is dangerous.

Once the initial plunge cuts have been made with the cone-cutting accessory, I make additional cuts, shaping the interior of the bowl, with a long round-nose carbide-tipped tool. After achieving the desired wall thickness and the maximum safe depth of cut, I separate the cone and remove it.

The interior of the bowl is finish-turned and sanded. I go back over the outside with a 6" foam back sanding disc and finish-sand the exterior to 320 grit. The bowl is then finished, using the methods described in previous sections.

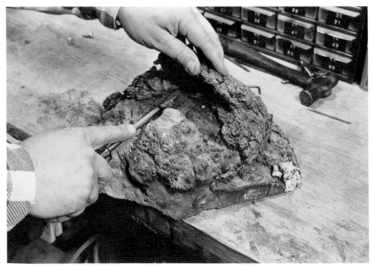

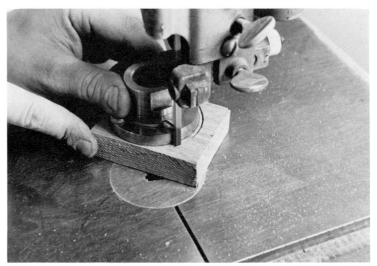

TURNING THE NATURAL EXTERIOR BOWL

To make a natural exterior bowl, leaving the outside of the burl as it grew, begin by cutting the rounded form of the burl off the tree section at an angle which creates the most uniform semi-sphere of the burl. Remove the bark from the burl and then lightly wire-brush the burl, removing grit.

In order to center the burl as accurately as possible so that it will be balanced on the lathe and to avoid the waste of some of the depth of the bowl by using screws, use the following method of wasteblock attachment for mounting the burl.

Screw the faceplate into a good piece of scrap stock. Then band-saw a quarter-inch around the faceplate. (The faceplate is attached to the board before it is sawn round so that the screws don't split the wood.) Mount the faceplate with the waste block on the lathe, true up and face off the block with a scraping tool, being careful to make a flat although not too smooth surface. Remove the faceplate with waste block from the lathe.

Find the center of the cut side of the burl (what will be the top of the bowl), drill a hole, and attach a screw center. The screw center, or stud arbor, is a handy way to quickly mount a burl or block of wood to face off the opposite side which becomes the bottom of the bowl. Mount the burl on the lathe. At the slowest speed, face off the bottom side of the burl creating a small flat surface. Turning the bottom of the burl in this manner assures that the bottom of the bowl will be parallel with the top with as little waste as possible. This is important because we want to keep the base of the bowl small.

Attach the faceplate with the waste block to a taper arbor accessory which fits in the tailstock. Apply glue to the waste block and to the flat of the bottom of the burl. Clamp the waste block and the bowl together by applying pressure from the tailstock. In the photos, I am using a Shopsmith, and applying pressure by extending the spindle of the headstock out towards the tailstock. Allow manufacturer's specified time for drying. I prefer to do this type of clamping after hours so that it's convenient to leave the blank on the lathe overnight.

Once the glue has dried, mount the faceplate with wasteblock and burl on the headstock spindle. Tighten the tailstock with the live center into the burl. Begin by turning the interior of the bowl, carefully checking to make sure not to go through the minimum diameter of the outside of the burl unless you want to make a hole through the outside of the bowl. (Often, such holes are attractive, but they don't usually work well in

shallow bowls such as the one in the photos.) Turn the burl between centers until the last possible moment, then snap the small cone off, and finish-turn the bowl interior. Once the final shape has been achieved, carefully sand the interior with a locking disc in the high speed drill.

You may finish-sand the interior of the bowl by hand-holding sandpaper sheets in successive grits with a foam backing pad. It's important to be very careful in this sanding process not to catch the paper on the edges of the bowl or to allow any part of your hand to come in contact with the edges.

Finish-sand the outermost edges, slightly rolling them over with a small foam back disc. Remove the waste block and finish using the techniques previously shown.

TURNING MASS AND AIR; PHANTOM FORMS

In the previous sections, two main approaches to the turning of burls were illustrated. First, in the turning of the small natural top bowl, a round blank was cut out from the burl, eliminating for the most part the natural irregularities of the burl surface except on the lip of the bowl. A relatively uniform cylinder for turning was produced. In the turning of the natural exterior bowl, the second approach was used: the natural exterior form of the burl became the exterior of the bowl. The unbalanced, irregular blank was centered as well as possible on the lathe, only the inside was turned, and the exterior was left untouched.

Between these two approaches exist infinite possibilities for turning a partially natural exterior vessel. The burl may be mounted on the lathe in its rough form and the turning tool used to turn down the areas of mass that extend outward, achieving a desired form which includes the gaps and dips in the natural form. The tool alternately cuts into the wood and travels through the empty spaces between the high points, in effect "turning mass and air." Doing this successfully requires complete control of the turning tool and an understanding of the visual effect of spinning on an irregular piece of wood.

When a non-round burl is spinning on the lathe, there will be an optical illusion of two forms, one within another. The opaque inner form is a close visual indication of the largest area of solid wood (of varying diameters along the length) that is possible for the burl as it has been centered on the lathe. Within this inner form, very dark areas will indicate bark inclusions or other irregularities. The fuzzy, transparent outer form is an illusion created by the rapid spinning of the varying protuberances (the natural formations of the burl) that extend beyond the maximum area of solid wood.

This phantom form will have tonal gradations, darker areas showing a more solid mass of material, lighter area showing where there is more space than material.

The burl, through its spinning phantom forms, suggests possibilities for form. The woodturner must first understand the limitations of a partic-

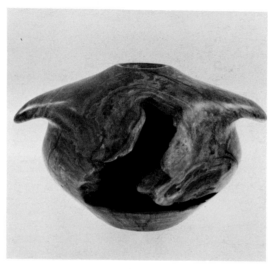

ular burl and then couple personal or classical form to the possibilities which the wood offers. By accepting voids and other irregularities as positive design elements, new possibilities exist for harmony between sculptor and material.

Partially turning the exterior creates a smooth round form with craggy indentations, gaps, or jagged voids. These spaces are as important as the form itself, like the silences in music. They heighten our awareness of the character of the form by allowing our imagination to fill it out, by emphasizing the contrast of the natural with the designed form. They become like the surface decorations of ancient Oriental pottery, yet with a depth that draws us into the piece.

Based on experience — understanding of the burl, and the suggestions of the phantom form — the turner must decide how far to go in turning the exterior, also considering his or her plans for the interior. The turner may decide to maintain a relatively uniform interior with no or few voids by keeping the hollow within the maximum solid center of the burl as roughly indicated by the visual opaque form. Or, the turner may decide that a larger diameter interior with voids and/or bark inclusions in it will enhance the piece being made.

The exploration of the varying possibilities for expression within the natural form of the burl is an exciting study, one which will teach the student much about technique, form and responsiveness to the material and the moment.

Top left: *Melvin Lindquist, Maple burl hollow vase with voids, 1984, 7" (18 cm) diameter. Collection, Mr. & Mrs. Charles Kerr.*
Top right: *Maple burl bowl with bark inclusions and voids, 1982, 12" (30 cm) diameter.*
Above: *Melvin Lindquist, turned and carved maple, burl, closed-mouth hollow form with void, 1981, 10" (25 cm) diameter.*

Above: *Melvin Lindquist, cherry burl natural top/ natural exterior vase, 1982. 6" x 7¹/₂" (15 x 19 cm). Collection, Bill Byers.*

TURNING THE PARTIALLY NATURAL EXTERIOR VASE

To prepare a blank for turning a partially natural exterior vase, my father cuts the log ends off an elongated cherry burl on his 12" capacity band saw. After studying the burl, he saws the bottom flat, eliminating the plain wood of the tree and establishing a parallel surface to the outer round of the burl.

When cutting the blank, the turner is faced with many decisions. Careful planning at this stage will create opportunities throughout the course of turning. Melvin prefers to incorporate the natural formation of the burl into the finished piece. He saws the turning blank partially round leaving two prominent areas where the burl recedes into the diameter of the blank.

The faceplate is mounted directly to the bottom of the vase and is attached to the headstock spindle. Melvin turns a small dimple in the top of the burl to receive the tailstock and secures the burl between centers using a live center in the tailstock. The bark is removed with a mallet to prevent its flying off during turning, and also to enable further study of the natural form of the burl.

Having studied the positioning of the natural burl irregularities within the saw blank, Melvin begins rough shaping of the vase, sensitive to the form of the burl and observing the phantom form as explained above.

Turning Burls

1

2

3

4

5

6

7

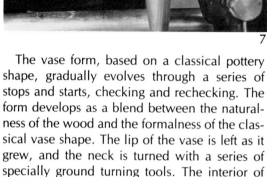

8

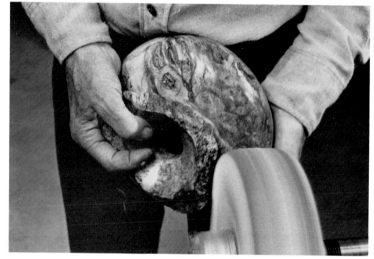

9

The vase form, based on a classical pottery shape, gradually evolves through a series of stops and starts, checking and rechecking. The form develops as a blend between the naturalness of the wood and the formalness of the classical vase shape. The lip of the vase is left as it grew, and the neck is turned with a series of specially ground turning tools. The interior of the mouth of the vase is turned between centers using the cone separation technique.

The interior of the body of the vase is hollowed by the blind boring technique (which will be more fully explained in the Chapter 18). First a center hole is drilled using a 1¹/₂″ spade bit held in the drill chuck in the tailstock. The tool rest is carefully repositioned so as not to touch the natural edge of the lip of the vase, and the interior is hollowed by turning with successive plunge and swing cuts achieved through the "feel" of the tool. The interior is hollowed to a consistent wall thickness based on the voids and bark inclusions and the proximity of natural recesses in the outer surface of the piece. Finish cuts are made to smooth the interior.

The exterior of the vase is sanded with the small 6″ disc sander and finish-sanded through successive grits. The faceplate is removed and the bottom is sanded first with the 12″ disc sander and then with the stationary flexible foam back. Melvin applies a tung oil and Japan driers finish, wipes off the excess, allows it to dry thoroughly and then buffs with Tripoli.

CHAPTER 18

Turning Vases

Melvin Lindquist has been turning for over fifty years. For the past twenty-five years he has concentrated on the vase form, working primarily in spalted wood and burls. After many years of practice, making a vase is routine, a form of exercise — a morning of turning after he walks his dog limbers up his hand and eye. After several pieces, the good wood — the wood that has been saved from forgotten years — is pulled out, old and dusty, and the tool is put to the noble substance to release the beauty locked within. By now, his turning is a fluid, accurate translation of an inner image. The piece simply and mysteriously takes shape. This process, seemingly intuitive and automatic, actually results from a mastery of techniques.

Of all turning, the vase form is perhaps the most difficult to understand. It is almost impossible to define or create a system of proportions that will work consistently. A very slight change in proportions may make the difference between a pleasing form and a form that disturbs the eye.

Creating a special piece is no accident, although it may appear to be. I have seen my father spend weeks exploring minor modifications in a lip or base, playing with the proportions of a particular vase form. Like the charcoal sketches a painter makes, these vases are alive, spontaneous, moving, as a result of the imper-

Left: *Melvin Lindquist, spalted white birch burl "Sung Vase," 1982, 8$\frac{1}{2}$" x 15" (22 cm x 38 cm).*
Right: *Melvin Lindquist, spalted maple vase, 1981, 5" x 7" (13 cm x 18 cm).*

Above: *Melvin Lindquist, spalted elm burl natural top vase, 1982, 9" (23 cm) high.*

fections. The final piece, the one for which the special wood has been saved, will be timeless and at rest.

Before turning a vase out of any wood, it is wise to study the vase form in a historical context, since practically every vase form has already been made. By accustoming the eye to the various vase forms created by masters, the turner may develop an intuitive feeling for form enabling good decisions that will result in a good vase.

The marks, lines and patterns in spalted wood become very much like the designs in the ancient Chinese and Japanese glazed vases: intricate, flowing and honest. Some potters used calligraphy or painted symbolic images. Some simply scribbled brushstrokes in a seemingly haphazard manner. Some carved through the top layer of glaze and/or clay exposing a different colored ground. This decoration is called sgraffito. The surface decoration of the zone lines and fungal patterns of spalted wood work in much the same way. Form and decoration joined in harmony reflect a magical truth: the union of complementary elements releases a beauty unknown to either.

Above left: *Melvin Lindquist, Spalted maple hollow vase, 1976, 12" x 12" (30 cm x 30 cm). Collection, Samuel and Eleanor Rosenfeld.*
Above right: *Melvin Lindquist, Butternut burl base, 1982, 11" x 10½" (28 cm x 27 cm).*

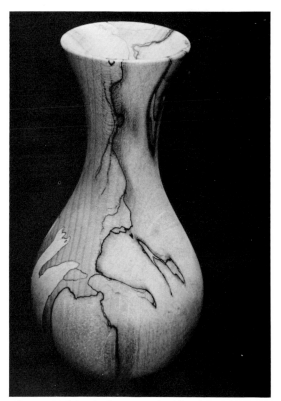

Above: *Melvin Lindquist, Spalted birch teardrop vase, 1967, 6" (15 cm) high.*

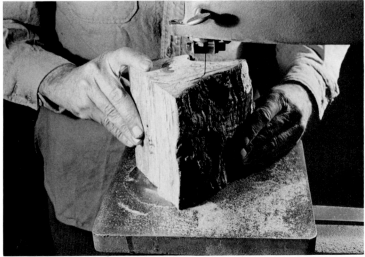

TURNING THE SIMPLE VASE

Turning vases of spalted wood presents the same problems as turning spalted bowls: the hard and soft zones, the pitting and torn end-grain, the lack of structural strength. But allowing the wood to suggest its natural form is the most difficult and important challenge in turning spalted vases.

First, Melvin selects a piece of good, dry spalted wood. He chain saws the block into pieces that will fit the opening of the band saw, studying the markings in each section to determine how to cut it in order to make the most beautifully marked vase possible. The blank may be sawn so that the vertical axis is cross-grain, parallel with the grain or on an angle to the grain. In each case, the choice is determined simply by which cut promises to unfold the best patterns of zone lines upon turning, taking into account the faults and weaknesses of the piece.

Once the blank is cut, it is attached to a screw center and held between two centers. The vase is turned to approximately an eighth-inch larger than the finished diameter (to compensate for the subsequent removal of the outer layer of chips and pecks by equilibrial abrasion). While the piece is still held between two centers, Melvin uses a small skew to remove as much wood as possible from the interior of the mouth of the vase. It is important not to make the wall of the mouth too thin, since the whole vase will require sanding. A center hole is drilled with the correct size drill to allow for a structurally sound

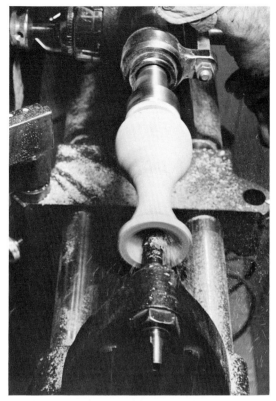

wall throughout the neck of the vase. For example, the vase in the pictures has a one-inch diameter neck. A $5/8''$ drill bit was used to allow for $3/16''$ walls in the neck of the finished vase. After drilling the hole, Mel turns the inside wall of the mouth down to meet the drilled hole, thus forming a continuous inner wall. The inside throat and mouth are sanded using a 60 grit $1/2''$ flap wheel mounted on an extension rod chucked in a high speed drill.

The outer surface of the vase is abraded with the disc sander with a flexible pad, using the equilibrial abrasion method.

After the inner and outer surfaces of the vase have been equilibrially prepared, Melvin hand-sands or foam pad sands while the vase is turning at slow speed, progressing from 100 grit, to 150 grit, to 220 grit, to 320 grit, to 400 grit (silicon carbide paper). At 320 grit, hand-sanding with the grain while the piece remains stationary sometimes produces the best finish. The interior of the mouth and throat of the vase are sanded by forming a cone with the sandpaper. After the vase has been finish-sanded by hand, wax is applied while the piece is spinning.

BLIND BORING

An old story goes: A student arrived late to his math class. Finding everyone quietly at work, he copied the two problems on the board and began seeking the answers. Unable to solve the problems during the class time, he worked all night and brought his paper to the professor the next day. "I'm sorry, I was only able to solve one of the problems," he told his teacher. Dumbfounded, his teacher explained that he had put the problems on the board as examples of unsolvable mathematical problems. Since the student had not known that the problems were impossible, he had approached them with a fresh mind.

Many years ago, a very special vase that my father had turned developed a big crack because of the thickness of the vase body. According to his usual practice, he had drilled a hole to the bottom of the vase, just smaller in diameter than the neck at its narrowest point. Naturally, the large bulk of wood in its body had caused the crack. My father began searching for a way to make vases with walls of consistent thickness, although it was a seeming impossibility. Any attempts to cut out the sides usually resulted in a smashed vase. After much experimentation, he developed an apparently simple solution to the problem: a technique which he called "blind boring" whereby the interior of a turned form may be turned out without seeing the surface being cut. By lengthening an existing carbide-tipped tool to approximately ten inches with a handle over twelve inches long and using a series of push/plunge cuts through the center hole, the inner mass of the first experimental vases was removed.

At first, blind boring was a frightening and risky proposition. I remember the first time I saw my father push the tool into a vase at a "backwards" angle. I was sure that he would throw the piece off the lathe. By now, however, he has refined the technique to the point that it appears just another automatic and effortless step in his turning.

With each obstacle overcome, continued discipline and daily practice perfect techniques. As each technique is mastered, it becomes precious to the artisan as one of many skills in a repertoire.

The tool for blind boring must be made of at least half-inch square stock and minimally ten inches long. The vase must turn at as high speed as possible, normally 1750 rpm. If the piece is in balance, this speed should present no problem, but if the piece is out of balance, it is better to run it a little slower. The turner must have considerable faith in his turning ability and a good deal of experience to back it up. The tool will be used in a full arc within the cavity, "blindly" cutting any surface with which it comes in contact. A three-faced carbide-tipped tool is helpful for this reason.

To blind bore a vase, Melvin begins by preparing a blank and mounting it on the lathe. He rough-turns to center the blank and turns the exterior vase form. Next, he turns the mouth of the vase as it is still held between centers. Once the form has been achieved, he replaces the live center with a 1" drill in the tailstock and drills a hole to the bottom of the vase.

Now, the blind boring can begin. Melvin makes push cuts successively in eighth- to quarter-inch increments. The mouth hole acts as a pivot point for the tool since the sidewards movement of the tool is limited only by the diameter of the opening and the length of the neck. That opening also acts as a fulcrum to dislodge the vase should the tool catch. It is important that only small amounts be taken out at a time. The tool must be allowed to do the cutting without being forced, and it requires a considerable amount of skill and strength to hold the tool steady enough to cut and shape without its grabbing.

After enlarging the hole by the push method, Mel employs the reverse, or drag, method. Instead of pushing, the tool is pulled toward the

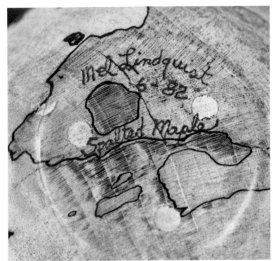

mouth of the vase so that the cutting face has a negative angle and is slightly below the center line. In other words, the tool is tipped downward to prevent its catching. Successive cuts, pushing and dragging, eventually rough out the hollow of the vase. As the interior is turned, the cavity fills with shavings which are removed by forcing compressed air into the hole.

A long round-nose scraper is used to form the consistent wall. When scraping the interior of the hollow vase, it is important to use a negative angle, lest the vase take off toward the ceiling. Of course, the tool rest must be as close to the mouth of the vase as possible, preferably at 90°.

The exterior of the vase is abraded using a 6" silicon carbide disc. For finishing the interior of the closed-mouth hollow vase, a flap wheel the diameter of the neck opening is used inside the stationary piece. Equilibrial abrasion of a closed-mouth vase is tricky since the vase has a tendency when spinning to grab the extension rod of the drill. Melvin hand-sands the exterior and the small amount of the interior that may be reached as the lathe turns at slow speed.

After removing the faceplate, the holes are plugged, and the bottom is sanded using the disc sander and the sanding jig. (See Turning a Spalted Bowl.) Then the vase bottom is finish-sanded to 320 grit on a stationary flexible foam back pad.

Melvin signs the vase bottom with a vibrating signature pen, then applies acrylic burnt umber, rubs it off, lets it dry and again lightly sands the vase bottom.

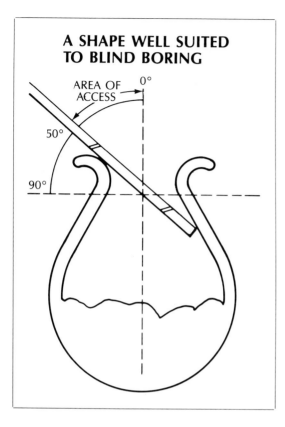

A SHAPE WELL SUITED TO BLIND BORING

AREA OF ACCESS

0°
50°
90°

BLIND BORING OF THIN WALLED FORM

30° 20° 10° 0°
40°
50°
60°
70°
80°
90°
5°

AREA OF ACCESS

A

B

AS DIAMETER OF HOLE A DECREASES, ANGLE B MUST INCREASE

USING A 1/4" BORING BAR AND A 1 1/2" ENTRY HOLE WITH A 1/4" WALL THICKNESS, THERE IS NO PROBLEM MAINTAINING 50° OFF OF FLAT. A SMALLER ENTRY HOLE MEANS A LARGER OFF-OF-FLAT ANGLE.

The vase is finished with a polyurethane and tung oil finish and, after thorough drying, is buffed with the buffing wheel and Tripoli.

As Melvin developed these blind boring techniques, it soon became obvious to him that he could help himself by turning shapes that were easy to bore. The thinner the wall at the entry hole, the easier it becomes to bore out the inside of the vase. The thicker the wall of the entry hole, or the longer the neck of the vase, the harder it becomes to bore out the inside. Also, the larger the hole, the easier it becomes to bore the inside, also facilitating chip clearance.

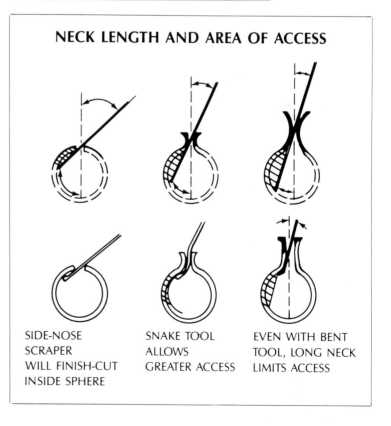

NECK LENGTH AND AREA OF ACCESS

SIDE-NOSE SCRAPER WILL FINISH-CUT INSIDE SPHERE

SNAKE TOOL ALLOWS GREATER ACCESS

EVEN WITH BENT TOOL, LONG NECK LIMITS ACCESS

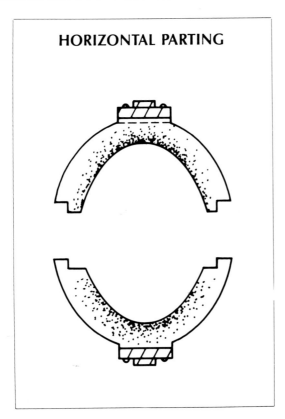

HORIZONTAL PARTING

OTHER METHODS
FOR TURNING A HOLLOW VASE

While developing and using the blind boring technique, Melvin has also experimented with other methods for hollowing out a vase. He found that he could horizontally cut a turned form in half, turn the inside out of each piece separately, and then glue them back together. Another way is by cutting the blank in half longitudinally on the band saw, carving out the inside and gluing the two sections back together. The most versatile method he has devised — the one that, next to blind boring, least disturbs the pure form of the vase — is to make a hole in the bottom of the piece, bore out the inside, then plug the hole, reverse the piece and turn from the other end.

The four methods (blind boring, horizontal parting, longitudinal parting and reverse turning), achieve the same purpose: a hollow form. Blind boring is the purest approach to turning, since the other methods involve joinery and glue.

Horizontal Parting

Melvin begins by turning a vase form while the piece is chucked between centers. Each end of the vase is squared up and enough material is left at the tailstock end so that another faceplate may be attached. He's careful to mark the center at the tailstock end. The piece is then either sawn in half on the band saw using a jig, or parted on the lathe with a parting tool. It can also be sawn on the lathe. Mel screws a faceplate directly onto the tailstock end (being careful to accurately position it) and each half is then hollowed out as though making two bowls. Corresponding female and male rabbets are turned and the pieces are checked with calipers and fitted together as in making a covered jar. The two halves are then glued together. The faceplate is removed from the mouth end of the vase, and the vase can then be re-turned, the mouth formed and the piece finished.

The vase is hollow; however, there is a line in the center where the pieces have been joined. One of Melvin's approaches to the problem of the center line is to turn a groove or grooves at the parting line creating a series of rings, after gluing the two halves together. In the late 60s, we made a series of turned and carved pieces where the center line is disguised through carving.

Longitudinal Parting

To hollow out some very tall vases, Melvin cuts the already roughed out vase in two on the band saw, the cut running in a diagonal direction from one side near the faceplate to the other side near the mouth. He then hollows out each section with a chain saw or die grinder and finishes the insides. To take up the saw kerf, he rejoins

Left: *Mark and Melvin Lindquist, hollow butternut carved vase, ca. 1968, (25 cm) high.*

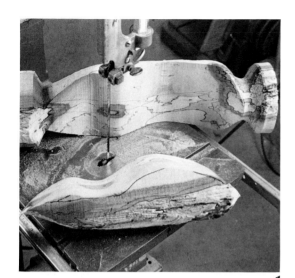

1

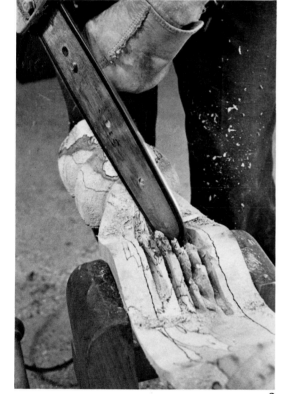

2

*Turning a
Hollow Vase*

3

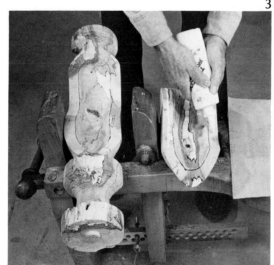

4

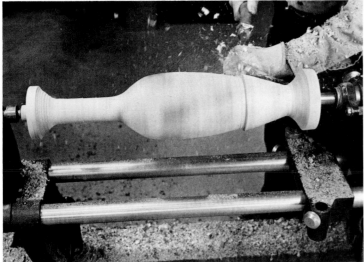

the two with a piece of veneer. After the glue is thoroughly dry, he remounts the piece in the lathe, turns the neck and finishes turning the mouth and outside of the vase. The neck is bored with the vase clamped in the vise.

Reverse Boring

One limitation of the blind boring method is that it cannot be used in turning some vases, because of the angles involved. So Melvin employs an ingenious system for hollowing out these pieces. He begins by mounting the faceplate on the mouth end of the vase (foreseen in the blank). He rough-turns the vase, backwards in position to the way a vase is normally turned. In other words, the mouth end of the vase is at the headstock rather than at the tailstock. The body of the vase is hollowed using the blind boring technique and the hole is squared off. The vase is then removed. He turns a plug to fit snugly into the hole in the bottom of the vase.

REVERSE BORING

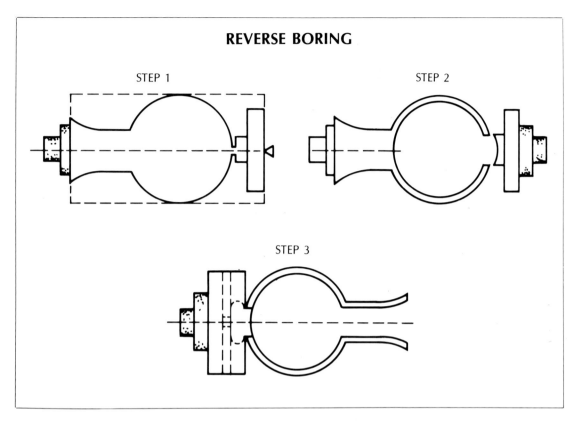

STEP 1

STEP 2

STEP 3

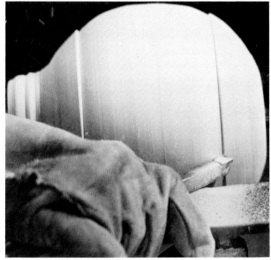

Leaving the plug on the lathe, he applies a liberal amount of glue and puts the vase on to the plug making sure that the grain matches. The lathe is used as a clamp by applying pressure from the tailstock, assuring proper alignment of the vase.

It is important to allow for proper drying time of the glue to insure that the pieces will stay together under the pressure of re-turning. The faceplate is then removed from the mouth end of the vase, and the vase is turned from the plugged end. The outside form is finalized and finished. Then Melvin drills a hole through the mouth and into the neck, opening into the hollow cavity of the vase. He uses a square-nose carbide-tipped tool (sometimes the heel of a skew) and tapers the inner wall of the neck to an even thickness.

The base where the plug fits in is sometimes turned to form a foot and the joint may be hidden by a "false bead." Often, however, Mel simply parts the plug at the base leaving a footless base showing a circle in the bottom which is the plug. Usually, it's difficult to find the plug when the grain is matched.

The vase is finish-sanded, oiled and buffed with Tripoli.

Melvin Lindquist is constantly seeking new turning techniques, both traditional and experimental. He enjoys the inventive process, finding solutions to turning problems. He will spend countless hours and much wood exploring a technical possibility. But, in the end, the skills, the tools and the methods he develops must serve to further his purpose: artistic self-expression through his wood. For, as he says, "Technique is not good by itself. A piece is meaningless if it cannot first lure a viewer by its presence, who then may wonder how it was made."

Acknowledgements

It's impossible to acknowledge all who have been involved in the making of a book which took fifteen years, since many have helped in ways not directly related to the actual book. Brad McCormick, patron and encouraging friend, helped in beginning stages to get me on track through his relentless uncompromising criticism. Robert Whitley, master furniture maker, has been and continues to be an inspiration and loyal friend. Dale Nish provided comments on the finished manuscript and wrote the preface for the book. Dale has been a model not only to me, but to many who want to express their thoughts and techniques in book form. My thanks also to Winslow Eaves, Bob March and Alphonse Mattia for their reviews of the manuscript. Jim and Dot McRae, and Bob and Jan Skinner have been loyal supporters, friends, critics, encouragers who have contributed in countless ways. Jan also gave unselfishly of her time and talents to "pre-edit" the book, creating a smoother, more readable text. Michael Bruss, our apprentice at that time, helped with many aspects of preparation for photography and logistics.

Also, I wish to acknowledge the help of two very much missed departed friends and mentors, Darr Collins and Will Horwitt, who each inspired my own pursuit of art. Countless other collectors and friends have contributed in various ways, from advice to encouragement and support. To all, I am deeply indebted.

It's strange to me how a seemingly chance meeting can have an impact on one's life; one in particular affected the outcome of this book. While speaking at the Connecticut Commission on the Arts, I met photographer Bill Byers, who told me he had done the photography for *Claywork* by Leon Nigrosh, and had enjoyed it immensely. I said to him, "You're going to do my book next; you're just who I need." He replied, "O.K., shall we start this week end?" After we both got over the shock of our first meeting, Bill showed up in his Volkswagen bus loaded with camera equipment and two loaves of fresh baked bread and we began working. Bill gave

Bill Byers

all he had almost every weekend for several summers. His professional eye and attitude have been a major factor in the development and completion of the book. I'm deeply grateful for his outstanding photographic work and support.

Special thanks go to my two sons, Ben and Josh, for their hard work in cleaning the shop for the photographs, and for their continued support and enthusiasm for the book.

My father, Melvin, continually encouraged me from start to finish, giving his opinions and criticisms. But most of all he has believed in and supported my work unconditionally from the beginning.

Wyatt Wade spent countless hours discussing and reworking the book. He has been a consistent, watchful, gracious editor. He was able to encourage and support where several other editors have lost patience and given up. Without his uncompromising and compelling influence, this book would not have been.

Finally, without my wife Kathy's constant vigilance, the book could not have been written. From the beginning, she has ordered, organized and edited each section, struggling to retain the meaning behind my often cumbersome statements, to plane down and shape them into graceful, concise sentences. Her devotion to the book, and to me, are deeply appreciated.

Photography Credits

Except for those listed below, all photographs are by Bill Byers.

Robert Aude, *p. 231;* Paul Avis, *pp. 227(B), 270, 273(R);* Courtney Frisse, *p. 86;* Bob LaPree, *pp. 28, 154(B), 272(R);* Kathleen Lindquist, *pp. 6, 23(TR), 29 (B), 31(T), 33, 88(B), 155(T), 163, 191, 194(B), 218, 219(TL&R), 226(B), 245(B), 253(T), 271, 230, 282(B);* Mark Lindquist, *pp. 8, 16(B), 18(T), 20 26, 27, 29(TR), 31(B), 37, 40 (TL), 49, 50 51, 53, 76(B), 79(B), 101, 121(B), 122, 129(B), 130(T), 147, 152, 154(T), 168, 175, 178(T), 181(BL&R), 195(B), 196(TL&R), 197, 198, 200(B), 210, 217, 220-226(T), 227(T), 229, 233, 252, 253(B), 265, 272(L);* James McRay, *p. 177;* Robert E. Mates, *p. 180(B);* Barbara Morgan, *p. 67(B);* N. Rabin, *pp. 40(R), 68(B);* John Russell, *pp. 17(B), 48, 105(T), 106, 112(B), 130 (B);* Tim Savard, *pp. 184, 198, 199, 200 (TL&R), 201, 274-276(T);* Robert Whitley, *p. 7.*

Key to Abbreviations

T=Top
B=Bottom
TL=Top Left
TR=Top Right
M=Middle
BL=Bottom Left
BR=Bottom Right

Index